BIG
BAD
GOD
of the Bible

BIG BAD GOD

of the Bible

LIVING
INK
BOOKS™
Writing Worth Reading™

MARK**LITTLETON**

Big, Bad God of the Bible
Copyright © 2008 by Mark Littleton
Published by Living Ink Books, an imprint of AMG Publishers
6815 Shallowford Rd.
Chattanooga, Tennessee 37421

Unless otherwise indicated, Scripture quotations used in this book are from The Holy Bible, New International Version (NIV). Copyright © 1973, 1978, 1984, International Bible Society. Used by permission of Zondervan Bible Publishers.

Scripture quotations marked NASB are taken from the New American Standard Bible®, Copyright © 1960, 1962, 1963, 1968, 1971, 1972, 1973, 1975, 1977, 1995 by The Lockman Foundation. Used by permission.

Scripture quotations marked KJV are taken from the King James Version of the Bible.

ISBN 978-089957-033-4

First printing—September 2008
Cover designed by Daryle Beam, Bright Boy Design, Chattanooga, Tennessee
Interior design and typesetting by Reider Publishing Services, West Hollywood,
    California
Edited and Proofread by Rich Cairnes, Dan Penwell, Sharon Neal, and
    Rick Steele

Printed in the United States of America
14 13 12 11 10 09 08 –B– 7 6 5 4 3 2 1

To Alisha, my second daughter, who in the last few years has made me think much about what it means to follow Christ. As a college student, you have a tremendous enthusiasm for God's Word and telling the world about Jesus. I hope that spirit never dies.

May this book be one that helps you in your faith and the faith of those you love.

Contents

Acknowledgments

Thanks to AMG Publishers, who took a chance on this book and made it work.

Thanks to my online critique group, fanstory.com, who read all these chapters and offered stout help and bold encouragement. I owe you all.

Thanks to my wife, Jeanette, who challenges my thinking on many issues. She made me think more clearly about these topics with her responses.

Thanks to my son, Gardner, who, although Bionicles are right now the passion of his life, still fires out a great insight now and then. God be with you.

Thanks to Elizabeth, my four-year-old, who inevitably toddles in with a request, need, or smile that keeps me going even when it's rough.

Why This Book?

I RECENTLY delved into a compelling quest—under, I hope and believe, the guidance of the Spirit of God. In short, I read a number of books by atheists. One by Bertrand Russell said little to me. Just intellectual garbage. Several others simply seemed angry and strident, like those by Christopher Hitchens, Carl Sagan, and others. But two stood out: *The God Delusion* by Richard Dawkins, the author of many books on his favorite subject, the evolution of the universe, along the lines of Darwin's *The Origin of Species*. And Sam Harris's book, *Letter to a Christian Nation*.

Both men said things that immediately showed me their purpose and intent: to obliterate Christianity, the Bible, God, and Jesus as fictions of the most poisonous kind. Their hope was to provide the "facts" available in our world in such a way everyone on planet Earth would be forced to admit that God, Jesus, and the Bible are nothing less than huge lies foisted on gullible people. Rejecting their arguments meant you were nothing less than a sanctimonious idiot, who really didn't deserve to live in our world.

Frankly, I found these writings superficial and full of holes wide enough to drive a universe through. Repeatedly, they relied on old arguments to prove their points, arguments that have been decimated by years of fact-finding and truth-telling on the part of the defenders of the Bible and God. When their arguments became tedious and laughable, they often pulled out so-called "facts" that anyone who knows much about the Bible could easily tear to pieces as "straw men" or "fictions."

I repeatedly came across passages like this:

Nobody knows who the four evangelists [writers of the Gospels—Matthew, Mark, Luke, and John] were, but they almost certainly never met Jesus personally. Much of what they wrote was in no sense an honest attempt at history, but was simply rehashed from the Old Testament, because the gospel-makers were devoutly convinced that the life of Jesus must fulfill Old Testament prophecies. It is even possible to mount a serious, though not widely supported, historical case that Jesus never lived at all . . .

Although Jesus probably existed, reputable biblical scholars do not in general regard the New Testament (and obviously the Old Testament) as a reliable record of what actually happened in history, and I shall not consider the Bible further as evidence for any kind of deity.[1]

I have to wonder what "reputable scholars" Dawkins refers to—the members of "The Jesus Seminar," who have been discredited time and time again as flakes with axes the size of Gibraltar to grind? Has he consulted any of the great names in Christian scholarship like Charles Hodge, Karl Barth, F. F. Bruce, Carl F. H. Henry, Charles Ryrie, Alister McGrath, or John Walvoord?

I also wonder about someone who so easily dismisses the Bible as an "unreliable" historical record, when anyone who honestly reads and studies it will soon find it the most accurate eyewitness report we have from ancient history. Especially when you compare it with other writings from antiquity like Homer's *Iliad*, *The Gilgamesh Epic*, or Caesar's *Gallic Wars*. The Bible instead is a book quoted and substantiated by numerous others who were not believers and who did not care a whit about it as the Word of God—Josephus, Tacitus, Suetonius, and many others.

A truth I discovered as a student in seminary is that at one time archaeologists set out to prove the Bible false in many of its historical details, especially in the nineteenth century when Bible skepticism rose to its heights. Today, though, renowned archaeologists like Kathleen Kenyon, Nelson Glueck, Frank Gaebelein, and Bryant C. Wood confirm the Bible's accuracy. For instance, Gaebelein writes, "The attitude of suspended judgment toward Bible difficulties . . . is constantly being vindicated, as archaeology has solved one Biblical problem after another, and as painstaking reexamination of discrepancies has finally led to answers."[2]

Their discoveries have proven over and over that the Bible is accurate down to the minutest details. Has Dawkins ever considered any of this evidence? Moreover, has he read Matthew or John, who were both disciples of Jesus? Where then does he get this idea that they didn't personally know him? Unless, of course, he's of the school that doesn't believe that Matthew wrote the book of Matthew or that John wrote the book of John. Like Mark Twain once quipped, "If Moses didn't write the first five books of the Bible, then it was another man by the same name."

But Dawkins just waves his hand and the whole Bible along with its portrait of Jesus is sent packing. Does he really think that will ride with people of the twenty-first century who actually appreciate dealing with the facts rather than a recitation of old and worn-out clichés? Does Dawkins really believe the worldwide prevalence of faith in God and Christ can be deconstructed by an argument he's put together from his own imagination? If the Bible is as replete with errors as he says it is, and if it's a complete hoax on the level of the Piltdown man, then why hasn't it been totally discredited to the point that its followers are reduced to a few churches in places like Podunk, Mississippi, and Fool's Haven, Texas? If this is all so obvious, why are so many of us so deluded? Basically, according to people like Dawkins, because we're nut cases, idiots, or both.

At another point, Dawkins writes that the God revealed in the Old Testament is "arguably the most unpleasant character in all fiction: jealous and proud of it; a petty, unjust, unforgiving control freak; a vindictive, bloodthirsty ethnic cleanser; a misogynistic, homophobic, racist, infanticidal, genocidal, filicidal, pestilential, megalomaniacal, sadomasochistic, capriciously malevolent bully."[3]

Frankly, when I read something like that, I have to wonder if Dawkins has ever given most of the Old Testament a fair and open reading. To be sure, there are problematic passages, with God exhibiting some hair-raising responses to sin and problems in his world. At times, he truly does look like "the big, bad God" of my title.

But from that I have to ask two questions: First, if the Bible is the Word of God, then why would God allow himself to be portrayed in such a terrible light, if not for some deeper purpose we should all long to discover? On the other hand, if, as Dawkins and others claim to believe, the Bible is just a book like any other written by fools and charlatans, then what does it matter? Why is he so strident about it? If the writers made up most of it, how do we know any of the things God supposedly did were really done by him in the first place? What basis does he have to quote it, let alone speak of its revelations as if they're even remotely true?

So on that front, it's a wash. Discard the Bible. It's just another book. Forget what it says. The God in it is an idiot, a miscreant, a bully, and no one anyone would want to know personally.

Regardless, I believe the Bible is God's Word, and all those horrid episodes a means to reveal something precious and wondrous about the God who wrote about them. Only an attitude that says, "Okay, I'm not sure I understand why God spoke of this, but I'll give him the benefit of taking a hard look at it just to see if there's anything deeper than a reason to reject him."

This book, then, is a discussion between myself and a number of unbelievers with serious questions like those these atheists and others raise. The person I introduce at the beginning, Doug (not his real name), was someone I encountered at a Christian writer's conference. We talked for quite a while and he proved to possess a clear-thinking, incisive mind well worth exploring. Those initial statements made me wonder where our discussion might lead if together we probed and found answers to the questions he voiced, the same kinds of questions any "seeker," atheist, or unbeliever might bring up if they had the chance.

The story line is pure fiction. The main character, Mark, is a fictional character in terms of the plot and dialogue. In that respect, this is an unusual apologetics book. Instead of the straightforward preaching you find in most of them, it's a story, almost a novel, in which Mark and various people discuss the great questions of our world and how the Bible explains them.

Thus, I hope you will stick with the story. I've tried to make the plot interesting and compelling, so that this is not just a preachy, formulaic apologetics book. However, my purpose remains to present real biblical answers for the "horrible" doctrines, events, and situations revealed about God in the Bible.

You either come to the Bible with the attitude of believing that all those terrible things God did have a definite purpose on his part to teach us something about himself and his world, or you come with the attitude of seeking to collect more ammunition for your discussions and diatribes against him.

Either way, I think you will find this a compelling read. I have found that God is not afraid of any question we might hurl at him. And he certainly does not shy away from revealing to us the stark truth, some of which may shake us to the depths of our souls. Much of it, though, becomes a source of real hope, joy, and peace in a trouble-filled world.

So, if you find Dawkins, Harris, and their ilk convincing, fine. But please give God a chance to answer from the pages of his Word. The risk of summarily rejecting him and his gifts is great.

Notes

1 Richard Dawkins, *The God Delusion* (New York: Houghton-Mifflin, 2006), 96–97.

2 Frank Gaebelein, *The Expositor's Bible Commentary* (Grand Rapids, MI: Zondervan, 1979), 1:31.

3 Dawkins, *The God Delusion*, 31.

CHAPTER 1

The God Who Befuddles Us All

Doug and I Meet

Amiddle-aged, quite intelligent man sat at my table that first morning to discuss Christian writing. The first thing he said to me when the Bible came up as a sourcebook for religious writers was, "I think the Bible is bunk."

Considering we were attending a *Christian* writer's conference, I admit he stunned me. I decided to press him about it, though, and he told me his name was Doug and he attended the conference because he wanted to write books for Christians. *Maybe diatribes for them about how stupid their faith is?* I wondered. He had to be in his forties, with neatly combed graying brown hair and stylish glasses. He looked intellectual to me in a way, and in another way, just an ordinary guy.

After studying him a moment, I said, "What exactly about the Bible do you think is bunk?"

"Everything," Doug answered, setting an elbow on the table and gazing across at me with deep blue, penetrating eyes. He had the kind of look that suggested he knew more about me than he let on. I had no idea why I might think such a thing, or how he could have such information—it was just a feeling, but a strong one.

1

"Genesis," he said. "Adam and Eve. The whole fruit tree thing." He frowned and his lips crinkled. "It's so stupid I want to spit."

"What's so bunkish about it?" I asked, now really curious. Of course, I knew multitudes of people who considered Adam, Eve, and, in fact, most of Genesis to be laughable lies concocted way back when around Jewish campfires by shepherds who had never heard of deodorant.

"It's ridiculous," he replied, his tanned face suddenly lighting up with passion. "The whole human race's future dependent on a decision about whether to eat a piece of fruit or not? That's absurd."

"Well, what would have been a better test?"

"Something significant," he said, his eyes glinting with fury. I wondered if he would stand up and start throwing things. "Something that makes sense. Something that would have taken some real grit and muscle. But it's something so foolish that anyone would have broken it just to see what was so great about this fruit. Curiosity. That's what the whole thing aroused. God should have done something else."

"Like what?" I pressed.

"That's God's business. It was up to him."

Okay, a bit of a dodge, but I could accept it. "Any other bunkish stuff?"

"Sure, that's only the beginning," he said, clearly rising to the occasion. "Why did God favor Jacob and not Esau before either was even born? That's totally unfair. And God's favoritisms are pretty rank when you look at the Bible. He spared King David, who had committed adultery and murder, but he took King Saul off the throne for making a little religious sacrifice that he probably had to make to keep his army from deserting because the prophet, Samuel, was seven days late. Seven days! Any modern CEO would have fired the guy—Samuel, I mean!"

I swallowed a little, thinking back through some of my own meditations about these things. Yes, there were times when the stories in the Bible astounded me. Some were even outrageous, and not in a good way. However, I was pretty sure without looking it up that

Samuel had told Saul to wait seven days, but I decided not to bring it up. I wanted to hear the whole litany, if there was more. Doug knew more about the Bible than the average Christian who was born into the church, taught Sunday school for eighty years, and read, meditated on, and memorized Bible verses since kindergarten.

Astonishing Favoritisms
from the Pit of God-Nature

He shrugged. "Any parent knows that showing favoritism to one child over another (as many of the Hebrews did in their families) is suicide. It leads to all kinds of problems. But God himself did it without flinching."

"Whom are you referring to?" I asked, wondering just how far I could push him about his Bible knowledge without revealing I had a master's degree in theology.

"Cain and Abel were only the beginning. God favored Abel. His sacrifice supposedly was better than Cain's? How so? We don't know. God always leaves out the important details so he escapes judgment by us. It's the old dodgeball routine. God's great at dodging questions, concerns, details, whatnot. He just sails along blithely like nothing's wrong, and then someone dies, or gets judged, or is thrown out of the coop. It just really cranks my chain."

I swallowed, amazed at how angry Doug appeared. But before I could speak, he went on, hands waving, eyes flashing: "After them, there were Isaac and Ishmael, who became the fathers of the Israelite and Arab nations, respectively. Because of God's favoritism toward Isaac, we have ended up with the Arab-Israeli conflict, which still boils over today as the world's greatest unsolvable political and ethnic problem."

I could agree with that easily enough. But Doug wasn't to be stopped.

"After that, we find Jacob and Esau. I said this earlier, but it bears repeating, it's so heinous. God rejected Esau before he was even born. In fact, the actual Scripture says—he pulled out a pocket Bible (something else that shocked me)—flipped through the pages, and read, 'Before the twins were born or had done anything good or bad—in order that God's purpose in election might stand: not by works but by him who calls—she [Rebekah, the mother of the twins] was told, 'The older will serve the younger.' That's Romans 9, verses 11 and 12, in case you haven't read it."

He smiled at me and I laughed. "I've read it."

"Good, then you know what I speak of." He smiled cryptically like he knew his words made me nervous. "So when you consider that Jacob, whose name means 'cheat,' was one of Israelite history's greatest schemers, scammers, and frauds, you have to wonder: Why this nasty favoritism from God? Didn't God realize how bad that makes him look, and also that such tactics create worse and more lethal problems down the road?"

I commented, "Some people write Esau off because he was immoral and godless and sold his birthright for a meal of stew—that's Hebrews 12:16, in case you haven't read it."

"I have. So it looks like we both know the same stuff. Except I'm agin' it and you're fer it."

I grinned. I enjoyed his sense of humor. Many people I'd talked to over the years with an axe to grind as big as Doug's never cracked the edges of their lips. I said, "I know from the Romans passage that God rejected Esau before he'd done any of this, before he was even born. I've wondered about that a lot, but it seems to me Paul's saying God does the same thing with all of us. Chooses us before he even created the world. All that. So it's not like it's a one-time case."

He clapped his hands. "Predestination? Another big problem. That eliminates free will, true freedom, everything. We're just puppets in his hands."

"Okay, God has done some things we don't understand," I said, getting a little antsy. "Is that all you have?"

Astonishing Responses to Problems

Doug shook his head, grinning at me under his thick hair, like he planned any second to deliver the true haymaker that would knock me out of Christianity for the rest of my days. "Favoritisms are not nearly as big a deal as God's incredible responses to various displeasing actions of his people."

He barely paused for breath. "Of course, the universal flood is God's first huge response to mankind's sin problem. Centuries pass from the time of Adam and Eve and mankind has gone terribly awry. Murder, malfeasance, and mayhem abound. So God decides to start over. He finds one faithful man, Noah, conscripts Noah's family to build an ark, and saves the situation from total disaster by wiping everyone else out. Noah is described using God's most praiseworthy terms—righteous, honorable, blameless—despite the fact that the first thing Noah did after the flood was get so drunk he passed out naked in his tent. Was God so bad at creating and leading that he couldn't work with anyone else on the face of the earth? And after the flood was over, what was there to prevent the same thing from happening all over again? Oh, right, it *does* happen again: At the end of Revelation we see God starting over for the second time in human history by turning planet Earth into a ball of fire along with the rest of the universe."

I had to laugh. "Man, you are on a roll."

"Yeah, well, I've thought about these things for years. Anyway, it just looks like this God is a major fumbler who can't seem to get anyone to truly follow him."

"Jesus did say it's a narrow way, and 'few are those who find it.'"

"Right, another big bugaboo. Why is God so content with bringing so few to himself? Why doesn't he want most of the people? Why doesn't he give all of them a chance at the brass ring? But no, he has to choose them first. And he chooses just a few. Guess his house in heaven isn't that big, huh?"

I grinned. "I think it's pretty big. The New Jerusalem is like 1,500 miles cubed, or something like that."

"He could do better, if you ask me." He looked into his lap, but jolted back up to me, his deep blue eyes glaring. "What is it about God that makes people turn away?"

I sighed and glanced out the window at the sunshine in the backyard of our church. Doug had thrown me, that's for sure. I hadn't met anyone quite as vehement *and* knowledgeable about the Bible at the same time.

He continued, "I mean, the same crowd that welcomes Jesus on Palm Sunday wants his head on Good Friday. Why does God make so many of us so mad?" He stared at me and I sensed he really wanted an answer. Why he'd cornered me, I didn't know. Did I look like "Mr. Bible" or something?

Somehow I stammered, "The Devil's trying very hard to convince everyone God is a loser and that we should all follow him—the Devil—who will give us what we really want. God offers holiness, the Devil offers pleasure. Which one is more attractive to you?"

"Yeah," he said and shook his head. "I know what you mean."

He went on, and I marveled at his ability to put words together. "The flood, though, huge annihilating response that it is, is small compared with some of the micro-responses we find later in Scripture. For one, in Numbers there's the case of Moses when he was told to speak to the rock to give water to his people. God busted him for striking the rock and refused to let him go into the new land with the people he'd led for forty years. For striking a rock! Give me a break."

"Maybe the break he was trying to give was to break the rock."

Doug laughed. "Good one. But it's a sad case just the same because we find similar actions when God kills certain people for their sins—the whole family of Achan in the book of Joshua, even though Achan alone committed the crime of taking things banned by God; the condemnation of King Saul for doing the very thing needed at a crucial moment when the prophet of God was purposely late in arriving to perform the sacrifice; the death of Uzzah, a priest, who steadied the ark of God on a cart when it nearly fell over—his crime not clear, except that God had prescribed a very specific way the ark was to be carried and it was not by oxcart; and the divine execution of Ananias and Sapphira because they had lied about the amount of money they donated to the church."

His stream of words made me out of breath! But I didn't interrupt.

"These all rank in my mind as responses far outweighing the sins which, in many cases, were overlooked at other times in God-history—like David and Bathsheba, Peter's denials, and Paul's blasphemies. But these are small compared with one other obliterating response I'd like to cite."

I couldn't help but smile. I liked Doug's passion. I knew plenty of preachers who could use a little of his "enthusiasm" for his subject in the pulpit. If most ministers spoke as straightforwardly and excitedly as Doug, the churches would be overflowing with people, instead of driving them away.

For me, a question occurred: Was I listening to a person steeped in the Bible who really knew what he was talking about, or was Doug just another skeptic who happened to remember a few stories from his youth that he could use as a dodge from real faith? I figured I'd have to plunge on to find out.

"So what is it?" I asked.

"When David numbers the people, taking a census in order to find out how many warriors he could count on, God reacted with fury and gave David three choices for punishment. David chose the one he felt relied on God's mercy rather than man's mercy—a plague—and seventy thousand people died in the onslaught. Please! David committed the sin! But seventy thousand innocent others had to die for his crime? And David goes off scot-free in terms of personal punishment? Come on!"

Yes, I myself had often thought about how harsh that one had been.

Doug shook his head and struck the table with his fist. I glanced around, but not one of the milling writers in the conference bookstore showed interest in what we talked about. "Once again," he said, "I see God acting in ways that seem to go far beyond the reach and culpability of the sin. Why does God react like this?"

I shook my head. "I'm not sure. I think there might be solid responses to your charges, but . . ."

"Charges?"

"What else would you call them?"

"This isn't a court."

"It's the court of your opinion, if nothing else."

He gazed at me, then suddenly said, "I'm not a complete unbeliever, you know."

I grinned. "I was wondering about that."

He shrugged, reminding me of that moment in *Butch Cassidy and the Sundance Kid* when Robert Redford and Paul Newman plummet down to a ledge on a cliff after being chased for days by a team of men bent on their destruction. A rattler sounds and Redford leaps, pulls his gun, and, falling backward, plugs the snake perfectly. He then looks at Newman and gives this amazing look of ambivalence, as if he did such things every day.

Doug said, "What's so funny?"

I told him. He laughed. "He's a great actor."

I nodded. "Anyway, you were saying . . ."

"Well, it's just that there are so many really troubling things in the Bible, and I don't want to sugarcoat it."

"I don't think you are. Do you have any other, er, charges?"

"Yeah."

Even More Problems, and Bigger Ones

Doug brought up what he considered manipulations of people, starting with Adam and Eve, and going on through King Herod's "slaughter of the innocents" in Matthew 2.

But then he said, "Perhaps the worst manipulation of all is that of Pharaoh when Moses beseeches him to release Israel from their slavery in Egypt. Throughout the story, we see a number of times when Pharaoh personally 'hardened' his heart against Moses. But there are also several instances in which God hardened Pharaoh's heart in order to multiply the plagues he wanted to send on Egypt.

"You find this hardening action in other places in the Bible," Doug went on, "but perhaps the most significant is found in 2 Thessalonians 2:11, where Paul says God will send a 'deluding influence' on the people in the time of the Antichrist so they will 'believe what is false.' This also proves not only is God not in the business of saving people, but in punishing and judging as many as he can. Does God really like sending so many people to hell? I think he relishes it."

He stared at me plaintively, as if for the first time seeing the magnitude of what he was saying. I sighed again for what seemed the millionth time. Doug hit on some of the bedrock issues I'd struggled with all my Christian life. But with hardly a pause, he went on to cite many of the genocides God ordered in the Bible, the vagueness of many of the prophecies about Jesus, and other problems you find in the Bible—"contradictions," he called them, then softened it to mere "obvious fabrications."

Then he struck what he thought was one of the biggest "slime-ball moves" in history: "The story of Job is the paramount case," he said. "In Job 1 and 2 the story unravels about a confrontation that occurred between Satan and God. God asked Satan what he'd been doing, and the Enemy reported he'd been 'roaming through the earth' (1:7). God then queried if Satan had noticed Job, one of the few righteous and good men on the whole face of the earth. Satan retorted that Job's faith was based on rewards God gave him, making him rich and protecting him from trouble through a 'hedge' Satan couldn't penetrate. But just take down that hedge and mess up Job's life, Satan said, and Job would 'curse you to your face'" (1:11).

I listened raptly, knowing the story well, having even written about it in one of my books. I looked forward to hearing his assessment of this situation, if it was at all like mine.

Doug said, "So God takes the bait and makes a wager with Satan: Job won't curse me and let's have a little contest to see if that isn't so. God puts Job in Satan's hands and takes down the hedge so Satan can do his worst. Job loses everything but his wife; however, he never curses God. In chapter 2, Satan returns to God, God asks the same questions again, and Satan retorts that if God will touch Job's body with disease, Job will most certainly curse God to his face. God again puts Job into Satan's hands and Satan inflicts Job with boils from head to foot. But even at this point, Job doesn't curse God. It's then that Job pleads with God to give him a reason for these sudden reversals and God remains quiet until the thirty-eighth chapter."

I gave him a moment to settle himself. I had to admit, this was the most fascinating conversation I had ever had with an informed, articulate unbeliever, if that's what Doug was. I sort of hoped he might be more of a seeker. I mean, why would he even raise these issues if he weren't? He seemed to want me to give him answers, real answers to these questions. I wondered if he'd read one of my books.

Doug continued, "What startles the reader here is this little wager between God and Satan at Job's expense. What kind of God lets his people be trampled on and destroyed in order to win a point with an enemy? It appears the God of the universe is just such a god. Or are we missing something?"

I rubbed my chin, thinking hard about this one, which had long rankled me. *Was that all it was—a wager? Wasn't there more to it? But if there was, why the bald fact of the wager? Why would God reveal something like this, if he wasn't afraid of what we would think about him?*

I said, "I'd like to hold out that we might be missing something."

"Perhaps."

More and More Horrible Things

He went on to catalog many more problems, from God's startling failures in human history (Adam and Eve, Cain, King Saul, Judas Iscariot) to more mundane problems such as how human work is so unfulfilling, how the world is so beset with problems, sins, famines, and murders, and the ultimate problem, death, which renders every "venture and hope finis. Unless, of course, you believe the whole resurrection thing," he added.

He paused, as if lining up his words in the right order. "Last on my list of ignominious God-events is the cross—Jesus valiantly and faithfully going to a brutal death to save humankind. God the Father and God the Son somehow became so separated that Jesus cried out from that very cross, 'My God, my God, why have you forsaken me?'" (Matthew 27:46; Mark 15:34).

He stared at me, his eyes two knots of fire. "I have to ask you: Wasn't there a better way? An easier way? Do you mean the only way God could truly redeem creation was to have his Son murdered? And not only murdered, but vilified, hated, reviled, tortured, and beaten as perhaps no other person in all of history has been vilified, hated, reviled, tortured, and beaten? All of it part of God's plan of the ages, which he crafted before the universe even began.

"What kind of person are we dealing with here? Is this God of the Bible a true maniac to do this to his own Son? If he would do this to him, what might he do to the rest of us at some time in the heavenly future?"

I gazed at Doug, feeling wrung-out and exhilarated at the same time. Yes, he had brought up many harrowing issues. But there were others I could think of: God's attributes and how in some way they contradicted one another—righteousness, justice, and grace, for instance. God's weirdest book of all—Revelation—that seemed so important, yet so useless as far as the modern world was concerned. There was also the continuing pain and suffering in the world—earthquakes, tsunamis, tornadoes, hurricanes—to say nothing of the many "ethnic cleansings" that seemed to be going on in various places, and the scourges of cancer, AIDS, malaria, and assorted viruses. Finally, the biggie, the way the world hated him so vehemently, and hated his people. If he truly was kind, loving, and understanding, why did so many revile him to his face, and get away with it?

A Kernel of Hope

Doug sat there very still and quiet, and I sensed he had poured all the acid out. But then he said, "Undoubtedly, I have sounded a little furious in some of my criticisms here, but I have tried to voice them with all the passion I think others through history have. These are issues I have pondered for many years. I have not gone off with theologians who try to explain them away or with those who offer fancy but ultimately unsatisfying solutions to these problems. At times I have wondered why I even give a minute of my time to this God I have painted with such stark strokes. But I *do* want to know the truth. And I would like to believe he truly is the compassionate and loving God of the universe. So this is my plea: Help me understand. Show me some answers, and I'll study them through myself."

I thought about what he had said, and then I replied, "Doug, I think the reality is that each of these problems is actually a means to know God more intimately and with greater love and understanding than we would get if God sugarcoated the whole thing. He dealt with rampant and irreconcilable problems. But, I believe, he also can show us he knows solutions that came in the process and that will lead us into a deeper love and trust of him than ever before."

"I'm sure you believe that."

"I do. Listen. He says in Isaiah 55, verses 8 and 9, 'For my thoughts are not your thoughts, neither are your ways my ways,' declares the LORD. 'As the heavens are higher than the earth, so are my ways higher than your ways and my thoughts than your thoughts.'

"This verse explicitly tells us part of the problem: We can't, or won't, or are unable to think like God and do as he does. Therefore, we might be missing a great deal when we try to apply human thinking to God's work in human history. Truly, as C. S. Lewis wrote in the *Chronicles of Narnia*—God 'is not a tame lion.'"

"Yeah," he said. "I'm sure that's a good way of putting it. But it seems like quite a mountain of evidence, er, charges, don't you think?"

"I think you've brought up just about everything." I waited, then finally I said, "Why me?"

He gazed at me, then smiled cryptically. "I'll reveal that later. For now, just say that I think you have a good mind and I'd like to hear you out on these subjects."

"That's fair. And thanks for the vote of approval."

He chuckled. "Believe me, I'm going to put you through the wringer."

"I look forward to it," I said. "I've always needed a good wringing out."

He smiled again, then stood, holding out his hand. "Monday afternoon. Say three o'clock. Starbucks in Gladstone. That's where I live. Can you meet me there, at the one on the corner of Antioch and 64th?"

"I know it well," I said.

"Good. I'll buy you a latte. If you really have some good stuff for me, I may take you out for steak and lobster at your favorite restaurant."

"That would be the Lonestar Grill."

He nodded. "Good, there it'll only cost me fifty bucks."

I took his hand and gripped it. He looked down at our hands. "You have a good handshake," he said. "I can trust a man with a decent handshake."

"Thank you again."

"Good. Go home and study your brain off. I'm going to come to Starbucks loaded for bear."

"I'll bring my shield of faith."

He leaned back and laughed. "Good one."

Then he walked away, and I wondered if he'd really be there on Monday.

CHAPTER 2

The Test in the Garden

We All Had It Perfect, and Yet We Rejected It Wholesale

A Look at Our Problem-Filled World

The daily news stresses me out big-time. In fact, not long ago my community *was* the daily news. In 2003, a mega-tornado tore through Kansas City. The sirens resounded in the air, and my family, as we always do, hurried down to the basement of our three-story house. My wife stayed a little behind, but when the tornado struck and she saw someone's grill revolving in the air over our backyard, she decided to join us. She even thought to bring down our two laptop computers, since we didn't have backups out in cyberspace somewhere. If the computers sailed away into the muck, we'd both be finished as writers.

We all prayed the whole time that God would spare our house and us. We even prayed that if it did hit our house, that God would not allow it to hurt the two cats hiding somewhere upstairs, we knew not where. I also mentioned my antique toy collection. (Not hiding, but up there.)

Jeanette prayed about her juke boxes.

Alisha asked that her CD collection would not go up in the air.

Gardner requested that his GameBoy games would all survive the impact.

Aren't we spiritual?

After that, we got it together and started praying about the neighborhood.

A sound like a freight train passing just feet from our windows made us all cower for a full minute. But then, just as suddenly as it had come, the sound and shaking stopped. After a few minutes of silence, we cautiously climbed the stairs and found our house intact.

Then we hurried outside.

Already, people filled the street. I saw that a tree from our front yard was now piled up against our backyard fence. Someone's roof lay in the street just yards from my minivan, which didn't have a scratch on it.

We started down the street. It was a true horror show. Just a few houses down from ours, we found a community laid waste. Many houses were reduced to piles of sticks and mortar. Some had parts missing, as if the tornado cleaved off one room and left the rest standing as if nothing had touched it. Down one street, every house had been smashed to bits. We learned later that night on the news that more than three hundred houses in our neighborhood were felled, to say nothing of the damage in nearby communities.

This was the closest I've ever come to losing everything. Fortunately, for us, it came out to only $1,600 in insurance damages (minus the $500 deductible). Three trees were torn from their trunks and lay all over our backyard. Neighbors with chain saws soon arrived and our beloved maple and apple trees were transformed into firewood.

I have to marvel at the power of nature. And I still wonder why we were spared and others weren't.

A few years ago, you will remember the great tsunami in the Far Eastern Rim nations. Hundreds of thousands of people died. All kinds of Christian groups rushed to the scene, bringing supplies, food, medicine, and so on. But still, millions were affected, their homes and cities wiped out, their families gone forever. Why do these things happen in our world with such startling frequency?

Next was Hurricane Katrina. I know you've heard enough about this disaster to make you start screaming. But for many people in the American South, it was a gigantic problem, and for some, it still is. And it could happen again this summer. And next summer. And the next. Many times over.

Every year we read about it: devastation from the latest hurricanes, earthquakes, mudslides, forest fires, and a multitude of other problems, to say nothing of plagues, famines, and food shortages in many places in the world due to lack of rain.

I look at such events and cringe. How does anyone, Christian or otherwise, who believes in a good, loving, and gracious God, reconcile these situations with him? How can he stand by and let his beloved planet experience such destruction and death? Is there something seriously wrong with his heart, or is it something else? Is he the vengeful Creator we find in some other religions bent on making us miserable? Or worse, is he some Nazi Dr. Mengele-type who loves experimenting on his children to see how far he can push them?

Some who experienced severe damage and losses in the tornado were Christians who gathered in their basements and prayed, even as the tops of their houses were being sheared off and dashed into the dirt. Few of these people deserved what they got in any justifiable sense. It was just an "act of God" or the "fickleness of nature," whichever way you want to put it. No one can control those things, and no one has any answers as to why they happen.

That's where Doug comes back in. He walked into Starbucks and sat down at my table. He looked weary and irritated, and I worried our conversation might be affected. To start off friendly, I asked him how the writer's conference had gone for him.

"I got what I needed," he said. "What do you want—coffee, frozen latte, whatever you wish?"

I spelled out an order for some strawberry-yogurt concoction I'd read off the large menu above the counter. He nodded, walked off, and soon returned with two of the same. "Thought I'd try it out and see what a real theologian drinks," he said with a grimace. "See if it does me any good."

I had a slug and it went down smoothly. I noted again that he appeared distracted, maybe even upset. I suddenly realized I had to deal with this if we wanted to proceed. "You look like you ran into a truck this morning."

"Yeah," he sighed. "Tough situation."

"Something I can pray for?"

He shrugged. "It probably wouldn't do much good. I have this client. He took out a million-dollar policy about a year ago, very expensive. He was only about sixty years old. Of course, we checked him all out. Now he's dead. The police have ruled it suicide, and that cancels the contract. I had to tell the widow this morning."

I gulped. "Man, that must be tough."

"You'd be surprised how many people try to scam life insurance companies." He leaned back in his chair. "Anyway, I met her in my office and explained things. She went ballistic. I had to ask the police to come and take her home."

"Whoa!"

"Yeah. Frightening. Anyway, I'm ready for our discussion, believe me."

I reflected on this a moment. "Just out of curiosity, how do you handle things like this? I mean, emotionally? And telling the person?"

He sighed heavily. "It's business. You tell them the facts. Lay them out. Show them the clause in the contract. It's pretty simple."

"Do you try to offer, uh, condolences?"

"Sure, but that's the least of it. I didn't hold her hand and tell her, 'Now, now, he's in a better place,' if that's what you mean. No, she didn't even seem to give a rat's behind about the guy. She just wanted the money." He gazed at me, searching my eyes. "Look, I never said I was a pastor. I sell life insurance, big policies. I never get emotional. That would be bad. And stupid."

"I guess." I looked down at my Bible.

He touched my hand. "Hey, I leave the tears and the compassion to you guys. Have to. I can't let things like this get to me. If I did, I'd be in a mental hospital."

I nodded, wondering how I could ever do a job like that. I decided maybe jumping back into our discussion would be best. I wasn't going to turn him into a bleeding heart anyway.

"Look, I've been thinking about all you said the other day. And, as the first matter of business, I'd like to talk about the sin in the Garden of Eden, and the curse that followed. It explains a lot about our world, why we have disasters like Hurricane Katrina and 9/11, and so on. I could start with Genesis 1 and the creation, but I really don't think we need to get into some big evolution riff. We can deal with that later perhaps, but let's just let the Bible speak for itself. The bald Bible."

He nodded. "I'm game."

I opened to Genesis 3 and moved my Bible between us so we could both read. "Go ahead," he said. "I know it."

"Good."

We Look at the Event That Started All the Trouble

He slid out his pocket Bible and opened it expertly to the passage. I was surprised a Bible this small contained both the Old Testament and the New Testament. I decided not to ask him yet why he carried one.

"Here," I said, "Moses records the fateful decisions of the first two humans, Adam and Eve."

He eyed me skeptically. "You believe they existed?"

I returned his stare. "Look, if you don't happen to believe they were the actual first parents, or that this is just a mythical kind of story to explain how evil came into the world, that's fine. Bear with me for the time being. Not only did Moses write about them, but several other books of the Bible refer to them as real people and the creation as a real event. Jesus even spoke of them in a way that shows he accepted the whole situation as a fact of history."

"I realize that."

"Good. But that's not the point. If you have a better explanation for our world gone seriously awry, then feel free to voice it.

Otherwise, you may want to think hard about the one I'm about to offer."

He nodded. "Talk."

I took a breath, then a sip of my drink, leaned back, and looked directly into his eyes. He appeared open and interested, and I relaxed now. I sensed he would not prejudge me as some flaming Christian idiot. In fact, he appeared to relish hearing someone offer reasonable answers to his questions.

Clearing my throat, I said, "Adam and Eve's sin in the Garden of Eden was a simple one. They had complete run of the place. God commanded them to take care of it. But he gave them one rule: Do not eat of the 'tree of the knowledge of good and evil' (Genesis 2:17). It stood in the middle of the garden, perhaps to make sure they recognized it and even had to think about what it meant. We don't know that it sprouted apples, but apparently some delectable-looking fruit hung from its branches."

He sipped his drink, but his eyes never left mine.

"Perhaps for a while, Adam and Eve just avoided the tree. But the serpent, taken over by Satan himself—and if you don't believe in him, either, just hang in there. Some things may start to make sense—arrived and talked to Eve about the fruit. He led her to believe that God had lied to them about the consequences of eating it—'You shall surely die'—and that he kept them from it to prevent them from becoming like him, wise and powerful. The serpent guided her thinking, she ate the fruit, and then gave it to Adam (who was right there with her the whole time apparently), who also ate. They immediately gained the 'knowledge of good and evil,' saw they were naked, and sewed fig leaves together to cover themselves. When they heard God walking in the garden, they hid themselves because they felt tremendous guilt at what they'd done, and also because they had died spiritually in their hearts, so God no longer seemed a friend, guide, and leader, but judge and jury."

Doug leaned back and put his hands behind his head. "Keep going."

The Magnitude of That Sin

For a moment then," I continued, "step back and consider how great that particular sin was."

"Seems a tad trivial to me," Doug countered.

"Perhaps. But hear me out. Adam and Eve were free in a way no one would ever be afterward. They lived in a lavish garden. They could eat anything they wanted. They had animals that obeyed their every whim. They ruled. The only person (boss, king, leader, whatever) they answered to was God himself. And he probably seemed more like a kind, friendly, benign grandfather (even though they had no idea about grandfathers at the time) who wished them nothing but the best.

"He gave them this one rule: Don't eat of this tree. As you said in our previous talk, with contempt I might add"—I grinned and he returned it—"'All of creation hinging on eating some fruit? Absurd!' But think of the beauty of this one rule. It was simple. It was easy to obey—just don't eat the darn thing. It sat in the middle of the garden so they'd constantly see it and notice it. And it would give them the knowledge of good and evil, either way (I'll get to that in a moment)."

"Not a tough rule," Doug agreed.

"Right. It wasn't as if God said, 'Go climb Mount Everest, dance on the summit, slide down all the way to the ground, and then I'll give you everlasting life.' Or, 'Build New York City from the ground up, and then I'll truly bless you.' They had already been summarily blessed. Or, 'Write a song the whole world will sing ever after.'"

Doug laughed. He sang, "I want to teach the world to sing in perfect harmony . . ."

"Right. You know Coke!"

"Drink it all the time."

"I drink Fresca."

"A Coke product."

"They own everything."

"They're God," he said with a smirk.

"Right. So I'm building up their account either way. Anyway, this test didn't require talent, brains, or incredible endurance, just plain ol', regular, stiff-lipped obedience. Can't you see that God had to be rooting for them to succeed? Isn't it as if God said, 'Look, there's just this one thing: Will you hang in there with me on this and obey this simple rule? It's a little matter, nothing stupendous. But I have to let you face it. Otherwise, you'll never be entirely free, or human.'"

Doug countered, "Why this test, though?"

"I believe God had to find out if these two humans would actually go along with him in this earthly adventure. He already had an angelic rebellion on his hands—more about that later. He didn't want a human one. But he had to know: 'Will you obey me in this very little thing?'"

"But why obedience?" Doug said, leaning forward on his elbows. I felt as if I had him pinned to his seat with interest. "Why was it even an issue?"

"Think of it this way. God had begun a grand experiment. He placed two freestanding humans in a magnificent garden. He gave them everything they needed. He even planted a tree in the garden called the Tree of Life. If these humans ate from that tree, they would receive eternal life then and there, never to die, no matter what they did with the fruit of the other tree. However, before God could let them dine there, he had to make sure they would go along with him in the venture. Would they listen to him? Would they consult him when they had questions? Would they obey him in a small matter?"

I could see a question in his eyes, and I continued, "You see, if these people refused to obey God but God gave them eternal life, he'd have eternal trouble on his hands, as he already had with the angels. So he had to test them, make sure they'd be loyal. Would they obey this piddling, trivial, almost stupid and incredibly simple rule? It was the only thing he required to pave the way to eternal life."

Doug didn't look convinced.

"Okay," I said. "Here's an illustration. Say you want to give your son a brand-new Corvette. He's been a good kid, no trouble, and you think you'd like to reward him. But you're not sure he can be responsible enough to drive around in a real Corvette. So you give him a test. You take him out in your Miata and tell him to drive. 'Just obey the rules of the road, and I have a big gift for you,' you tell him. You get out there. But the Miata just goes to his head. He drives over the speed limit, sails through stop signs, and doesn't obey red lights. It's crazy. What has happened to this kid? You don't know. But would you give him the Corvette now?"

"Heck, no!" Doug roared with a big smile.

"Well, that's the scenario. God couldn't give them the Corvette—eternal life—if they couldn't obey some of his very simple rules. So he gave them one to test them out, see what they'd do."

"Yeah, I can see it now," Doug said.

I told him, "There's a verse of Scripture that has always struck me: 'Whoever can be trusted with very little can also be trusted with much, and whoever is dishonest with very little will also be dishonest with much.' It's in Luke 16:10."

"I think I've read it. One of those Scripture passages that's just plain common sense."

"Good. God gave Adam and Eve a chance to be faithful in a very little thing so he could be sure they would be faithful in much bigger things—when they received eternal life after passing the test and needed to be trusted about everything else. You ask, 'Didn't God know what they would do? Isn't God all-knowing?' Certainly. That's revealed throughout the Bible. But this situation had to be worked out in a real time and place, and in that sense God's test was a real test. It wasn't a manipulation or a taunt. God wanted to show them who they were and what they were made of, something he has to do with every one of us sooner or later.

"In fact, Scripture reveals that in some sense every person in human history was 'in' Adam at that time. We all voted with Adam whichever way he chose. Our destiny was wrapped up in that moment, too. Take a look at Romans 5, verses 12 through 14."

I flipped pages and was amazed how quickly Doug found the passage in his own Bible. I said, "You are a very adept student of the Bible."

"It's been the most interesting and the most infuriating book I've ever read."

I laughed. "I can ID with that."

He grinned and we went on, reading through the verses.

"Adam represented all of us, and we were all, in some sense, with him in this test. There's some disagreement about that among theologians, but at least that's what I believe, and what makes sense to me. Even if you don't happen to believe that, ask the question: Who has obeyed God perfectly in anything since? If you're mad at Adam and Eve for blowing it, just consider how the rest of us are doing on 'do not steal, do not lie, do not covet, and do not commit adultery.'"

He nodded, finishing off his drink. "Okay, I think it's a good explanation. I'm impressed, at least on this one point."

Feeling buoyed up by that remark, I said, "Well, it gets hairier along the way."

"I expect it does. Go back to the test."

"Well, seeing it that way, you realize this was no trivial, unreasonable test. It was an easy thing to obey, and it was an easy thing to succeed in. God didn't make it tough, or painful, or even stressing."

Doug blew frustrated air out between tight lips. "Then why didn't God help them pass it?"

I cocked my head with surprise. "Don't you think he tried to? He told them what the test was and what the consequences of failing were. He walked with them every day in the garden. Presumably they could discuss it with him. 'So why can't we eat of the tree again?' 'And what happens if we mess up?' 'And what's the point? It's such a little thing. And that fruit looks so good.'

"Looking through the whole Bible, you find that God is like this: He wants a relationship with those who believe in him. That means conversation, questions, arguments, if necessary. God is not afraid of anything we throw at him. So if other passages are any indication, and even though we don't see it in the stripped-down passage here, it's probably true that Adam, Eve, and God talked about many things. And that they could raise any issue they wanted."

"I find that amazing about God," Doug said. "At least what Christians tell me about this so-called relationship."

"That's the God who wants us to know him—intimately, personally, eternally. Don't you think it's a good thing?"

"Sure. But . . ."

"But what?"

"It just seems so impossible. Why would he care that much about you or me?"

"A great question." I thought for a second. "Why? Because that's the way he is. That's the real God of the universe. Do you know anything about Islam?"

"Allah? Sure. He's this aloof potentate way up there whom no one can see or know or talk to or anything."

"Right. Would you find such a God worth following or even interesting?"

"Not really."

"So you can see why God values a true relationship and fellowship. And because he's eternal, omnipresent, all-powerful, he can maintain those relationships with everyone at once."

"It blows my mind," he said. "But then again, it's a very attractive element of Christianity, I have to admit."

I liked his honesty. "Good. So you see, with Adam and Eve, while God might have offered explanations and answers to their questions, the one thing God couldn't do was force them to do the right thing. That would have taken away their real freedom and rendered them little more than robots. But they had to be tested in this arena, the core element of their morality and values: Would they obey God? Even when they didn't fully understand why he had made this order? Even when it seemed like such a harmless little thing to do? Even when they had no idea what real death meant, and all it entailed?"

"So it really is quite a large matter?" Doug eyed me with interest, and I could see the lightbulbs going off in his mind. Glancing around, I noticed several others sitting in the store, working at computers, tasting their drinks, and paying no attention to us. That was fine with me. Doug was certainly enough to tango with. I didn't need someone else horning in with his two cents' worth.

"It *is* a large matter," I said. "The most important matter in the universe. It's what every one of us faces every day, over and over."

"I'm beginning to see it."

"And isn't that the essence of faith and obedience? To go with God, to take him at his word, to follow him even when we can't comprehend all the small print and complex details? Isn't the most basic expression of faith trusting God at the core of our beings, even when he seems a little strange, or tough, or demanding? Just take the issue of sexual immorality. God has made it clear: Sex is allowable only in the context of marriage. No fornication. No adultery. No sex with same-gender people. No animals. Et cetera. God has even told us why—because it defiles us, fills us with guilt, and further separates us from him. But what do we do? We say, 'So what? I'm doing it anyway.' The problem isn't us not comprehending the truth. It's simply that we refuse to listen to him and obey him, even when we realize God's intent is blessing, not stealing from us something pure and valuable."

He looked a little uncomfortable, and I wondered if he had some sin issue that kept him from God. But I decided not to probe that. Not yet.

"So our problem is the will, not the head?"

"Right." I nodded sadly, once again reckoning with the implications of what that little test had done in human history. "So Adam and Eve failed along with all the rest of us. We couldn't obey God in this very little thing, and we certainly haven't in the big things that have followed."

He looked a little grim, but I plodded on. "God tested humankind and found us wanting. We weren't even willing to obey him in the easiest matters of life."

"Pretty bad foul-up," Doug said.

"To be sure. We had it all—a perfect environment, all our needs met, a lovely marriage, a God who cared—and we threw it all away because we wanted something more. We wanted to be like God. We wanted to rid ourselves of him and take over everything ourselves."

"Sounds like what's wrong with the whole world today," Doug said. "I mean everyone I know is like that. We all want to be the boss, the big honcho, to call the shots. We don't like anyone telling us what to do."

I laughed. "Think about it. Isn't this a perfect picture of what it's like to be human? Doesn't it ring true to reality? It's a universal thing. It's not like this is some weirdo story no one can identify with. It's all of us at once. Do you see that?"

He nodded. "I never thought of it that way. But I can see it."

"The truth is, Doug, you find this over and over in the Bible. The stories, the events, the situations—all of them are pictures of us. Take any one of them, and you can find yourself in it somewhere. That's why I believe God—not just some human—is the author of this book. He crafted it so we could all see who we really are and hopefully to point us back to himself."

Doug shook his head sadly. "So we had it made, and it wasn't enough."

"Exactly. One of the great principles of living life on planet Earth. We're never content. The other side of the fence always looks greener. That's a basic principle of Satan's approach to temptation. He tells us this about drugs, illicit sex, driving too fast, whatever: 'Hey, look at this. It's great. Don't you want some of this?' We may know God's rule about such things, as I said: 'Do not steal. Do not take God's name in vain.' But many times, we just don't care. We go for it, to our peril."

Doug stared down at the table. "I've seen it over and over in my life."

I sensed the pain beneath the surface here, and I said gently, "Maybe that's why we're here right now, talking about it. So God can help you start making better decisions and ultimately to begin a relationship with him."

He looked up, curiosity in his eyes. "You think so?"

"I think everything in life is orchestrated by God to get us moving in his direction."

He sighed. "I hope so. And at the same time, I'm terrified."

"Good. Because it's going to get worse."

He grinned. "So what's next?"

"We'll look at what happens when God responds to Adam and Eve's sin."

"Let's get on with it."

CHAPTER 3

The Curse on the Serpent Explains Satan's Hatred for Humankind and God, and Why He Does Everything to Mess Up Our World

God Deals with Satan's Sin

I pressed on, glancing at my watch and amazed that already an hour had passed. "When God found the two of them, asked them why they were hiding, and the whole thing came out—he saw they had failed the test. And with one rather amazing sequence of explanations: Adam told God that the woman *he'd given him* had gotten him to eat the fruit of the tree. So Adam's basically saying, 'It's your fault, God.' And then God turned to Eve, who immediately blamed the serpent. The serpent turned to his left and right, and just mumbled, 'Uh-oh.'"

Doug smiled. "You bet that's what he said."

"Yeah, the whole blame game began at that moment, and it hasn't stopped since."

"Been there, done that," Doug said and gave me a little thumbs-up. "Used it many times with great effect."

I chuckled. "So at that point, God pronounced this curse on them, the serpent, and everything else, and it's this curse that is important here. Let's read the words of the curse carefully:

> So the LORD God said to the serpent, "Because you have done this, cursed are you above all the livestock and all the wild animals! You will crawl on your belly and you will eat dust all the days of your life. And I will put enmity between you and the woman, and between your offspring and hers; he will crush your head, and you will strike his heel."
>
> To the woman he said, "I will greatly increase your pains in childbearing: with pain you will give birth to children. Your desire will be for your husband, and he will rule over you."
>
> To Adam he said, "Because you listened to your wife and ate from the tree about which I commanded you, 'You must not eat of it,' cursed is the ground because of you; through painful toil you will eat of it all the days of your life. It will produce thorns and thistles for you, and you will eat the plants of the field. By the sweat of your brow you will eat your food until you return to the ground, since from it you were taken; for dust you are and to dust you will return." (Genesis 3:14–19)

"It's pretty astonishing. But why such an all-encompassing curse?" Doug asked.

I took a breath, thinking it all through one more time. "Because God saw that in order to get people to obey, love, and follow him, which he had hoped would happen with Adam and Eve but didn't, he realized something else would have to be done. Their actions not only cut them off from God, but they caused a total spiritual destruction of planet Earth. This is how Paul put it in Romans 8:20–22:

> For the creation was subjected to frustration, not by its own choice, but by the will of the one who subjected it, in hope that the creation itself will be liberated from its bondage to decay and brought into the glorious freedom of the children of God. We

know that the whole creation has been groaning as in the pains of childbirth right up to the present time.

"What's that saying to you?" I asked.

"Sounds like the creation was messed up pretty badly."

"Exactly. This whole world, which God had taken such care to create, was now doomed. He couldn't let it go on forever because the evil that now infested it would not just die out, but it would become a juggernaut of evil for all eternity. God had to destroy it entirely, and that was the whole reason for the curse that follows. In effect, our first parents messed it up for good by allowing this evil presence to take over. In fact, John says in 1 John 5:19 that Satan became the ruler over the whole planet at that time. How would you like to live in a world run by him and never be able to escape?"

"Probably a little like living under the Taliban on steroids," Doug said with a smirk.

"Far worse. So it couldn't be fixed simply by rewinding the tape or wrapping something in duct tape. No, one day God would have to redo it all, with people who would obey, trust, and truly love him. Peter refers to this in 2 Peter 3:13 when he says, 'We are looking forward to a new heaven and a new earth, the home of righteousness.' Goodness, kindness, doing what's right all went out the window with Adam and Eve's sin. A whole new universe would have to be created and populated with people who truly would obey God. But to get them to that point, God had to curse the earth and its inhabitants in a way that he knew would ultimately turn them around. We'll get to this a little later."

Doug still looked confused. "Wait a second! I still don't see why God had to go to such an extreme. A curse? Wasn't that jumping to conclusions?"

I stopped to think. "Okay, here's another example. When Adam and Eve refused to obey this one rule, something intrinsic and eternal happened to them, in their deepest, most personal and precious humanity. They experienced spiritual death. They lost their sense of God and his love. They cut themselves off from him. He was still there, but they felt distant, forsaken, and above all guilt-ridden, to say nothing of angry, bitter, and out to get some payback. In addition, their bodies became infected, and one day they would die physically. That spiritual and physical death has led to every sin every person ever committed."

For a moment, I tried to think of a way to make it plainer. "Here's a thought," I said, something coming to me. "Think of the original creation as a beautiful house. Everything was perfect, just, truthful, and righteous. But with the sin in the garden, they razed the house on the inside. The outward façade looked okay, but step inside and it's a burned-out mess. No commitment to God and his truth. No belief in doing what was right and good. No desire to follow the principles of holiness and righteousness. It's so bad, it can't be rebuilt or rehabilitated because what had happened inside would spread to the outside eventually, and then it would have to be torn down. The only thing left to do is for the builder to condemn it and eventually start over.

"For a second, look at what follows this wrong turn. It wasn't like several people just got nasty over dinner conversation. No, Cain murders Abel in the next scene. Others follow, like Lamech, who boasts he'll avenge himself sevenfold for anyone who does him wrong. In Genesis 6:5, we see how really bad it became: 'The LORD saw how great man's wickedness on the earth had become, and that every inclination of the thoughts of his heart was only evil all the time.' We don't know everything these people were doing, but Paul gives us an inkling in 2 Timothy 3:1–5, because the Bible sometimes compares the 'last days' of the world to Noah's time:

> There will be terrible times in the last days. People will be lovers of themselves, lovers of money, boastful, proud, abusive, disobedient to their parents, ungrateful, unholy, without love, unforgiving, slanderous, without self-control, brutal, not lovers of the good, treacherous, rash, conceited, lovers of pleasure rather than lovers of God—having a form of godliness but denying its power. Have nothing to do with them.

"How do you think you'd fare in conditions like that?"

Doug shook his head. "But it really doesn't look that bad today. I mean—"

"Hey, you have to realize this—we live in a world that God has transformed. He has done millions of checks and balances to change our direction. The Bible, Jesus, Christianity, have influenced and rebuilt billions of people. Governments like our own were fashioned based on the laws and truths of God's Word. The Spirit of God works through Christians and others the world over. It's not as bad as it could be because of factors like that. But sooner or later God will still have to start over with a new world inhabited only by people of faith if he wants the kind of righteousness and holiness in it that he longs for."

Doug shook his head. "But if God knew this would happen, if he's omniscient and saw every decision any of us will ever make before he even created the world—I think it says that somewhere—then why? Why didn't he create Adam and Eve so they wouldn't make this mistake?"

"We'll get to that," I said. "But realize, even though God is omniscient, in other words, knows all—the past, present, and future—these events still had to be worked out in real time for all the participants. God relates to them not as this person who knows all and sees all, but as a Lord, Friend, and Guide who must help them wade through the real problems of everyday life. The Bible was written as history unfolded, not as God wished it might have been, or as if he were high above it all just watching. He has been involved in it from day 1. And he acts, speaks, and reacts as a person who deals with things as they happen. Just think how weird it would get if God had said to Adam and Eve, 'Look, I knew this would happen. Sorry I let it go that way. But that's part of my plan, so you'll just have to live with it.'

"So Adam says, 'You mean you planned this to happen? You mean you could have stopped us? You mean—'

"'Hold it, hold it,' God cries. 'If you want to see things from my perspective, you'd have to become like God. And that can't happen.'

"'But . . . but . . . you betrayed us. You're a crumb. How could we ever trust you after this?'

"You see, even though God had a plan before any of these things happened, even though he in his omniscience can work around and within events, he still can't force autonomous creatures to do whatever he wants. Imagine if every time you were about to do something wrong God jumped in front of you, whacked you across the cheek, and said, 'Hey, idiot-boy, that's not a good idea. I can't let you do that.' It would get impossibly complicated, to say nothing of violating our autonomy."

"Almost like the U.S. government."

I laughed. "You bet. So the reality is that God is in one sense above us all and working behind the scenes in his own way, while at the same time letting us all do as we please. He warns us when necessary. He speaks to us through our conscience. Sometimes he orchestrates circumstances to help us or preserve us—how many times do you think you might have been killed by a drunk driver if God didn't occasionally work to prevent such things in this world? But on the whole, God has chosen to let circumstances unfold as they would naturally, without his constant intervention. He deals with it step-by-step, but never forces anyone to do his bidding. Otherwise, he'd have to turn us all into robots, punch in the numbers, and we, like little computer programs, would do what he wanted. Who wants a world like that?

"So we as God's subjects have to look at this as if he is just another player, rather than from a divine standpoint, which is impossible for us to fully comprehend."

"Okay, I think I get that. But I still don't see precisely why God had to levy this incredible curse. It seems like overkill to me."

I sighed and searched for another answer. "Good question. But the truth is God couldn't repair what had happened to his world, as I've tried to show. Adam and Eve's disobedience made them slaves to Satan and corrupted the whole universe. It was like letting botulism into a can of beans. You don't try to fix them. You can't put the beans through a sieve or through some process. They're ruined. You throw them out—eventually. At the same time, though, unlike a can of beans, the world had many valuable elements that could be used for a good purpose until the 'throwing out' time came. Certainly, God didn't want to send Adam and Eve off to hell and be done with them. Didn't he owe it to them to offer his help, to figure out a way to get them back to being blessed, to enable them to find a way back to him and back to that eternal life they must have sorely wished for? Certainly he did. As a result, he would have to do something else."

"What?"

"Redeem it. Save it. Find a way for the people of earth to come back to him and have another chance at hope and joy and eternal friendship with him before he completely destroyed the old creation."

"Jesus?"

"Correct."

"Which is why things today aren't as awful as they could be."

I nodded, looking down at my Bible. "Anyone who reads much of this book will see that God has always tried to find creative ways of preserving those who would be faithful to him. I mean, think of what he might have done to Adam and Eve and the whole universe at that moment. He could have killed them on the spot and sent them off to hell or whatever and been done with it, then tried again. But who's to say the same thing wouldn't happen all over again?

"You have to remember that somehow every person who has ever lived was in Adam and Eve in some sense from the start. So to kill them off would be killing off the whole future human race. Why would God want to do that, when he knew he could use this horrible downturn to engineer a situation that could lead to great good? You know that verse, Romans 8:28—'God works for the good of those who love him'—so God never just destroys something like we do when some project doesn't work out. Scripture reveals that God always finds ways of preserving the faithful and getting good out of the bad.

"As a result, he chose to make a way for people the world over to escape from their destroyed planet and come to a new place, where everything would be perfect again, better than the first model, a place where virtue and goodness would endure and never crash again. But first, each of those people had to pass another test."

"What was that?"

"Faith. Being born again. Starting anew. Being made new on the inside. That's what being born again is all about. Jesus starting over on our insides so we could inhabit that new world he planned to create. But that's getting ahead of things."

"Sure is," Doug said. "I'm not ready for that yet." He smiled. "You ask me to walk an aisle, and I'm out of here."

I laughed. "Believe me, I will never ask you to do that. Not in Starbucks. It doesn't even have an aisle."

He leaned back and laughed. I really began to like this guy.

I said, "Okay, let's take a look at the curse on Satan."

The Curse on Satan

In order of their respective sins," I continued, "God started with the serpent first. God blasted him several ways:

He cursed him above all animals.

He would crawl on his belly and eat dust all the days of his life.

God would put hatred between him and the woman.

He would also put hatred between the serpent's "seed" and her "seed."

The "seed" of the woman would ultimately kill him after he managed to wound that seed on his heel.

"Heavy stuff," Doug mused.

"You bet. But you have to remember that this curse was not just on an animal, but on Satan himself, who had possessed the rather innocent serpent. We know that from Revelation 12:9, which says, 'The great dragon was hurled down—that ancient serpent called the devil, or Satan, who leads the whole world astray.'

"In that regard, I believe the original serpent, a 'beast of the field' according to Genesis 3:1, being more 'crafty' than any other wild animal, could talk. That might have been how Eve was so easily beguiled. The serpent acted as her friend and comrade before Satan ever possessed him, so she probably trusted him.

"The important thing, regardless of whether that's true, is that this curse would have tremendous consequences for both Satan and our world. Consider some of the problems that resulted."

Doug listened intently and I could see his bright eyes fixed on mine as if I was telling him things he'd really never heard before.

I took a deep breath. "First, Satan would hate God above everyone else, even more than he already did. God turned him into something despicable and ugly in the real world (a snake) and presumably that same transformation happened in the spiritual, angelic world that Satan inhabited. He had once been an 'angel of light,' but God stripped that guise away. God judged him with an ugliness he would certainly have found humiliating."

"I'm not exactly fond of snakes myself," Doug said.

I laughed. "Slimy, nasty, poisonous. Yeah, I'm sure Satan really tracked with that getup."

We both smiled. "The second thing is that Satan would 'eat dust.' He would never have any satisfaction in the things of this world or his world. His thirst would only grow, and his hunger would never be satisfied. This would magnify his hatred for God even more, and make him want to destroy God and all that belonged to him."

"I never thought about that," Doug suddenly said. "Very good. A true insight. So Satan could never experience a single pleasure ever again?"

"Right. I think that's it. Here, Satan probably thought he'd made the heist of the millennium, and now he ends up choking on dirt."

"That put a chink in his armor."

I laughed. "I bet right now he's sitting out there somewhere just wishing he could have a decent drink of water."

"Please. Beer or something. Michelob. Not just water."

"Fine." I grinned and pressed on. "Third, God would put 'enmity' between the woman and Satan. This part of the curse is interesting in two ways. It explains the natural revulsion that most women have for snakes. And it also explains why many women often exhibit a greater spiritual development than men—because they hate Satan and all he stands for—lies, distrust, dishonesty, and trickery. Who of us who are married doesn't recognize how much women revile these tactics, which they often find in their men?"

"Oh, yeah. I'm married to one of them," Doug said with a chuckle.

"Aren't we all?" I nodded knowingly. "Fourth, there would be enmity between 'his seed' and 'her seed.' What is this?"

"Her children and his?"

"Yes, 'seed' normally referred to progeny, the children of the woman's womb. But why 'her' seed, not 'his and her' seed as is the reality?"

"An interesting sidelight," Doug said.

"It's an important point, and why we have to see Scripture as inspired by God. Otherwise, we could just say it was an oversight by the writer. But if God really is the author of this book, it's there for a purpose. But what purpose?"

"Well," Doug said, squinting, "Jesus was born of a woman, supposedly, without the 'seed' of a man."

"Precisely," I said, nodding. "I see this statement as a prophecy of the virgin birth of Christ and his battle with Satan many centuries after this event. Christ is the special 'seed' of the woman, not the man, and that is how the Bible says he came into the world. His war with Satan is well documented in the Gospels."

"Amazing. Even back then, right at the beginning, God's talking about Jesus."

"Yes, and think of it coming at that moment. What a puzzle that must have been to Adam and Eve and all the people after."

"Wouldn't be figured out till Jesus came, I guess," Doug said.

"Now you're thinking like a believer."

He laughed. "Don't give me that much credit, please!"

"The fifth thing is that Satan would 'bruise' him on the heel, and he would 'bruise' Satan on the head. What is this but a reference to the battle between the two in which Christ mortally wounded Satan by rising from the dead, while Satan only sent him into the grave for a weekend?"

"Really heavy stuff," Doug said.

"Right, and it all happened as a result of failing the test in the garden and fouling up God's plan for a happy, healthy humanity."

"I can see it having far-reaching consequences all the way down to today, actually," he said. "It explains a lot."

"It really does. And you can see from this that these horrific consequences of the curse on Satan led to such things as his great enmity for Christ and the Jews, his hatred of all those connected with God—Christians—and his determination to lead anyone astray who is allied with Christ. In fact, I believe that the great horrors the world has inflicted on the Jews throughout history stem from this satanic anger. The Jews gave the world the Bible and Jesus, the two things Satan most despises. So he turns his ire toward the Jews at every turn. What better way to explain the fact that the Jews remain a separate race, hated and rejected by many in the world, even though for centuries they were scattered throughout the earth, with no nation to call their own? Their survival to this day is a testimony to God's love, and their persecution to this day is Satan's furious answer to that love."

Doug's lips crinkled with thought. "Interesting. I never realized that, either."

"Wow! I must be a genius," I said with a grin.

"I wouldn't go that far."

"The thing is, this curse on Satan touches every one of us, especially those who have become Christians. Satan despises God and anyone allied with him, and he will do all he can to destroy those people. I don't know that Satan can manipulate the weather, but according to the book of Job, chapter 1, he can. And it may be that many of the scourges we see in the world today are his direct hits on the people he abhors, whether they're Christian or not."

"You're saying the weather is a result of Satan's manipulations?" Doug queried, his eyes narrowing.

"No, I'm not saying all disasters are satanic. I have a better answer for that later on. But it's clear in the Bible, from Job and the fact 'the whole world lies in the power of the evil one,' according to 1 John 5:19, he may have some power there."

Doug nodded. "I have to admit, it's a very interesting take on things."

"Good." I paused and thought maybe something more down-to-earth than all this theology would break through.

"Perhaps a personal story will help you understand what I mean here. When I became a Christian over a weekend in August 1972, I discovered an intense inner sense of God's presence, joy, and love unlike any other I experienced before that time or since. On the drive home that Sunday night I confronted my parents about what had happened to me. When they refused to accept what I told them, I became angry and jumped out when we pulled into our driveway, and walked away. At the time, I had recently graduated from college and was living at home that summer logging some extra credits toward attending medical school.

"As I walked up the street, I pulled out my wallet and dropped it on the ground. I emptied my pockets as a symbol of leaving my old life and joining a band of Christians somewhere on the planet. My father followed me up the street, arguing with me and trying to persuade me to talk more, come home, and act civilly. I told him, 'Your face and your heart are filled with Satan. I can't go back.' When he looked into my eyes as I said this, I actually thought I saw the image of Satan glaring back through him at me."

"This really happened?" Doug said.

"Absolutely."

"I would have slapped you."

"I think my dad almost did."

His eyes widened. "So what happened then?"

"He left me at that point, and I continued up the street, confused and wondering what God wanted of me. I didn't realize Satan was trying hard to keep me on this crazy kick about finding a 'Jesus Freak commune' somewhere.

"That night, I walked to the house of the folks who put me on the journey toward Christ in the first place. When I got there, they thought I was high on drugs from the way I looked—hair every which way, dirty, barefoot. But I convinced them I had met Jesus. When I told them all that had happened, they called a friend in to counsel me. This friend, named Betsy, led me through the 'Four Spiritual Laws' from the Campus Crusade for Christ booklet of the same name. I told her accepting Jesus like that was what I'd done a few days before. When I informed her I had a job to report to that morning, and that I had walked out on my parents, she turned to the Ten Commandments and read me the fifth one, about honoring your parents. She asked me point-blank, 'Do you think what you did tonight honored them as God says we must?'

"Pricked in heart, I shook my head. Betsy counseled me to go home, apologize for my impetuous actions, and 'to live a truly godly life before them that would make them want the God I believed in.' She also said I had a responsibility to report to my job, and she showed me other Scripture passages about how God wants us to obey his laws and live out his truth before the world."

"You were the classic fanatic."

"Until that moment, I guess. But I knew she was right and I sensed that Satan had been trying hard to derail me from doing the things that would win God's favor and stop the Enemy's influence in my family, if there was one.

"My friends drove me home, and at three in the morning, I found the back door unlocked. I walked in, my heart pounding, and knocked on my parents' bedroom door. My dad jumped up and hugged me, telling me, for the first time in my life, that he loved me. He and mom got me into bed. After they went back to their room, I found a Bible and hid it under my pillow. I felt as if I'd just faced off a direct attack of Satan trying to steer me into something crazy that would leave me bereft of my family."

"Amazing story," Doug said.

"I really believe I was under attack, Doug, a kind of attack that would happen many times in my life thereafter. Satan is real. He hates God and Jesus and his people. And he will do anything to hurt, frustrate, and defile them in the eyes of the world."

"I believe it," he said. "Jimmy Swaggart. Ted Haggard. Those guys."

"Right. Satan tries constantly to get believers to commit sins in order to bring shame to the name of God. That's exactly what the Bible says, and what Paul also says in Romans—that the Gentiles blaspheme the name of God because of what we believers often do."

"Interesting," he said. "I never thought of that."

"Well, neither did I till right now."

He grinned. "You're lying."

"Yes, actually, I had that one down seven seconds after I became a Christian at the age of twenty-one."

"You're cracked."

"Look, I'm not going to snow you. I study the Bible all the time. It's probably my highest passion in life."

"I believe it."

I regarded his wide eyes, his concentrated manner, and in my heart I just prayed, "God, you have to bring this guy into your kingdom. I won't be able to stand it if we lose him."

Doug regarded me curiously. "What?"

"I'll tell you about it later. The point is, we can't put everything off on Satan. Many times our own choices and actions cause our biggest problems. But there are times in every life when he tries to lay us in the dust."

"I've actually seen it," Doug said. "Many times."

"I bet you have. And it all goes back to this curse. Satan and one-third of the angels, who rebelled with him, create havoc and trouble all over the world. In the Bible they're called demons, and they're everywhere. The Enemy lashes out to this day, and he will do anything to dethrone God and gain the right to rule himself."

"But if that's the case," Doug said, "we really *are* doomed."

"No. All this would lead to God's plan for buying it all back— redeeming it—from Satan, evil, death, and all that, and giving it all a chance at new life."

"How?"

The Curse Broken

I took a breath. "God does not want us to fear Satan. When Jesus died on the cross and rose again three days later, he summarily defeated Satan. Sin, used by the Devil to destroy and deter God's people, was forgiven. Death, which Satan employed to stoke fear into the heart of every person, was terminated, at least in an eternal sense. Jesus fixed both problems in one swift blow, and Satan could do little more than run for the hills.

"That doesn't mean he isn't still active. Clearly, all over the world, he uses his tools of lying, deception, trickery, and thought control to lead people into all sorts of crimes. But for the Christian, Satan's power is broken. He can no longer slay us with guilt over sin, or terror in the face of death. Jesus set us free from the curse that turned Satan into a monster. We can spit in his face all we want. He is little more than a straw potentate, with no real power to hurt us."

"I never saw it that way," Doug said, rubbing his chin. I was glad I'd gotten to him.

"But that's only one-third of the curse," I reminded him.

CHAPTER 4

The Curse on the Woman Caused the Whole Battle of the Sexes That Rages in the World Today

How God Dealt with Eve's Sin

It was past five o'clock. We'd been at it more than two hours. "Do you need to go home?"

"I can get a sandwich. Let's keep going."

"It's your life," I said and he smiled.

"You're an interesting guy," he said, and I found myself praying again for his salvation as we spoke. "You talk like it's so natural and real. I never heard any preacher talk like you."

"I'm not some magic person. There are many people smarter and better explainers than me."

"Still, you make it easy to understand. But don't let me interrupt you."

"It gets more interesting as you move on to the second part of the curse, the one God pronounced on the woman. Genesis 3:16 says, "To the woman he said, 'I will greatly increase your pains in childbearing; with pain you will give birth to children. Your desire will be for your husband, and he will rule over you.'

45

"Take a look at that. From this, we see several specific consequences of Eve's sin:

"First, God would 'greatly multiply' her pain in childbirth.
Before this, a woman bearing a child apparently would not have
experienced much pain. But afterward, it became part of the fab-
ric of all of life. Why did God inflict this agony on women forever
after?"

Doug's lips crinkled. "I think when I discipline my kids, I sometimes give them some long-lasting element of the discipline, so
they'll be reminded of what happened and motivated not to do it
again."

"Very good," I said. "I think that part of the curse would
remind each woman when she brought a child into the world of
that initial sin. He wanted her to think long and hard about what
had happened, and this would be one vehicle that would provide
that memory and the reflection that could come with it. It would
also remind women to want something better in the future, a new
world, a place where pain wouldn't exist."

"I can see that."

"Did you know that most animals have little to no pain in
birthing? Only when there're complications and such?"

"I've heard it."

"Women stand alone in this matter."

He nodded. "It's an interesting point. I've heard it many times,
but never thought of it that way."

"The truth is that just about everything God does in life is
meant to point us to the need for salvation. But even more than
that, isn't it amazing the Bible offers this testimony, whereas, to my
knowledge, no other religion does?"

His eyes narrowed. "So what are you saying?"

"One of the things I'm going to bring up over and over is how
God embeds in the Bible so many things that point to him. This is
one of them. How did Moses happen to know this? Why would he
think it anything other than normal? God revealed it to him. And
we all know now that a woman giving birth is not just a human
act, but God reminding us all again that he's behind it all, nothing's

an accident, nothing happens just because evolution made it that way or something."

Doug scratched his nose and sighed. "I guess it does make sense. But why so much pain?"

I laughed. "Would a little have had any effect?"

"Yeah, I see your point."

"Good." I paused and gazed at the passage for a moment. What I needed to say next might be the biggest mindblower of all, and I wanted to phrase it carefully. "Now the second thing about this curse: God says Eve's 'desire' would be for her husband, but he would 'rule' over her. What do you think that's all about?"

"She'll still want her husband, even though she knows having his kids will cost her."

I nodded thoughtfully. "That's what some think. But this is a very interesting expression, found only in one other place in the Old Testament: in the story of Cain and the rejection of his sacrifice to God. God told Cain in Genesis 4:7, 'If you do not do what is right, sin is crouching at your door; it desires to have you, but you must master it.'"

Doug's brow crinkled. "So this desire is not a good one?"

"No. In fact, consider the situation for Cain. Sin, temptation, and evil itself 'crouched' at his door. Sin 'desired' to control and overwhelm him, but he had to master, or rule, it—'crush it down and bring it under control.'"

"That changes the whole tenor of the curse," Doug said.

"Right. On first reading, it sounds like God means a nice thing—the pain would not keep her from loving her husband. But in reality it's not. Some have tried to say the second part of the curse on Eve mitigates the first part of the curse, the pain in childbirth. Yes, she would suffer great pain, but she 'would still desire her husband' sexually, like you just said.

"But this doesn't wash. Of the three curses in Genesis 3, none of them offers words of consolation after the harsh, stark statement of the blight in the first part. If this is a curse, then there has to be something else here.

"What that is becomes apparent from the Cain passage. God is cursing woman with the whole feminist/male chauvinist conflict. Forever after Eve's sin, women would 'desire' to 'rule over and control' their men. They would seek to dominate them and lead them around by their noses. Women would regard them as pigs and chauvinists and talk about them like they were dirt.

"Nonetheless, it wouldn't work. In the end, the men would crush and rule and 'break' the women who tried to rule over them. They would (most of them) dominate the women in their lives, and the women would just have to live with it. In other words, God is cursing women to living in an environment where they would cease to be the complete and fulfilled persons they might wish, because the men, in seeking to overcome the women's influence and attitudes, would crush them down to dust."

Doug eyed me with amazement. "That's incredible. But it really does explain a lot in life, why women are like they are, why men are like they are. Not you and me, of course, and our wives, but everyone else."

I laughed heartily. "This explains the whole male-female controversy that continues to rage in our world. God didn't create man and woman that way. When Adam and Eve came into existence, they lived in perfect harmony. They were partners, team members, lovers, perfectly complementing each other. But their sin rendered their relationship dysfunctional.

"As a result, women have to fight for every right, break, joy, and hope in this world. In most of the earth, apart from the United States, women are readily and completely crushed into total submission. They can't do anything unless the men say they can do it."

Doug nodded sadly.

I said, "Think about Islam. In it, women are little more than third- or fourth-class citizens, if not outright slaves. Their husbands 'own' them. They have no rights. Their husbands can divorce them simply by saying three times, 'I divorce you.' In most countries dominated by Islamic principles, women can't vote, drive a car, go to school, teach men or boys, or wear normal clothing. They are completely subjugated. Many other religions are like that, too, and even in some supposedly liberated places in the world, women are mistreated and broken people. Of course, I'm sure Gloria Steinem would say this is precisely the way it is in the United States."

He smiled. "There are many like that."

"Right. But here it is, in the Bible. Long before twentieth-century America, God turned women into rabid feminists and men into heavy-handed male chauvinists. It goes right back to the beginning."

"It is amazing. But why?"

"Again, it goes back to God's plan. When women get out there in the world and look around and see how hard and awful it is, they'll have to hark back to that day when Eve committed her sin. They'll have to admit they blew it and that will drive them to seek forgiveness from God and to trust him that things can get better."

Doug sat very still. "Okay, this sounds really bad. Where's the hope?"

Hope for the Oppressed

Good question." I began slowly, picking up steam as I went along. "As with the curse on Satan, there is a real promise of hope. In Christ, the curse is lifted. It doesn't apply to the pain of childbirth—that remains. However, in Christianity, women are granted full citizenship and heirship to the kingdom. Paul says in Galatians 3:28, 'There is neither Jew nor Greek, slave nor free, male nor female, for you are all one in Christ Jesus.' This truth imparts equality of purpose, status, life, and freedom to all persons, including women. Husbands are told in Ephesians 5:25 to love their wives 'as Christ loved the church,' sacrificing himself for her. And Peter commanded husbands to treat their wives as 'heirs with you of the gracious gift of life' in 1 Peter 3:7. That's to treat them as mates, equals, with respect and deep love. Women don't have to become demanding, domineering feminists to get what they want. And husbands don't have to beat them into submission. In Christ, the curse on women is lifted and broken, and they can find true fulfillment in life."

Doug held up his hand. "But I thought the Bible supported subjugation of women."

"Where?" I asked.

"Christianity has suppressed women for centuries."

"Not *real* Christianity. I already mentioned part of what Peter says in 1 Peter 3:7, but here's the whole verse: 'Husbands, in the same way be considerate as you live with your wives, and treat them with respect as the weaker partner and as heirs with you of the gracious gift of life, so that nothing will hinder your prayers.' For a man to crush down, dominate, and debase his wife as anything less than a full citizen of God's kingdom invites God's censure on him, hindering his prayers from being answered."

Doug stared at me, clearly incredulous.

I went on, "I see this reality every day in my church and community. Women teach children, boys, and men, speak up in classes, and lead in worship. Women wear clothing that is modest but fashionable. Women walk beside their husband arm in arm, at his side, a coleader of their home and their place in the world. Women can take on any job they desire. It's not by accident that in Christian countries where the Bible has had a strong influence, women are regarded as equals of men, with the same rights and freedoms as their husbands.

"To be sure, women have had to battle for these rights. It wasn't until the early 1900s that women received the right to vote in the United States. It hasn't been until the last few decades women have won the right to work in the career they most desire. But Jesus himself was the first true great liberator. Women enjoyed a high and positive role in his ministry. Women were the first ones to see and report his resurrection. Women have often been the leaders in the compassionate ministries of the church. And it is women who have become the heart of the church and of many communities.

"But only in Christ, Doug. Remember that. For those outside his kingdom, though they may reap the benefits of biblical truth in their cultures (as do women in the United States, Europe, and many of the Catholic-oriented countries), they will not experience the personal benefits of harmony in the home, joy in life, and hope of a better world ahead.

"Though the curse on women produces trouble with everything from childbirth to male-female relations, from dysfunction in the home to the political climate of a nation, God has not left us without hope. In Christ, the curse is broken and real freedom results. It's all meant to point us back to him, to point women to him. 'Trust me,' he says, 'I will give you what you really want.' I'm not saying the world has always treated women properly. But true Christianity, as it's read in the Bible, supports the kind of principles we have seen coming about in the United States for many years. Sure, there have been problems, even in the church. But you look at the words of Jesus, the words of Paul, even the women of the Bible, and you see a very different picture."

Doug nodded. "I see it. I guess it's another deception of Satan to make us think Jesus was some domineering male who didn't care about women, and Paul a chauvinist of the highest level."

"It is. Everything they said and did liberated the women of their time. That the church messed it up in later years is the fault of the church, not of the Bible, or Paul, or Jesus."

"Interesting," he said. "You continue to blow my mind."

"There's still one more curse."

"Let's hit it. But meanwhile, I'm getting a sandwich."

"I'll have to call my wife, too. Tell her I'm out evangelizing the masses and not to wait up."

He laughed. "I'm the masses?"

"You're bigger than most guys I know."

"Okay, now you're getting personal."

We walked over to the counter, and one more time I prayed for Doug's redemption. This was the part that always killed me: not being sure whether my efforts like this would lead to a person's salvation, or just a sigh of "nice-answers-but-I'm-not-going-to-cross-the-line. Have a nice life."

I shuddered at the thought, but knew I had to keep with it and not give up.

CHAPTER 5

The Curse on the Man Demonstrates Why Life in This World Is Such a Struggle, Even Though Again It Points to Redemption

We Look at Adam's Sin

We sat with our sandwiches—which Doug paid for again—and before we dug in, I said, "Would you mind if I offered a blessing?"

About to bite into the sandwich in his hand, Doug paused and pointed to me. "Got me, Preach. Go ahead."

We bowed our heads, and I prayed, "Lord, thanks for this fine food and Doug's generosity. I hope he will continue to feel that way as we go on. But I ask in particular that you help me give him factual answers. If I'm wrong about anything, alert him to it, and make him come back with more questions. But when I'm speaking your truth, I pray he'll listen to it and believe it as I do. Thanks, Lord, for this time with him. I pray you bless him and his family with happiness, prosperity, and fulfillment. Amen."

I looked up and he stared right into my eyes. "You really mean all that?"

"Sure. What wouldn't I mean?"

"I've never had anyone pray those things for me. You sound like you really know the guy."

"Who?"

"God."

"I do."

He laughed. "That always kills me about you Christians. You talk about knowing God personally like it's just a regular thing."

I picked up my sandwich. "Doug, if you never learn anything else from me, get this: God is real. He cares about every one of us. And he wants us to know him personally, intimately, like best friends, like we plan to spend a lot of time together and look forward to it every day as we wake up. God is more real to me than you are. I don't mean that as an insult. I just mean he's inside each of us. He knows all our thoughts, ideas, hopes, dreams, feelings of anger, whatever. And he doesn't condemn us for them. He corrects us, sure. But believe me, he's the truest friend you'll ever have. That says nothing about him also being our Lord, Master, King, Savior, and so on."

"But he's not your *buddy*?"

I smiled ruefully. "I know a lot of us sound like that. But no, he's not the heavenly Buddy, for whom I guess I'd have trouble having respect. I don't see him hanging around the house over beers, watching Monday Night Football. Rather, he's someone I love and worship, someone I listen to and obey, someone I value and want to tell others about. He's the greatest person in existence. And he doesn't abide fools. But he's also patient, kind, understanding, and gives each one of us all the time we need to find out about him and decide whether we want to be part of his family."

"Like me?"

"Absolutely."

He flinched for a second, and I sensed some deep emotion hit him then, but I decided not to say anything about it. I didn't want to embarrass him.

We finished our sandwiches and then I said, "Okay, we come to the curse on Adam. This is what the Bible says:

> To Adam he said, "Because you listened to your wife and ate from the tree about which I commanded you, 'You must not eat of it,' Cursed is the ground because of you; through painful toil you will eat of it all the days of your life. It will produce thorns and thistles for you, and you will eat the plants of the field. By the sweat of your brow you will eat your food until you return to the ground, since from it you were taken; for dust you are and to dust you will return." (Genesis 3:17–19)

"You ever hear that joke?" Doug gazed at me, mischief in his eyes.

"No, tell me."

"Kid hears the pastor say the thing about Adam being made from dust and returning to dust. One day, he runs downstairs to his mom. 'Mom,' he yells. 'A whole lot of Adam is under my bed, and I don't know whether he's comin' or goin.'"

I laughed heartily. "Great one."

"See, I paid attention at least once in church."

We both grinned. I had begun to really like this guy and something within me longed deeply that he would take the step of accepting Christ soon.

"To me," I explained, getting back to the curse on Adam, "this is probably the harshest of all the curses above. Satan we have no feeling for, so his is quite deserved. Woman escapes not too badly. But 'male-kind' reaps a heavy blow. Let's look at several things God says here."

Doug leaned forward, his head down slightly, looking at his Bible.

"First, it says the ground is cursed. In the agrarian society that Adam would soon begin to build, he would struggle. In the Garden of Eden, his job was a joy. He tended the garden, ruled over it, and it yielded to him every good thing. Because of the curse, this would no longer be normal. The earth, though cultivated and planted, would largely bring forth thorns and thistles. He would sweat as he worked the land, facing harsh seasons and harder times.

"I don't believe, though, that the curse meant only weeds would grow in among the real vegetables. The whole earth was cursed. God didn't spell out all the details, but I think this intimates that weather would go awry. Earthquakes would occur. Volcanoes would sprout in the land. All kinds of disasters would befall humankind because the whole earth was now under God's censure. It was no longer an endless playground for us. Instead, we would have to fight for our survival, and even then it would be a lifelong battle."

"Amazing," Doug said. "You see all that in there?"

"Figuratively. Just because God didn't give us every little detail doesn't mean it's not implied. I think God is basically saying, 'Life on this planet will be tough, and anything can happen at any time.' I get that idea from other passages. If you want me to show you—"

"No. Keep going."

"So why do you think God did it that way?"

Doug scratched his eyebrows. "I guess to get us to realize what we'd done, and also to make us, like you said, want and long for a better world, the world God would promise later throughout the Bible."

"Precisely. But also this was designed to get people to look back to him for help, guidance, power. You see God's trying to tell these people, 'The only way you will get through this alive is by coming back to me, depending on me, trusting me. Otherwise, you're going to face fear, worry, terror in the night, and every other insecurity.'"

Doug shook his head. "It's amazing what's really there when you look at it."

I gazed at him solemnly. "It's another reason you can bet your money this is God's Word, not just the writings of some crazy Jews. It goes far beyond a cursory reading. There are depths here it takes years of study to penetrate."

"I'm beginning to see that."

I bent down and read the words again. "Next we see God cursed human work as a whole. Humankind would no longer derive meaning, fulfillment, and pleasure from their work. Instead, it would become a grueling, joyless affair, full of discouraging setbacks, and constant struggle and hardship to produce even the most simplistic foods. The world would provide a steady source of trouble and complications. Though we live in a day when our parents have told us, 'You can do anything you want,' polls still reveal that more than 80 percent of the U.S. population does not like or enjoy or feel fulfilled by their daily work. Résumés fly around, everyone's looking for the greener grass.

"But it isn't there. God has cursed human work because of Adam's sin, and we all are reaping the consequences. We will get no real pleasure out of much of our work, no matter how hard we try."

"I've enjoyed my work, though," Doug said.

"Okay, but think about it. How much of your day is really fulfilling and enjoyable and how much of it is problems, headaches, scares? Like the one we talked about earlier about the million-dollar policy guy who committed suicide?"

He frowned. "Yeah, there's a lot of it."

"Also, think of the fact we live in the United States, have the greatest economy on earth, and have more freedoms than any other country—much of it because of the teachings of the Bible? We also live in the twenty-first century, a time of great prosperity and every pleasure you can imagine. But how many other nations are like that? How many people the world over live lives of 'quiet desperation,' as Thoreau wrote?"

He nodded. "We are mightily blessed."

"Don't answer, but think about why that is, Doug. Why is the United States, of almost all the nations of the earth, blessed the way it is? Just think about it." I paused.

Then I continued, "We'll talk about that later. Let's get back to the curse on work. Let me give you an example. My father-in-law worked in a paint factory all his life, for low wages. At his funeral, we met some of his coworkers, who talked about what a practical joker he had been, pulling all kinds of stunts during his shifts just to make it interesting. He was faithful to his family to provide for them. But it was hard work, and from my talks with him after I married his daughter and he had retired, I discovered it was a tough, demoralizing lifestyle. He found his greatest relief in bowling, winning trophies, and recreation after his hours in the plant. He managed to inject some laughter into it with his practical jokes, but he still had to stand at that machine day in and day out, performing boring tasks that seemed to offer little sense of accomplishment.

"I also recall my own summers working in a box factory. I helped out on different machines spitting out a hundred or so boxes a minute, piling up skids with a stack of the things tied neatly in groups of twenty or twenty-five. It was hard, sweaty work in the summer in a factory with no air-conditioning. The people I worked with seemed ignorant and were foul-mouthed, talking about sexual escapades endlessly. I wondered how they could live like that, year in and year out. I was just a college student employed for the summer, and I wasn't even a Christian then, but I couldn't imagine a life of this spiritless work that seemed to fulfill no one.

"Just the same, people in offices didn't seem to have it much better. When I worked a white-collar job as a customer service manager in a machinery company, I remember the boredom I faced every day answering phone calls from cussing customers who wanted results pronto. I found out that one manager in a customer's plant had many choice names for me when I failed to give him what he wanted. I couldn't imagine making a life of that.

"But many people do. They toil, fighting the boredom, fighting the hangovers, fighting the headaches and sore backs and screaming muscles. And they do it for a lifetime. Why? To survive. They must provide for their families. They have to support their drinking, their bowling, their golf jaunts. But they are cursed, just as Adam was, and they will find no relief in it. I remember reading about a guy who had the words chiseled into his gravestone, 'Bowled 300 in 1962.' Imagine that being the sum total of your life. When I was a pastor, one of the older men I tried to reach with the gospel walked into my office to announce he'd retired, bought an RV, and planned to crisscross the country, playing every golf course in the land. He said it had been his dream for years. It struck me as such a shallow ambition. But that's the story of many people.

"They'll live lives of quiet desperation, and one day, if they're lucky, most of them will retire on Social Security and whatever they might get from their company, and eke out a life until they die. I think that's what I see in life in most people: just trying to get through the night, as the Beatles once said."

"It's really pretty grim," Doug said with a pained look on his face.

"But why did God make it that way?"

Doug smiled. "Same answer: God was trying to get people to come back to him and say, 'Hey, this stinks. How can I make it better?' To depend on him, to trust him, and to look to him to actually make things better for them."

"Precisely. And that's why there is hope." I tried not to sound perky, but always ready to offer that dash of realism that would give Doug a sense that in my worldview all was not lost, even with the curse.

Once Again—the Curse Lifted

Hit me with it," Doug said. "We come to the great promise of the truth of Christ's kingdom," I said. "In him, the curse on work is lifted. You no longer feel the futility of your labors. Instead, he says, 'Whatever you do, work at it with all your heart, as working for the Lord, not for men, since you know that you will receive an inheritance from the Lord as a reward. It is the Lord Christ you are serving.' That's in Colossians 3, verses 23 and 24."

"I think I recall it. Thought it was just more simplistic Christian platitudes at the time. But I can see it's more than that."

"Correct. In Christ, the curse is finished. A Christian can find joy in his work, because he's not serving that vengeful, cold boss who seems determined to make his life miserable. Instead, he knows he labors with Christ, by Christ, through Christ, and one day he will be rewarded in heaven for his honest, faithful work by that same Christ."

Doug rubbed his eye thoughtfully. "So you're not even working in this world anymore. You're seeing yourself as if you were in heaven?"

"In a way. Good thought. I remember when I caught a vision of this. As I said, I was a customer service manager in a machinery company. Every day, I woke up with a headache, feeling exhausted and beset. But I would pray about it on the drive there, and God just changed my outlook. When I got to work, my brain filled with ideas, with innovative thoughts, and I began writing memos and shooting out improvement ideas that led to many great changes in the company. I really believed I served Christ, not my boss, who unfortunately was a cussing, harsh, driven man. When he yelled at me, I saw it as the discipline of Jesus. And when he commended me, I knew it was Jesus talking there, too. My work improved because I caught the vision of the curse and how God had lifted it for me in Christ. I could look forward to a heavenly paycheck one day, far beyond anything I could earn in this world."

"You really felt that way?" Doug asked.

"It was a daily battle. I had some bad moments, and when I got into writing Christian books and that started taking off, concentration came hard. But as I saw how my work suffered, I prayed for God to let me make my living from my writing, and in a short time that happened."

"You feel fulfilled now?"

"In ways I never have before."

"And you believe God did that?"

"Definitely."

He fixed his stare on me, and I sensed he was searching for the truth. Did he think I was painting too rosy a picture? Did he think, like so many of us do at times, that I was sugarcoating it?

I said, "Don't get me wrong, Doug. There are many times in my life as a freelancer, working out of my home, all that, it's not pretty. It seems I'm nearly always strapped financially. But God takes care of us. There are books I've written that I didn't much enjoy. But that's the reality of work. I don't think anything in this cursed world is meant to be perfect. That's heaven. Not here."

"I can see that. Okay, what about this other stuff?"

The Second Part of the Curse on Adam

I looked down at my Bible. "The second part to God's curse on Adam is that he would die, for he was made of dust, and 'to dust he would return.'"

I looked up at Doug. He said, "The biggie."

"Right. Death is the ultimate consequence of the curse. God did not want it to be that way. He originally envisioned a world like a garden in which his citizens would labor with joy, freedom, and exuberance. But Adam and Eve dashed that world to smithereens when they sinned. Now, they would live in a world of struggle, pain, never-ending internecine fighting, and death."

"It really sums up a lot."

I felt my lips slip into a grim line. "I don't know what Adam might have felt with this Sword of Damocles called *death* hanging over his head, but it must have been discouraging every day. All he had to look forward to was struggle, struggle, struggle, and then death. As one of my friends puts it, 'Life stinks, and then you die.'"

Doug laughed. "Yeah, I've said that one."

"So have I. But it seems to sum up the whole rotten scenario. No matter how hard we work, no matter how much we build or gain or gather, we still face the ultimate enemy. We will all die, and everything we've lived for will be passed to our children, however foolish they may be."

"Yeah," Doug confided, "I have a kid, don't know what I'll do with him."

"You want to talk about him for a second?"

Doug shrugged. "He's eighteen. I made a mistake and gave him a motorcycle when he was sixteen. Now it seems he's married to the thing. He's in this group, a bunch of kids on bikes. They motor all around. He has no interest in college, no interest in working in my company. He dresses like a dirtball, has long, greasy hair, and I'm ashamed to go to any family gathering with him."

"I didn't know."

"I don't talk about him much." He peered down at his lap. "It really hurts," he said.

I suddenly felt a wave of compassion shoot through me. "It's not over, Doug. He has a lot of years ahead of him. Right now it looks bad, but it won't always be that way. Why don't we stop and pray for him? And for you and your wife, and your other kids."

He just nodded, his head still bowed.

I ducked my head again and spent the next few minutes asking God to help Doug and his wife be patient and loving, and to turn his son around. It was pretty simple, but I quoted a few verses and reminded God it would mean a lot to me to see Doug filled with news about his son's big "turnaround."

When I was finished, Doug looked up. His eyes appeared a little wet, and suddenly I felt the emotion welling up in me. "My wife and I had a prodigal," I said. "I'll tell you about her sometime."

"Want me to pray for her?" he asked, breaking the tension.

I grinned. "She's back to normal. Just pray that she doesn't get any new tattoos."

"Ah, one of those," he said with a chuckle.

I sensed he felt better so I turned back to my Bible. "Okay, about the problem of death. I remember hearing a speaker talk about how death drills its fear into you more and more, the older you get. He said, 'Imagine an organ with a stuck key. That key is death and it reminds you it's always there, watching, waiting, making its sad music. But you can play around it when you're young and full of ideas. You can work it so that you hardly hear the death key at all. It's just there, and you know you'll make a life regardless. It seems like just a little bump out there, a tiny voice you can drown out with other activity.

"But as you grow older, that key gets louder. Soon, when you get into your fifties, sixties, seventies, you can no longer just play around it. It's always there, reminding you of doom. Soon, all you can hear is that key. Every day. Every minute reminding you, 'I'm coming. I'm hungering for you. One day I'll be there, and there's not a thing you can do about it.'

"Then the preacher said, 'That, my friend, is what it's like to live without Christ.'"

"Now you're scaring me," Doug said with a slight grin.

"Just trying to keep it real."

"Pretty graphic."

"We don't like to talk about it. We decorate funerals with flowers. We embalm the body, make the corpse look as if he's at peace. But deep down, I think everyone fears death like nothing else. Not all the time. Not when you're young. But sooner or later, you have to reckon with it."

"I'm thinking about it right now," Doug smiled grimly. "So where's the hope this time?"

Once Again, Enter Jesus

The basic fact is that Jesus has conquered death," I said. "We no longer have to fear that final outcome, but can labor with joy and exhilaration because this world is not the end. Listen to what Paul writes in 1 Corinthians 15:58 after a long passage about how Jesus has conquered death once and for all: 'Therefore, my dear brothers, stand firm. Let nothing move you. Always give yourselves fully to the work of the Lord, because you know that your labor in the Lord is not in vain.'

"For me, that's the ultimate joy of being a Christian. Your work, whatever it may be, wherever it may be, 'is not in vain in the Lord.' Nothing is lost. All is conserved. Your achievements, whatever they might be, are not meaningless or futile. Rather, they are recorded in heaven. They are not 'for nothing,' and one day you will reap tremendous rewards on the basis of them. Death is the doorway to God's perfect paradise."

Doug sighed. "I want to believe it, but . . ."

"It's okay. There's time. You need to think through these things. They're not easy issues to deal with."

He scratched his chin. "Some time ago, I read the best seller by Mitch Albom, *The Five People You Meet in Heaven*. I don't think it's a Christian book, but I found several things in it that really sounded inspiring. One of them concerned the main character's feeling his life had been a waste. A World War II vet, his war crimes haunted him, small as they were. Also, he worked all his life as this maintenance man of a boardwalk fun park with Ferris wheels, Tilt-a-Whirls, and so on that he constantly repaired. He had done his work faithfully, but he felt a terrible lack of meaning as a human being. He believed his life had been a big zero."

"Interesting," I said, thinking of how Doug had said the same thing.

"And it does look like a big zilch, until he meets this little girl in heaven he had saved in the accident in which he died. This little girl informed him that his life had not been a waste. Why? Because he 'had kept the children safe' by his vigilance and care in repairing the park equipment. She reminded him that what he'd done for all the children who ever went into that park was something worth applauding."

I thought it sounded like a book I should read.

Doug went on, "For the first time in his existence, this man suddenly saw his life had not been a colossal bummer, but something to be proud of. It really got me. I want my life to be like that. But . . ."

I could feel the emotion rolling through him. "But you don't feel like that now?"

"Not really."

"Why not?"

"I sell life insurance. How lame is that? I had to tell a lady today she wasn't going to get her retirement because her husband's death was really a suicide."

"People need that insurance, though, many of them. It helps people when bad things happen to them."

"Sure. But all I'm ever concerned about is the next sale. Hard enough to admit, but I don't really care about those people. I put on 'the face.' I nod when they tell me their troubles and concerns.

But getting them to sign on the dotted line is about it for me. I hate my callousness sometimes, but that's it. There's not much real fulfillment in that."

I thought about it. "Then you're experiencing the curse yourself, right now. You can say, 'Yes, God, I see how this curse deal is pointing me to you. I want life to be better. I can't believe this is what it's really all about.' That's what I think God is trying to do in you through that, Doug."

He stared at me, then he sighed. "You make it sound like it's good."

"It *is* good, Doug. If it leads people to God, it's very good, the best thing in this world. I remember one of my professors telling about how he visited India and this woman who had leprosy stood up and held up her hands. Nothing but stubs by then. This woman said, 'I praise God I had leprosy. I praise God I lost all my fingers, because he used it to bring me to him.'"

"Wow!"

"Yeah. But that's it. I think God uses all kinds of bad things in life to get our attention, to point us to himself. Some people become bitter, though. They look at some tragedy like leprosy or whatever as God being mean, nasty, judgmental. Others, though, can see it for what it is—God trying to get them to look to him."

"Are you saying God caused the leprosy?"

"No. That's part and parcel of living in a fallen world. God didn't cause it, he used it for good. I'm saying God took that bad, evil thing in her life and focused her in a new way, so she could see that it had turned her to Christ."

He nodded. "You've got me thinking. But it's late, and I'd better go. So do you have a parting shot?"

I smiled, thinking through all we'd talked about. "So why do you think God cursed it all in the first place?"

He shook his head. "To punish us. To make us realize we'd messed up big-time. To get us to look to him."

"Yes, but the main thing is that God wants every one of us to so puke on this world, to be so disgusted with it by things going wrong, and lack of fulfillment, and pain in childbirth, and weeds growing in the garden, that we finally throw up our hands and cry, 'This can't be all there is. This can't be what life is all about. It stinks. There must be something better. It should not be this way.' Then God walks over and says, 'Good. I'm getting through. Let's talk.'

"That's what God is trying to do in us every time we go into our offices and sit down, stare at our coffee and think, 'I can't take another day of this.' That's what he's trying to tell us as we see our friends die, and we sit in the chairs at the church or funeral home or whatever and think, 'Where is my friend now? Is this what we all come to?' It's God at his teaching best."

God Gives Back with His Left Hand

Doug stared at me. "I can't believe this."

"What?"

"You've just made the worst thing that ever happened to the human race sound like the greatest thing."

"It is, if it leads people back to God. I really believe that."

He shook his head and stood. "You're certainly standing on its head everything I've ever believed."

I had to chuckle. "Another question, Doug: From what we've discussed, why is our planet so messed up?"

He looked off over the coffee shop, then returned to me. "Adam and Eve disobeyed God, I guess."

"More than that. Think about it. Adam and Eve didn't just break a little law. Study the Genesis 3 passage. The serpent led Eve, and Adam there with her, to think they could defy God, go their own way, do their own thing, and ultimately take over for him. They were saying to God, 'We don't need you. We'll run things from here. Get lost. We think you're a liar and a cheat, and we want nothing to do with you. We're going with the serpent guy.' In effect, they gave God the finger."

Doug hung his jaw a second. "All that?"

"Sure. Listen. Our world is messed up for three very basic reasons: One, we kicked God out of our lives. Two, we gave Satan complete leadership and control to deceive and lie and cheat and trick us. And three, then God cursed it so everything spun out of control. Ultimately, we brought it all on ourselves. But here's another thing: What would you have done if you were God and you got that big finger in your face after all you'd done for them?"

Doug laughed. "It wouldn't have been pretty, believe me."

"Right. But God did something to redeem it: He cursed the whole thing, but he didn't curse us. He didn't say, 'Begone you little jackals, into the pit with you.' No, he said, 'Okay, you're going to be stupid about this. Fine. Then I'll do something that forces you to take another look at me. I'll do things that will make you look up at heaven every day and say, 'Please, God, make it better for me. I'll do stuff that will make you realize I'm not the bad guy you think I am.' So God only cursed their world to try to get us back on course, point us to the truth, and ultimately lead us to Christ."

He shook his head. "And it's all right there in Genesis."

"It's brilliant, isn't it?"

He nodded. "I have to confess, the way you put it there, it's stunning."

I looked up at him. "There's a lot more. But one of the strange things I find about God is how he gives back with his left hand what the right hand has taken away. Let me tell you another story before you go. A number of years ago when I attended college, I bought a 1965 cream-colored Mustang that I loved. I drove that car everywhere. But one winter, I cracked the car up. It was my fault, and the insurance company didn't cover my part of it. It was some $275 in damages, and at the time, in 1970, that was pretty big bucks for a poor college stiff such as myself.

"I deliberated over the estimate and lay it on my desk in despair. I didn't have the money. But I certainly couldn't afford to junk the car. There seemed no way out until my father stepped into my room. He picked up the estimate and studied it. 'Pretty hefty price,' he said, looking at me lying on my bed, deeply depressed.

"'Yeah,' I muttered.

"'Tell you what,' he said. 'I'll go halve-sies with you on it.'

"I stared at him and sat up, hope surging into me. 'What?'

"'I'll pay for half if you pay for the other half.'

"'Really?'

"'Would I kid you about money?'

"I whooped. And I never asked him why. I never had to. I knew the answer. Because my father loved me. He did many things like that throughout my life, which in retrospect amazes me to this day.

"I think that's the picture of God here, Doug. 'I'll go halve-sies with you.' Except God said, 'I cursed the world, but I'll give you a way out. I'm going to send you a Redeemer. He'll get everything fixed. Be on the lookout. Trust me, and I'll get you where you really want to go.

"In a way, it seems beyond belief. Why would God do this? The answer should be quite evident, but I'll repeat it: because despite the fact we are mostly ornery, disobedient, foul-tongued creatures, most of whom still give God the finger many times a day, he still loves us enough to send his Son to die for that orneriness and to keep trying to turn us around.

"We don't have to suffer in the shadow of our guilt from the garden, the power of Satan, or the effects of the curse for another minute. In Christ, God gives it all back to us: joy, fulfillment, life, and life eternal."

Doug shook his head, his eyes looking as if he was amazed and maybe even happy. "You're hitting me hard, but I'm getting it, I think. Now—"

"One more thing, Doug," I said, walking with him to the door. "I want to give you an assignment."

"Good. Better not be a term paper, though."

"No. I want you to ask several people you trust why they think our world is so messed up. See what kind of answers you get. Even from Christians. See what they say."

We reached our cars. "I'll do it," he said. "First person I'll ask is my son. He'll probably say, 'What's messed up? I got a Harley, leathers, and a chick. What else is important in life?'"

He said it all with this tone of rank sarcasm. I laughed. "Funny."

"It's a good assignment. I will get some answers for you. I'm curious myself."

"So you want to meet again?" I said a little nervously.

"Maybe Monday afternoon is our day. Meet here at three again?"

"Fine with me."

"I'll be here," he said, as he climbed into his shiny new silver Lexus.

As I walked back to my seven-year-old Oldsmobile minivan, I silently said to God, "So he's an unbelieving insurance guy with a Lexus, and I'm a believing writer writing books about you with this piece of junk. God, this does not compute."

I chuckled as I got in, and it seemed the Spirit whispered in my heart, "Remember, your minivan is paid for, too. What kind of payments do you think he has on that sleek new Lexus?"

"Yeah," I said out loud. "Guess it does compute. But I wouldn't mind trading cars with him for a couple of decades."

"Wait till you see what you drive in heaven."

"Yeah, that's what you always say."

"It's true."

God always has a sense of humor. So I sped off, feeling positive and hopeful about what had happened with Doug, asking God again to open Doug's heart to the truth, praying that Doug's son would come around, and that Doug would find some real fulfillment in his work this week.

CHAPTER 6

The Cause of Most of the Evil in Our World Is Nasty People Doing Nasty Things and Not Caring about Those They Hurt

Doug Reveals Some Personal Problems

When I walked into Starbucks the next Monday, Doug already sat there with two of the same drinks we'd had the previous Monday in front of him, one at my place. He also had his Bible open.

"Hey, I meant to pay for your frozen strawberry concoction this time," I said, feeling like I really needed to do that more than ever.

He smiled. "Don't worry, I'll let you buy sometime. But since you're a poor writer, I'll have mercy on you."

I sat down. "I'm not that poor. Anyway, what're you reading?" I noticed the Bible open to the Psalms.

"Psalm 23. You know, the one about the shepherd. I thought I'd renew my memory of it."

"It's a good one."

He gazed at me. "Don't you think it's sometimes a little too incredible, though? Nice rosy picture and all, but is it true?"

I took a sip of my strawberry whatever-it-was. "It doesn't mean things won't go wrong in your life. We live in a fallen, cursed, Satan-led, and God-hating world. But I've seen it work out in my life exactly the way the psalm says, many times."

"Name one."

I regarded him with interest, wondering where this came from. "Okay, just this morning, in the paper I read about a triple murder, rape, sodomizing, you name the evil, of some doctor's family in Connecticut. It was awful, though they got the killers. I looked up at my wife, Jeanette, with tears in my eyes and said, 'We better make sure our doors are locked at all times, honey.' She agreed, but then she said, 'I don't think we should live in fear of this kind of thing, honey. God does protect his own.'

"I thought about how easy it would be for me to be paralyzed with terror just about every minute of the day. Drunk drivers crossing lanes right into your car. Stalkers out there after my kids. Terrorism. The bomb. But I really don't think about it much. Why? Because I know God's there, he's in charge, he's watching over me and my loved ones, and he's always assuring me simply to trust him to be there. Even if we do die horribly, it's all taken care of. God will get us to heaven safely."

Doug gazed at me evenly. I couldn't read anything in his deep blue eyes, but something about them was so skeptical and yet at the same time hopeful that I knew there had to be more than what he said: "It must be a nice feeling."

"It is. I never really had that inner security till I became a Christian, though. Before I met Jesus, I faced terrible self-esteem problems, a desperate terror of death, and constant worry about whether I could make my life a success. Meeting Jesus changed all that. And look at me now! Books, a wife, kids, bills, bills, bills. It's just a wonder."

He grinned.

But I added most seriously, "I don't think that's something God gives to people without them trusting him."

He sighed. "My mother's sick," he said suddenly and his eyes flickered away.

I sensed he felt deeply about this. "What's going on?"

"Colon cancer. Very developed. She and I are close. I don't know what to say to her."

"Does she have any beliefs about God, Jesus?"

He hung his head slightly. "I don't really know. I mean she goes to church, but I'm pretty sure the Methodists don't believe like you believe."

"You never know, Doug. But let's pray about her, okay? Prayer does things. You might be very surprised."

He looked away.

I asked him, "Man, is there anything else?"

He shook his head. "It's tough," he rasped. "She's very afraid. I thought maybe I'd send her a card with Psalm 23 on it. I know she'd probably laugh, it coming from me. But I'm serious."

"It might speak to her—you just never know how God is working in someone." I took a deep breath. "Are you all right with this?"

"No."

"Yeah. Look, let's pray. Then we can talk more."

We prayed and he even added an "Amen" at the end. Then he wiped his eyes, and said, "Okay, I don't really want to say any more right now. It's too close. So what's up for today?"

"I thought we'd talk about what causes most of the evil in the world."

"Like my mother's cancer?"

"Just like it."

He shrugged. "God's cursed our planet. I guess it goes back to God."

"Does it really?"

"Okay, fine, we sinned and brought it on ourselves. Is that more theologically correct?"

I paused and realized he felt a lot worse than he let on. "I sense some real bitterness here, Doug. Should we address that first?"

"I just don't get it. You talk about Jesus, he's going to make everything perfect. But what about my mother? You know anything about colon cancer?"

"A little."

"It's a tough way to go." He looked away.

I touched his shoulder. "I want to give you something to hang on to, okay?"

He came back to my eyes. "Fine."

I opened my Bible to Isaiah 43:1, 2. "This is a message God gave the people of Israel when they went through some really tough times—total destruction of their nation, their leaders murdered, their women raped, all the young people taken off to slavery in Babylon. I think that ranks up there as pretty bad circumstances."

He gazed at me with skeptical eyes. "Go ahead. I'm listening."

"God says, 'Fear not, for I have redeemed you; I have summoned you by name; you are mine. When you pass through the waters, I will be with you; and when you pass through the rivers, they will not sweep over you. When you walk through the fire, you will not be burned; the flames will not set you ablaze.'

Doug laughed. "Okay, all this has happened to them and this is what God says to them? It's got to be a joke."

"No. It's tremendous truth. It's the truth we need most in this world. It's that God is with us here and now, no matter what we face. His presence, even if we end up dead, is powerful comfort. Moreover, he's saying, 'Ultimately, though all has gone wrong, this isn't the end. You are mine, and I will take you to my heaven where you will experience joy, peace, and love on a level not possible in this world. Don't look at this world. Look to me. I'll get you where you really want to go, and that's all that really matters in the end.'"

"You really believe that, don't you?"

"It's a sacred promise I hold onto all the time."

"But my mother—"

"Doug, if your mother's a Christian, there's nothing to worry about. She's in God's hands. And no matter how she leaves this world, all that she goes through here will seem like nothing compared with the joy and greatness of the next one."

He sighed. "I thought I had you. I thought I had you nailed."

"It's not me. God wants you to believe this stuff. It's the only thing that will get you through the terrors of this world. The *only* thing."

He nodded. "I'm beginning to believe it. Okay, I feel better. I guess I just have to make sure my mom's a Christian."

"And you, too. And your family."

"Yeah." He smiled that big grin of his. "Hey, I'm working on it."

"That's all I can ask."

We both chuckled and sipped from our drinks.

I was about to start in on it, but Doug said, "Wait a second. Don't you want to hear about my assignment, O great and wise teacher?"

I shook my head. "You know, you're getting a little uppity these days. I may have to cut you down to size and steal that Lexus of yours."

"Oh, you noticed that?"

"I don't think it's the kind of car that slithers unmentioned through the night."

"Yeah, well believe me, it's not that great. And the payments are brutal."

"I bet."

"Anyway, about the assignment." He rubbed his brow with his hand. "I talked to three people—my wife, my partner at work, and my secretary."

"Great."

"Claire—she's my wife—said the world wouldn't be so messed up if she wasn't married to me. I had pretty much bungled everything up for her. If only she had married the other guy . . ." He laughed. "She has a good sense of humor. Then she said she thought it was messed up because we couldn't elect a decent president. That was as far as she would go."

"So it's the government. If we just didn't have such bad governments, we'd all be fine."

"I'm not sure that's what she meant—I kind of think she really didn't want to deal with the question."

I nodded. "Lots of people like that."

"Right. So, next I asked Len, my partner. He had some jokes, too, but I said I was serious and I told him a little about my talk with you. Not much. But he almost had a seizure. 'You start getting into religion, Doug, it'll be over for you in this industry. You can't become a religious fanatic and sell insurance effectively.' I asked him why that was and he just said, 'You know the scene. You can't really be honest with people about this stuff. If you told them the truth, they wouldn't buy a single thing. All the little clauses and outs for us. You know that. You get religion like some people I know, they stop being salespeople and start being their clients' friends. And that's the end.'"

I had to think about that one. "So he's basically saying, who cares what's wrong with the world, but if you want to know the truth, I think it's religion. Especially Christianity."

Doug frowned. "Yeah, I think that sounds like a good assessment."

"And your secretary?"

Doug smiled. "She's this very pretty, very available single girl, just out of college, all gung-ho, wants to move up, wants to land some charming, hunky guy, all that."

"So what did she say?" This was getting curiouser and curiouser.

He took a breath. "She said it's because of the *thetans* who filled our world with some kind of gunk that makes everyone sick emotionally, but if we'd just accept the teachings of L. Ron Hubbard, we'd all get it together."

"So she's a Scientologist?" I said with a chuckle.

"Oh, yeah, totally into it. I had no idea. And she really gave me a talk about it, invited me to one of their meetings." He shook his head. "Man, I'm getting hit in every direction."

I suddenly fixed on Doug with my gaze. "Be prepared, my friend. Satan's going to be throwing a lot of lies at you. He wants to prevent you from listening to any of this, and he'll do anything to derail you. It could even involve your mom, your son, everyone in your life."

"I'm beginning to believe it. So anyway, it was a total whack job. Not one of the three I asked knew anything about what the Bible says. And I suspect if I talked to more people, I'd get even more bizarre answers."

"Our world is in deep trouble, isn't it?"

He leaned back and really laughed it up. "If you weren't so funny at times, my friend, I think I'd just write you off as some stiff, humorless Jesus freak. But you're really not."

"Thanks for the compliment, if that's what it is."

He took another drink and smiled at a passing couple. "Okay, so what's this evil in our world stuff?"

The Whole Free-Will Problem

Basically, it comes down to the kinds of decisions people make," I told him. "I think you'd probably admit most of the evil in our world is done on people by people. Sure, there are great disasters—the tsunami, Hurricane Katrina, but those are minor compared with murders, rapes, thefts, terrorism, wars, and so on. Wouldn't you agree?"

"Yes. I really would."

"Now the question is, 'Why is there so much evil in people?' I'm not saying there's no good, either, but when you look at even the little things all of us do almost without thinking—harsh words, bad moods, gossip, talking behind people's backs, secret stuff like sexual dalliances, porn, overeating, overspending, greed, all of it—we're a pretty sinful bunch."

He nodded. "Okay, you're not going to hurl some hellfire at me now, are you?"

"No. But really, it's pretty obvious. There's not one of us on earth who's perfect, who never makes mistakes, who never hurts those we love, right?"

"Of course."

"So the question is 'Why'"?

He smiled. "Don't keep me in suspense, just spit it out. I don't know the answer to this one."

"First, there are many things that influence our decisions, both the good choices we make and the bad. Let's make a list. Can you name a few?"

"Sure," Doug said. "Genes. They say there're all kinds of genes that make us do things. An alcoholic gene. You drink, you have that gene, you're done for. A fat gene. A gay gene, though I think there's a lot of disputing about that one." He nodded to me and I smiled.

"Yeah, you'll get a fight on that one."

"Sure. But that's just the beginning. What about your family's influence? Your mom, dad, siblings? They all molded you in all kinds of ways." Doug chuckled. "Take me. I had a brother who was a great athlete. All my life, I've wanted to be as good as him at sports. But he whips me every time. I've even decided at times to work out simply to beat my bro."

"Me, too. Not with my brother, but other things." I picked up my cup. "In my family, there were certain ways to do things. Manners. You picked up a cup this way." I showed him. "And drank it this way. That was mannerly. Now I get out in public in a restaurant I'm thinking what slobs these people are around me because they don't do it that way."

Doug laughed. "Yeah, and there're our personalities, too. I'm just laid-back and easygoing most of the time. But my wife is high-strung, stressed, always on edge, always having to be the best, wearing the most with-it clothes. It blows my mind that she even cares about those things. But that's her outlook, the way she's made."

I shook my head as I saw so many of my relatives in the same light. "Right. And what about peer pressure? You can make decisions and choices that are bad, wrong, or even harmful to you simply because your friends are all doing it. I remember how my best friend worked on me for months about smoking pot. Then one night I got into a car, and they're all toking up. I felt tremendous pressure to conform. And that's exactly what I did, not something I would have done on my own, if I had been completely free at that moment and unafraid of what everyone would think."

Doug leaned back and shook his head. "Everywhere you look, there's something. Advertising. They're always saying TV violence doesn't influence anyone, but I ask, Why do all those people advertise on TV? I bet that Marlboro man led more young guys into smoking than anyone else in history."

Sighing, I said, "So what makes us what we are? What forces shaped and developed our personalities so that one of us chooses to pierce her belly button and another colors her hair purple and a third rides a motorcycle in the rain?"

"Cool. Never did that one."

"The piercing, the purple hair, or the motorcycle thing?"

He laughed. "Definitely the third. The other two are out of the question."

"Okay, few people want to say anything against the idea of freedom of will in our world. Especially Christians. We want to believe that everyone has the freedom and right to choose any which way they want, especially when it comes to things like sexual identity, drinking alcohol, using drugs, who you sleep with, all that. But it's crucial stuff, and it leads to all kinds of bad stuff for people. We can steam all we want about AIDS, STDs, and so on affecting everyone. But the Bible clearly says God sends judgments, disciplinary efforts to turn people around, to stop such behavior, which he says is wrong. And I'm not just talking about homosexuality, but the whole spectrum of sexual sin—adultery, fornication, sodomy, sex with animals, all of it. The only kind of sex the Bible approves of is in the context of marriage. But I guess a lot of people have to learn it the hard way."

Doug looked uncomfortable for a second, and I sensed I'd hit another nerve. But he quickly recovered. "I get you there. I have a friend who got herpes because he slept around. He went around cussing the girl, saying what a slut she was. And he's bedding down with every babe he can talk into it."

"We're often blind to our own responsibility for our own problems. But we have to ask, What does the Bible teach? Is that where we truly find ourselves? And is that what we even find in experience?"

"You're going somewhere," Doug said, "and I'm fixed to my seat here, so out with it. I can take it."

The Power of the Past

Good, but as Yoda said, 'Don't be frightened.'"

"Love those movies."

"The best. Anyway, anyone with at least a smattering of knowledge about personality and psychology will readily admit each of us has been shaped by our past experiences, our genetic makeup, the people we hung with and hang with now, TV, advertising, peer groups—it all comes at us and many times we don't even know why we did something. People who suffered abuse as children—sexual, emotional, physical—often end up being abusers themselves. Why?

"Researchers tell us that people act as they have been taught, and use what they've learned. If they obeyed their fathers because he beat them up when they refused, then when they grow up and have their own children, they will often use the so-called tried and true methods of their youth. They beat their own kids because that's what worked with them.

"Cigarette smokers often have kids who eventually become smokers themselves. Not in all cases, of course. Sometimes those very kids so hate cigarette smoking that when they grow up, they wouldn't think of touching a cigarette. But isn't that the same kind of shaping, in the reverse direction?"

"Sure." Doug rubbed his nose. "You're saying although we have freedom of choice, our experiences and all these other things, our past, and so on are going to influence us, no matter how much we might like to think we're totally free in that decision."

Deeper

But let's go a little deeper," I suggested. "Let me tell you about something in my makeup, my penchant for lying as a child. I learned early on (though I don't know where) that lying when trouble struck, when I wanted something, or when I just needed to wriggle out of a tight spot worked. Most of the time anyway."

"Where did that come from? Why is it that my four-year-old stands there in the kitchen with a busted glass and spilled milk at her feet and I can ask, 'Who did this?' And she can say, looking right into my eyes, 'I don't know.' Or, 'Gardner did it.' That's her brother, but he's outside in the backyard with the dog. Where does that come from? I never taught her to lie. I haven't sent her to lying school. I really don't think she learned it from her Barney videos, either."

Doug eyed me uncertainly. "What are you talking about? Original sin or something?"

"Think about that for a second," I said. "Do you know what it is?"

"Like you said the other day, Adam and Eve and all of us turned against God in the garden. We went our own way. We gave God the bird. Isn't that it?"

"A big part of it. But something happened to us when we shoved God out of our lives."

Doug leaned forward on his elbows. "I'm listening."

I glanced to my right, and noticed a big guy with a beard, wild brown hair, and jeans and a work shirt sitting in front of a laptop. He appeared to be listening to us, and I wondered if he was.

I shrugged it off, though, and continued. "Let me give you an example. In high school, I found my first girlfriend. She was great, and we fell in love quickly. Of course, I began trying every move I could think of on her. She was Catholic, though, and would just remove my hand from whatever part of her body I went after at the time. Her main goal in life was to be a virgin when she got married. I brought up every argument, every '60s 'truth' I could think of, but she wouldn't budge.

"Eventually, it got to be a problem. She didn't understand why I wouldn't simply accept and honor her beliefs. I couldn't understand what she was so uptight about. My question is this: Why did I have to ruin so many evenings trying to wangle her into sex? Why did I just ignore her thoughts, beliefs, rebuffs, and plug on, determined to get what I wanted, showing no real respect for her as a person?"

Doug sighed. "It was the same for me, only I usually got what I wanted."

I smiled wryly.

"I never felt good about it, though."

"Right. Why is that?"

He rubbed his brow. "Conscience? Human nature?"

"Good. Now we're getting to it. There's something very basic and wrong about us ever since that first sin. You can call it original sin, but it simply means we went on tilt from that moment on and became dysfunctional, rebellious, uncaring, selfish creatures. God had warned Adam and Eve about it. Do you remember what he said?"

Doug nodded. "They would die if they ate the fruit."

"Correct. There are three kinds of death in the Bible: physical death, the one we're most familiar with. Eternal death—that's going to hell after you die physically. And spiritual death."

He gazed at me thoughtfully. "The first two make sense. But what's spiritual death?"

"Let me quote a couple of passages." I riffled through my Bible to a passage in Ephesians: 'You were dead in your transgressions and sins' (2:1). Dead. That means somehow, even though you are alive in body, your insides, your spirit, your soul, are somehow gone. Broken. Finis."

"Really?"

"Listen to this one. This is from Jesus: 'What comes out of a man is what makes him "unclean"' (Mark 7:20). Jesus was talking to his disciples, trying to make them understand it wasn't outer things—dirt, muck, etcetera—that made them sinful in God's eyes, but these things: 'For from within, out of men's hearts, come evil thoughts, sexual immorality, theft, murder, adultery, greed, malice, deceit, lewdness, envy, slander, arrogance and folly. All these evils come from inside and make a man "unclean."'"

"Where is that?"

"Mark 7, verses 21 through 23."

Doug wrote it down on a pad he had by his Bible.

"Then listen to this one from Paul again. It's in Romans 7, verses 14 and 15: 'We know that the law is spiritual; but I am unspiritual, sold as a slave to sin. I do not understand what I do. For what I want to do I do not do, but what I hate I do.'"

Doug blanched. "Sounds like me."

"Right. It hits hard. Paul is talking about how he tried so hard to obey God's laws and truths. But he failed. He couldn't keep them. He even agreed God's laws were good. He saw the sense in them and thought they were wise and helpful. But then he went out and did the exact opposite. Why?"

Lights came on in Doug's eyes. "I think I get it. He said in that passage he was 'sold into bondage to sin.' It's like when Adam and Eve sinned, they left us in this terrible state where sinful desires, lusts, addictions, and so on control us. We know intrinsically what's right—through our conscience and so on—but we can't do it."

He laughed. "Am I right? Is that right?"

"You hit the nail on the head, man. That's the whole issue. When we ditched God, told him to get lost and all that, we put ourselves into this condition where we couldn't even be what we knew we should be, what we wanted to be. So we eventually gave up and just let the bad stuff rule our lives."

"Addictions," Doug said. "Mental diseases. Racism. Murder. Mayhem. Sexual craziness. Drugs. People destroying each other. All of it. It all comes from that."

"Precisely."

Doug sat back, a satisfied look on his face. "I'm not so dumb."

We both laughed, and I was about to move on, when I noticed the guy to my left get up. He sidled over, his thumbs hooked in his belt. A shiny buckle with a Confederate flag on it seemed to push right in our faces. "Couldn't help but hear what you were talkin' about," he said. "You talkin' religion?"

I looked up at him. Mountain Man was the only way I could describe him. I held out my hand. "I'm Mark. This is Doug."

"Jesse," he said.

"Why don't you haul your drink over here, and your computer," Doug said. "You can listen in. But remember—he's the teach. I'm mostly here to listen to him and shoot spitballs when he gets totally off the wall."

Jesse sat down and looked at both of us. "Well, do it," he said. "I've got duct tape on my lips."

"The more the merrier," I said, and proceeded.

Two Examples

I looked from face to face. I couldn't believe we were talking about these things in a local coffee shop. But where else would we? And why not?

"Let me give you two personal examples," I said. "The first happened in high school. I had taken the PSATs and got my numbers in the mail. I had a 63 in math—you may remember the PSATs were two numbers, the SATs three, from 200 to 800."

Both men nodded. "So that was pretty good, that 63, but on the bus, I noticed I could turn the 63 into a 68 simply with a little pencil mark."

"O-o-o-h, you were a bad boy," Jesse said, and we all laughed.

"It was pretty typical for me back then. Anyway, that weekend, Dad came up to my room with my scores in his hand. He said, 'I want to show you something.' Then he proceeded to set down the booklet, point to the 68 and then erase the part I'd added. I sat there numb, my heart pounding. Dad said, 'Now how do you suppose that happened?'

"I couldn't believe I'd been nailed like that. But I just stammered, 'Someone must have done it on the bus.'

"Dad gazed at me. 'You really think that?'

"'Sure, guys are always doing those things.'

"He pressed me a little more and soon I named several friends who might have done it. He knew the truth and I knew the truth. But I couldn't say it out loud. Finally, he just said, 'Okay, you think about it and if you want to change your story, come and tell me.'

"He walked out, leaving the incriminating evidence on my desk. I sat there, my mind whizzing with every possible new excuse I could think of—but not the truth. It took Dad about a half hour of grilling later to get me to admit the truth and even then it was bitter and I hated him for it."

Jesse laughed. "Hey, I shoulda thought of that. Except mine was a 33 instead of a 63. I got a 63, my parents woulda flown me to Harvard for immediate entrance."

We all laughed. "Okay, contrast that with this one: My friends are with me at my grandmother's house in the mountains on a lake in Pennsylvania to have a bachelor party for one of my friends getting married. We're all sitting on the swimming dock there, boating and having a fine time. My friend Jon casually asks my father if he has a knife in the motorboat. He needs to cut something. My Dad pulls out a brown-handled tri-bladed knife and sets it on the dock.

"Jon picks up the knife and gazes at it curiously while my mouth drops open in abject horror. I know instantly why he's looking at it so carefully. The knife had once belonged to him. Years ago when we were youngsters, he had lost it. Or should I say, I had stolen it."

Jesse and Doug stared at me like I'd just sprouted spiders on my forehead, and I wondered if they thought this was trivial, or something worse. But I had to go on now. "In juxtaposition to that searing moment was the fact that two days previous I had become a Christian. For the first time in my life I felt free—forgiven—for years of mini- and maxi-wrongdoings. In less than twenty-four hours I shed years of guilt, fear, worry, and self-loathing, and found new hope and happiness in Christ.

"I was a changed person, and I knew I couldn't excuse the knife problem away, or lie, or just hide the truth somehow. God was there with me, watching, encouraging me to come clean. I'm literally shaking all over, but I say to Jon, 'Do you recognize that knife?'

"He shrugs, probably trying to play dumb so as not to point any fingers. 'I'm not sure.'

"I take a breath and say, 'You should. It was yours. I stole it from you when we were kids.'

"The dock becomes still as a morning glare. Jon won't look at me. I can feel everyone staring at me in amazement, all my best friends from my youngest years, my parents, my grandma. They all know I've gone through this transformation the last few days, but this is the first sign of anything about it that was real.

"I don't know how I did it—God was giving me the strength I know now, but I went on, 'I'm sorry I did that. It was wrong. You can have the knife back.'

"Jon waves his hand. 'It's all right. Don't worry about it.' Then he turns to me, 'Man, Littleton, you are a little too honest!'

"I start to protest, but he adds, 'Hey, it's good. I wish I could be that way.' Everyone relaxes and it's over. We all go on to other subjects.

"But later, as I reflect on it, I come to a realization. Knowing God personally does far more than simply wipe out guilt; it frees us to face the truth about ourselves. Because I knew I was forgiven, because I felt free, because I knew the truth then, and that Jesus stood there with me, I no longer feared exposure. That mountain of ragged disgusting clothes—my past sins and mistakes—no longer worried me, thinking I'd be found out, but they were opportunities to tell the truth about myself, about God, about life. It was a moving moment for me."

"That's incredible," Doug said. "I wish I could do that with . . . well, some things."

"Yeah," Jesse confessed. "I got a lot of crap in my life, excuse my French."

"It's okay. I know what you mean. But what made the difference for me? Do you see it?"

"God. Jesus," Doug said. "Nothing else."

"That's precisely it. That's why a relationship with God is so essential. Without him, we're strung up by our past, by our deceits, by our lies, by our inner deadness. God can't just give us some rules to follow. That doesn't work. We don't follow them, and we mostly don't care. But when he steps in and says, 'I'll give you the power not only to obey, but to want to obey,' that's different. That's why having him in your life is so essential.

"I think of O. J. Simpson, how he just couldn't admit the truth, if he did commit those murders. Think of how people go to court to defend their innocence, and even keep proclaiming it all the way to the chair, even though the evidence against them is overwhelming. Think of President Clinton with all the lies he told, under oath. Why did he do such things? He had to know he'd be caught. But Satan tricks us into thinking a little lie will send everyone packing. Like all of us, until we're set free by Christ, we have to hide the truth, to lie about it, to cover it over, to pretend it's nothing, to talk ourselves out of it.'"

Some Biblical Examples

Continuing, I said, "When we first talked, Doug, you revealed your anger at some of the things God did in response to human sin. You thought they were over the top. Let's take a couple of them. First, the temptation of Eve."

"Good one," Doug said. "I mean, God lets Eve fall into the hands of the greatest trickster in history. It seems unfair."

"Right. But look at it more objectively." I looked from Doug to Jesse and quickly went through the scene, just to make sure Jesse was up to speed on it. He had read it before. "It's a simple command: Don't eat the fruit or you, Eve and Adam, will surely die. Simple, right? Not complicated. Not like God said, 'Look, you eat this fruit, a worm will get into your gut. It'll eat its way out. If you talk to the worm when he gets out, he'll lead you into worse things. But if you squash him on the spot, he will still come back and back and back. Each time he'll offer you bigger and bigger things until he's offering you the whole universe if you'll just call God a joke. You do that, that's the end. I squash you.'"

"Sounds like a comedy routine," Doug said.

"Sure. But God made it real simple. 'You do it, you die.' But look at what the Devil does. He gets Eve to focus on the fruit. He asks a question: 'Did God say you couldn't eat fruit from any of the trees in the garden?'

"A no-brainer, right? Eve answers correctly, but look at her answer. She got it all messed up. First she says, 'From the trees of the garden we may eat.' Fine, not bad. But what did God say originally? Look back at Genesis 2:16. Notice any difference?"

Doug flipped a page and read the verse. "Not to question what you're sayin' here, but there is a one-word difference."

"What?"

"'Freely.' God said they could eat freely."

"What's the difference from what Eve said?"

Both men sat very still, and I could almost hear the wheels turning. Jesse spoke first. "Well, it's kinda like God said, 'Hey, there are all these fruit trees, all over the place, and you can eat as much as you want. No restrictions. No Atkins diets. No limits.' But the way Eve says it, it's like she's bored with the whole thing. 'Oh, we can eat from any tree we want.' I mean, I bet that fruit was awesome, better than any today. And she's like, 'Ho-hum, this is all such a joke.'"

I stared at him. "You might be a Bible scholar someday, Jesse. Billy Graham, watch out."

"You really think that's good?" he asked.

"Definitely. Now notice another thing. She goes on and says, 'But from the tree in the middle of the garden, God has said, "You shall not eat from it . . ."' Stop there. What do you notice here?"

This time Doug spoke. "I'm not going to let Jesse here get out ahead of me on his master's, so here goes. She should have said, 'From the tree of the knowledge of good and evil,' but she garbled it, I don't know why. Maybe because she had to learn all about it from Adam, and like most men, he probably said, 'Just don't touch it or go near it.' So she didn't know the details. But it's as if she really didn't understand what this was all about. To her, it was just a tree in a certain spot. But God had called it something significant—'the tree of the knowledge of good and evil'—so this was an important tree, not an ordinary one. And she just didn't think about the meaning or what it was really about. Like she didn't even care."

I nodded. "You guys are killing me here. Am I not supposed to teach you?"

"Hey, we're no slouches," Jesse said.

"I see that now. So she says, 'God said you shall not eat from it or touch it.' Look at that. What's going on here?"

"He didn't say not to touch it," Jesse said.

"Exactly. What was she doing?"

Doug looked deep in thought. "She was actually making it worse than what God said. He just said not to eat it. But she's really scared of this or something."

"Precisely. And what do you think God wanted them to do? What was the whole point of this tree?"

"Question him about it. Find out why it was so sinister," Doug said. "God undoubtedly would have welcomed their questions, engaged them a little. But they were too shy or something."

"It's clear later that God came walking in the garden every day," I said. "And what did he do? He talked with them, answered questions, discussed all kinds of subjects. 'So how're the cows doing, Adam?' And, 'Eve, did you have fun with the lions the other day?' He wants a relationship with them. But it's like they don't get any of it."

"But why not?" Jesse said. "I mean, they were smart, weren't they?"

"Sure. But they had to choose to talk to God, learn, grow. That's a choice we all have to make."

"Amazing," Doug said. "It's like God's right there, and they don't want anything to do with him, and this is all before they've even eaten the fruit."

"We don't really know what went on," I told them, "but we do know humans are a stubborn bunch. So look at what happens next: The final thing from Eve is that she says, '"Don't eat it or touch it, or you will die."' Look again at God's directive to Adam. What does he tell him?"

Both men bent to their Bibles. Jesse looked up first. "I don't know if this is much, but God said they would 'surely' die. It's like there's no question there. It's absolute. But for Eve this wasn't that big a deal."

"Correct, again. You have all my seminary teachers beat any day."

Both men grinned.

"So the serpent at that point just says outright, 'You will not surely die. For God knows that when you eat of it your eyes will be opened, and you will be like God, knowing good and evil.' What is this?"

"A total lie," Doug said with a sad nod. "He knew she was an idiot regarding God's command, so he figured he could lie to her without question."

"An A-plus for you, Mr. Doug."

"Well, what about me? I had some good stuff!" Jesse countered.

"You get an A-plus, too. But don't let it go to your head."

"You know," Doug said, "I never saw any of this. It just sounds like God created the garden, and then, bang, they've sinned and they're thrown out."

"Right. But the reality is they probably had a lot of time to learn the ropes. And I really believe God wanted them to come to him with their questions. You know the craziest thing of all?"

Both men stared at me.

"They would have gained the knowledge of good and evil if they obeyed, too. They would have understood the meaning of it and how it affected everything. They would have remained in that perfect place, raised their kids there, and it would be a completely different world for all of us."

"Amazin'," Jesse said. "They were just stupid."

"No, like many of us, they were tricked, deceived into think-ing God withholds the really good stuff from us, has no good rea-sons for his commands, and that *he's* really the enemy."

Jesse shook his head. Doug just stared, then sighed. "It would have been a very different place, you know?"

"It would have."

I turned a page. "You want to look at another one?"

"Definitely," Doug said. Jesse nodded.

Cain and Abel

Just turn the page. This is the story of Cain and Abel. In it we see just how messed up Adam and Eve's mistake made everything. Cain ends up murdering his brother. Let's look at it."

I read the passage and both men looked up. "It says that in the course of time Cain brought an offering of the fruit of the ground. Why would he have done this?"

Both men looked stumped. Then Doug said, "Well, after the sin in the garden and Adam and Eve did the fig-leaf bit, God made skin garments for them, so I presume God had to kill some animal. Maybe from that . . ."

Jesse broke in. "It's just a natural thing to do. You have good product, you get blessed, you wanna thank somebody. They must've known it was all from God, so they wanted to thank him."

"Good." I looked from face to face. "There's a lot of argument about this incident. I'll clue you in in a second, but let's read on. It says Abel brought an offering, too. What was it?"

Both men read. "'The firstlings,' it says," Jesse said. "What's that?"

"From the meaning of the Hebrew, we know a firstling was a way of saying it was the best, the first ones, the most perfect animals Abel had. What does that say to you?"

"Abel brought God the best lambs he owned," Doug said.

"But what did Cain bring?"

Both men looked back at the passage. Jesse said, "It don't say he brought his best veggies. He just brought an offering."

"Think about that, and let's see what's next."

We all bent to our Bibles. Doug looked up first. "It says God had 'regard' for Abel's offering, but not for Cain's."

"What then do you think is the issue?"

Jesse jumped in. "I think it's obvious. Abel brought his best. Cain just threw somethin' together. Maybe he even collected the veggies he didn't really want that much."

Doug laughed. "Kind of like when the school takes up a food collection, and we give them all the cans of stuff we don't really want."

"Exactly!" I said. "Great illustration. And that's what I think happened. Undoubtedly, Adam and Eve taught these boys about being thankful to God and all that. They knew about bringing offerings. God must have told them about it. I mean, if you look at the Bible as a whole, God speaks a lot about what he expects, what he commands, what kinds of choices he wants us to make. He's not this strong, silent type who expects us to get it by osmosis. So I'm confident that even though Adam and Eve had lost the Garden of Eden, God hadn't abandoned them. He kept in touch and helped them as was necessary. That was the whole point of the offerings. When you have a relationship with God, you want to thank him for his blessings. But it's like Cain just resents the whole thing."

"So he ends up killin' his brother," Jesse stated.

"Right. And notice that God warned him. He tried to show Cain the way to get back in his good graces. He didn't just swat the guy and say, 'You're out, you idiot.' No, he tried to help Cain think through what had happened."

Doug sighed again. "It's amazing how communicative God is in these episodes. I always thought he was this far-off, uncaring, aloof person no one can really understand or know. But it's like he's real to these people, and not a bad person at all."

"You got it. And you can look at the majority of the situations in the Bible where something went haywire—murder, adultery, whatever—and you should assume God tried to warn those people before they did it. Through their conscience, through the Spirit, through friends, through the Bible itself. God warned David through his Word about adultery and murder in the Commandments. He spoke to David again through Joab in the numbering of the people in 2 Samuel 24. God cautioned Samson repeatedly about his sins with women and so on. Even in the case of Noah's flood, during the building of the ark, God must have used Noah to admonish the people and tell them to repent or death was coming. In so many cases, the problem isn't God's uncontrollable anger, as some would have us believe, but those people: They just wouldn't listen. You see it all through the Bible."

Doug rubbed his chin reflectively. "So what you're saying is that an awful lot of the evil done in the world is done because people simply won't listen to God, to the truth, or to whatever?"

"Absolutely."

Bound by Our Spiritual Condition

And that's the ultimate problem with everything in life. Because of our sin nature, the fact that our disobedient, rebellious side controls us, we reject God and Jesus, we try to make our own way in the world, and we lie and deceive and hide the truth about our real selves from each other, when if we'd just be honest, admit to the truth, we'd feel free—guilt-free, and worry-free, too.

"It doesn't mean a person can never do good, even heroic, things in his life. But the general pattern of all people, before they reckon with God's love and forgiveness—is that they're unable to hear the voice of God, unwilling to live up to what God wants."

I turned to my Bible again. "This is how Paul says it looks in Ephesians 4:17–19:

> So I tell you this, and insist on it in the Lord, that you must no longer live as the Gentiles do, in the futility of their thinking. They are darkened in their understanding and separated from the life of God because of the ignorance that is in them due to the hardening of their hearts. Having lost all sensitivity, they have given themselves over to sensuality so as to indulge in every kind of impurity, with a continual lust for more.

"Look at the list:

"Walking in the futility of their thinking—they keep trying to figure out life, its meaning, if there's a God, if evolution is the truth, if other religions are the truth, if Jesus really existed—but without the Bible, without accepting that it's God's Word, it's futile. They keep searching and searching and never find the answers till they turn to God.

"Being darkened in their understanding—they can't see the real world as God created it; rather they see darkness and can't understand who God is or that he cares for them. They don't even understand each other, or evil, or why they do the bad things they do.

"Separated from the life of God—life, real life, is in Christ. Joy. Peace. Love. Hope. It eludes them. I've been reading the life of the Beatles and it amazes me how lost they were, trying to find enlightenment in drugs, in music, in debauchery. But they couldn't find it. What they were living was death, despite the money, fame, and power, they were/are living dead persons who cannot fully appreciate or enjoy God's world.

"Because of the ignorance that is in them—they don't know the truth and therefore can't live it out. They don't know what they don't know, and they don't even know they don't know that.

"Because of the hardness of their hearts—they have a conscience, but through repeated wrongdoing and denial, they have turned it to rock. They can no longer even hear it warning them of destruction and death.

"Having lost all sensitivity—they don't care about doing what is right and good. They're totally uncaring, selfish, self-absorbed.

"They have given themselves over to sensuality—look at our world today. Everything is about sex, lust, looking good and young, and getting pleasure. People become totally out for themselves and the next kick, the next high."

"What a list!" Doug exclaimed. "I almost feel like, wow! That's the world I'm living in."

I looked from Doug to Jesse and back. "Right! That's the condition of the lost person. It's what it means to be bound to your sin, unable to live the life you really long for. It doesn't mean you automatically go off the deep end. But it does mean you're bound by your sinful inner nature. You can make free decisions, but you cannot make them freely. Your natural thoughts and concerns would guide and ensnare and trap you into doing the same old things you've always done."

It astonished me how Doug and Jesse were concentrating. Here were two very different men whose beliefs, to some degree, I didn't know about, and yet they appeared absolutely transfixed. I knew it was the Spirit of God speaking to them right there, and I knew it had little to do with me.

I plunged on again when no one said anything. "Here's another example. I once met a man who was addicted to heroin. The only way he could be set free was through taking another drug, methadone, which didn't have the kick of heroin, but relieved the hunger for it. I asked him what it was like. He said, 'You don't feel anything'?"

"'Nothing. Not love. Not happiness. When I make love to my girlfriend, I don't even feel the orgasm. It means nothing to me. I just do it to please her.'

"'What keeps you going?' I finally asked.

"He gazed at me strangely, a haunted, despondent look in his eyes, then shook his head. 'I don't know. I just don't want to die, so I keep hoping it'll get better.'

"I shared the gospel with him. He thought it was interesting, but at the time did not trust Christ."

Jesse hung his head. "I know where that guy's at," he said to the table. "I been there. Not as bad maybe. But there."

I put my hand on his shoulder. "When I attended college, I recall one day when a friend named Debbie came to me and said, 'You're the only happy person I know, Mark. Why are you happy?'

"I remember staring at her and laughing. 'What makes you think I'm happy?'

"'I can tell. You're always in a good mood. You're nice to people.'

"I shook my head. I had not yet become a Christian, though I had been reading about it. I said, 'I don't know that I'm happy, and if you knew me really well, you'd know that I'm not. But I want to be. I'd like to be. I just don't know where to find it.'"

I looked from Jesse to Doug and back. "I think that's the condition of a person caught in this life of futility, ignorance, and hardness. They're striving. They're trying. At times they catch a glimmer of something good and beautiful, perhaps when they have sex with the one they love, or look at their daughter's face as she sleeps, or when they play on the lawn with their new puppy. But the general tenor of their lives is one of darkness and coldness. Because of something called God's 'common grace,' the blessings he gives to everyone regardless of their faith, everyone receives a measure of good days. But in the end, it's not enough. They will continue to make bad decisions and go the wrong way until Christ turns them around."

We all stopped and stared into our drinks for a second. I finally broke the silence, saying, "Okay, what have you gotten out of this? What do you have for me?"

"We're screwed up," Jesse said and smiled grimly. "And screwed, too."

Doug didn't answer for a long time. "I think what you're saying is we're not horrible people, but we make choices based on bad influences. We're like sailors lost at sea. We don't know where to go, how to get home. So we just keep paddling, hoping something will change. Then maybe one day we hear about God and Christ. If we let them help us, lead us, change us, we find they actually want the best for us. We start to experience what God really wants for us. And things get better."

I nodded, for a moment struck so strongly I couldn't speak. I so wanted both these guys to find the truth. I said, "Listen to this list, guys. Just take in the words." I read from Galatians 5:22, 23: "'The fruit of the Spirit is love, joy, peace, patience, kindness, goodness, faithfulness, gentleness and self-control.' What would you give to have those kinds of qualities in your life every day?"

"All I'm worth," Doug said.

"Same for me," Jesse added.

"Contrast that with this list just a few verses before: 'The acts of the sinful nature are obvious: sexual immorality, impurity and debauchery; idolatry and witchcraft; hatred, discord, jealousy, fits of rage, selfish ambition, dissensions, factions and envy; drunkenness, orgies, and the like' (vv. 19–21). Think about this: Whom would you rather live with—people characterized by the first list or the second one?"

"It's a no-brainer," Doug said. "But I just don't see how it's possible."

I gave them a solemn look. "Believe me, it is. That's the kind of new world God is building. He's inviting people into it who want that quality of people around them. That's what the gospel, Jesus, God, the Bible, are all about. 'Come,' he says, in effect, 'trust me and I'll get you to a new place where you'll marvel for all eternity at how great it is.'"

Doug shook his head. "Well, once again, my friend, you've blown my mind."

I sensed our meeting was over. I glanced at Jesse. "You're welcome to sit down with us anytime, Jesse. Thanks for being here."

"My pleasure," he said.

Doug clapped him on the back. "Bet you didn't know what you were getting into."

"Nope," Jesse said with a grin. "But it was good. I learned somethin', 'n' I'll be back. Mondays at 3?"

"Right."

"Okay," I said. "Assignment for next Monday."

Doug groaned, but Jesse looked intrigued. "Study your choices and decisions this week. See if you can pinpoint what influences cause you to go one way or another. Especially look at things like doing good in contrast with doing something questionable."

"Oh, now you're getting personal," Doug said with a smile.

"Christianity is about real stuff, guys. It's not theoretical. It applies to the most basic things in life. God's in the business of changing lives, not giving us knowledge we can't use."

Jesse held out his hand. "Thanks. Don't know if I'll be here next Monday, but I'll be here when I can. Gotta drive a big rig."

"I'll be here," Doug said. "Until then, I'm off in my Lexus. Don't be jealous, guys, it's a sin."

We all laughed again as we walked out together.

In the parking lot, I said to them, "One more thing. Next week I'll plan to talk about the next logical step: We see the evil in our world, but how did it get here originally? Where did it come from? Think about it. See if you can find out any theories, or what others say. Be prepared to be amazed."

"I'm there," Doug said.

Jesse walked off to his Harley. I put my hand on Doug's shoulder. "I'll be praying about your son, and your mother, and anything else you give me. I really believe prayer does things, Doug. God answers in amazing ways for me all the time. So don't discount it, okay?"

"I appreciate it," Doug said. "I know I'm not there yet, but if I begin to see God working in my family and around me, believe me, I'll tip my hat to him."

"Great. And think about those verses I referred to. You might even memorize them."

"Where were they?"

"Isaiah 43, verses 1 and 2."

"Great." He walked away. As I climbed into my minivan, I prayed about all these things again, feeling as if we were all on the cusp of something incredible.

CHAPTER 7

God Is Not the Reason Evil Came into Our World

A Quick Trip through Explanations of the Origin of Evil

I remember the class and professor vividly. We called him "the hanging doc" because of his sudden skewering thrusts of logic. We learned it wasn't sensible to argue with him, for he always found the hole in your system and made you look the fool. Most of us simply hoped to get through the class unscarred.

Then there was Howard. He struck me as the proverbial "glutton for punishment." He always had an argument. Strangely, his words were often tinged with references to faith in God. That set the good doctor off like nothing else. Religion was, to him, the absolute inanity.

One day the professor said, "If God is good, why is there evil and suffering? If God is all-powerful, why doesn't he do something about evil? If he truly loves us, as the Bible purports, then all the more reason to do something final and complete about the evil in our world. But the truth is that he's neither good, nor all-powerful. He's nothing at all."

Howard raised his hand. "Then why *is* there evil?"

Doc smiled. "Like the evil that you have in your mind right now—that you can outwit the professor?"

The class laughed.

But Howard didn't. "No, how can there be evil if there's no such thing as God or good? Evil only exists because good exists. If good exists, who made the good?"

The hanging doc licked his lips. "You'll read about it in Hume. Have you ever read Hume?"

Howard shook his head.

"I thought so," said the professor. He turned to the class. "Here he thinks he can come and argue about evil and he hasn't read Hume. That's like thinking you can kiss a girl without lips."

The class chuckled again. Then the prof deftly reeled off a series of logical ifs, thens, buts, and hows and stunned us all into believing there was no reason for faith in Scripture or anything else, except human logic. From his words I got the impression the hanging doc didn't give Satan, God, Jesus, or anyone else in the Bible much credence. They were all myths, lies, made-up stories, and so on. I never understood it all very well, but at the time it was most impressive.

People have offered many theories on the origin of evil in the universe. Many scoff at the idea of a being named Satan and a God named Jehovah. But we find in our world today a rising interest in angels and their counterparts, demons and devils. September 11, 2001, changed the thinking of many. Could there be an evil force or even an actual person or persons behind the carnage created by suicidal extremists who believe their god sanctioned the bombings? Otherwise, how could anyone explain this insanity? Especially when they're taught by their religious leaders that they will be rewarded for such deeds in their heaven?

How can we call this anything other than "pure evil"? Or "evil personified"?

Who is behind such actions? Is it really a god named Allah?

And what about the many evil things done by others in this world, including so-called Christians? I remember reading of a pro-life activist named Paul Hill who believed God wanted him to assassinate an abortionist. He followed "God's" directive and was brought to justice by execution a few years ago.

Others like David Koresh, Jim Jones, and Charles Manson have used biblical verses to justify their evil actions.

Still, just look at our world. Simply scanning the headlines today on a Web site I visit, there is news of . . .

> A suicide bombing in Baghdad that killed sixty-three innocent people.
> The conviction of a man who raped and murdered a small girl.
> A judge who gave a serial sex offender nothing more than three months' probation.
> A diatribe against Christian family clinics (called *crisis pregnancy centers*) that try to help unwed mothers bring their babies to term and put them up for adoption rather than abort them.
> An editorial calling our president a liar and a fraud.
> And on and on.

Are such actions evil, guided by personal forces that swirl around us every minute of every day, or are they just "stuff" that happens?

So what are the theories about evil in our world? And what does the Bible say about it? What is this thing we call "evil"?

Evil Locked in a Death Grip

Some say, for instance, that good and evil have always struggled, with neither outwitting or destroying the other. They will fight for all eternity.

This is the answer of Taoism and numerous other religions, including Zoroastrianism and various cults. Its most basic definition is dualism. Black and white wrestle together. They have equal abilities and power. Therefore there will never be any resolution. Ever.

The classic expression of this idea in modern times is George Lucas's Star Wars movie series. In them, the Force can be used for good or evil. Neither has the upper hand. The Force simply exists, waiting to be tapped. But it can lead people like the Emperor and Darth Vader into evil, or people like Luke Skywalker and Obi-Wan Kenobi into good. Many, like Han Solo and his friends, remain on the sidelines, supporting neither side, and in fact doubting the existence of the Force. But by the end of the series, the viewer is convinced of one basic fact: There is good, and there is evil. You can join with either one, and use it for your success. But beware: It could eat you up.

The primary problem with this idea is that it doesn't explain reality. Regardless of whether evil wins in a certain scenario, or good, all of us have a basic conviction that it's right and best that good triumphs in the end. It's the stuff all our hopes and dreams are pinned to. If good can never ultimately overcome evil and vice versa, then the old expression, "Let us eat, drink, and be merry for tomorrow we may die" is the only worthwhile answer to the question of how to cope. What's the point of ever doing anything good or bad? It doesn't matter what you do, so do what you want. In such a system, the cold-blooded murderer has as much right to his murders as Mother Teresa to nurturing the lepers of Calcutta.

But there's something worse here. This view implies that evil is a condition to be accepted. There is nothing to be done about it or against it. This is the view of Hinduism. The law of Karma is always in operation. You reap in this life what you sowed in the last. If you experience pain and degradation now—you're a leper, or poor, or you lose at everything you do—well, you've just gotten what you deserved. If your neighbor's lot is bad, don't help him—you'd be fighting against an eternal law. So why help another? Why fight wrong? Why invent a Superman who fights for truth, justice, and the American way? Anything he does goes down the toilet. Get your kicks and get them now. Tomorrow the gettin' may not be so good.

You can see the problem with such a belief system. Anything is justified. Nothing can be rationally condemned. There's no reason to feed your children let alone the hungry around the globe. Anyone who truly believes this is the right explanation of evil, where it came from, and where it's going, has no reason for doing anything but what he wants when he wants to. Such a theory becomes the ultimate reason for evil to flourish even more than it does.

Evil Is an Illusion

Another answer is that evil is an illusion. We simply aren't seeing things right. It's really no concern of ours, for it doesn't even exist. This is the view of Christian Science and some Indian sects, as well as several Buddhist teachings.

The idea involves the supposition that evil itself is not the problem. It's the illusion we see, but it's not the bedrock issue. The real problem is our desires. If we could simply rid ourselves of all desire, we'd be at peace, happier, and better able to cope with the world. Say "Om" a million times a day, rid yourself of hunger, lust, hope, needs, and so on, and you have it. You're headed for nirvana, where you'll experience "true nothingness" for all eternity, and be at peace.

But such a view is an illusion. Who can read a daily newspaper or drive through a city without recognizing that evil exists? As one of my friends puts it, "I can see people not believing in God. But I can't see anyone who reads the daily newspaper not believing in evil!"

Moreover, who wants to live without desires? It's the inner need and motivation to survive, to eat when hungry, to drink when thirsty, to procreate, to succeed in life, to help others, and to aspire to be a good, decent person, that compel us to make our world a better place to live, and to leave a legacy worth remembering.

It's also evil desires that lead to all the bad things in our world—greed, lust, hatred, prejudice, pride, and so on. Truly, desire makes nearly everything that happens in our world on a human level happen. Without desire, good would never be accomplished. Without desire, evil would never have a foothold.

God calls us to control our desires and channel them for good things, not forsake or eliminate them.

God Himself Blew It!

Others venture that the problem is God himself. Though he is very powerful, he still has limitations. Evil is the result of his creation going off course. He simply couldn't stop it. It's just a fact of nature. God wants to get it back on course, but so far he's failed.

This was the view of a popular book some years back, *Why Bad Things Happen to Good People* by Rabbi Harold Kushner. God wants to help, but he's hampered. We'll just have to hang in there until he gets himself together.

Is this the answer? If it is, it's a dismal one. Who could trust a God like that? Who could worship that God? To the contrary, we'd pity him. He becomes little more than a supernatural wimp, the divine victim of victims.

Moreover, this is not the God of the Bible on any level. The psalmist writes, "The LORD is compassionate and gracious, slow to anger, abounding in love . . . He does not treat us as our sins deserve or repay us according to our iniquities" (Psalm 103:8, 10). Take Psalm 33:9–11: "For he spoke, and it came to be; he commanded, and it stood firm. The LORD foils the plans of the nations; he thwarts the purposes of the peoples. But the plans of the LORD stand firm forever, the purposes of his heart through all generations." Does this sound like an impotent sissy? A person who can't do anything for anyone?

If Kushner is right that God is just not strong enough to solve the problem of evil, then frankly, I couldn't worship him. I want a God who can step in, guide me, empower me, help me solve my and others' problems, and make life better on our planet. That's a God worth following, loving, and worshipping. But not this weak-kneed fraud some truly believe the real God is.

It's the Law of the Jungle

Still another answer comes from the scientific realm. All nature includes evil. Animals kill, maim, wound, and deceive. People are little more than animals with big brains. Thus, they shouldn't be expected to act any better. It's part of nature. It's the result of time plus chance making you and me imperfect and full of problems.

This is the evolutionist's response. We are nothing more than the result of billions of years of random changes and natural selection. If I defeat you, it's because I'm a superior product of the evolutionary process. If you destroy me, well, so what? It's all just part of the dance.

An insight into what some scientists say about the origin of evil actually comes from an interview/debate Dr. Richard Dawkins had with geneticist/Christian believer Dr. Francis Collins in *Time* (November 13, 2006). Collins says at one point, "Evolution can explain some features of the moral law, but it can't explain why it should have any real significance. If it is solely evolutionary convenience, there really is no such thing as good or evil. But for me, it is much more than that. The moral law is a reason to think of God as plausible—not just a God who sets the universe in motion but a God who cares about human beings, because we seem uniquely amongst creatures on the planet to have this far-developed sense of morality. What you've said implies that outside of the human mind, tuned by evolutionary processes, good and evil have no meaning. Do you agree with that?"

Dawkins replies, "Even the question you're asking has no meaning to me. Good and evil—I don't believe that there is hanging out there, anywhere, something called good and something called evil. I think that there are good things that happen and bad things that happen."

In other words, real good and evil, one force or person representing each and opposing the other and waging war to gain adherents and followers in the world, do not exist in Dawkins' universe. There is nothing really to separate them. Everything is gray, with occasional spurts in one direction or another, but none of it attributed to a battle of wills on some giant spiritual plane, as the Bible depicts the war between God and Satan, God and evil, in its pages.

A Logical Explanation?

But does this actually explain reality? Do we not see every day the struggle between good and evil—in Iraq, among races, between people in the same families? Look into your own heart and what do you see? If you're like me, you see a constant struggle of different forces, one telling me to do bad things, another telling me to do good. As Paul wrote, "For our struggle is not against flesh and blood, but against the rulers, against the authorities, against the powers of this dark world and against the spiritual forces of evil in the heavenly realms" (Ephesians 6:12). And in Romans 7:15, Paul details his own internal struggle: "I do not understand what I do. For what I want to do I do not do, but what I hate I do."

If evil and good don't exist in some cosmic sense, then why does the battle swirl all around us, every day, even inside our own hearts and souls?

Regardless of how you believe evil came into our world, the fact is that evil permeates everything, with good constantly working to right us, guide us, and get us back onto the path of decency, humanity, and righteousness.

Beyond that, the bigger problem here is when you believe evil forces don't exist, that there's no real battle going on behind the scenes, it dismisses all responsibility on anyone's part. We're just doing what we were programmed to do. If Charles Manson murders Sharon Tate, who has a right to protest? He was just following what evolution and "Mother Nature" put into his heart.

What, then, is the answer?

We Talk about the Devil—
Satan—the Enemy of God

As Doug and I talked, I spelled out these ideas to him in detail. We paused, though, and I said, "Look, let's talk about some personal things, now that I've completely blown you away with my erudition about good and evil. How's your mom?"

"Same," he said with a sigh. "You know, tests, more tests. Everyone's on pins and needles. No big breakthroughs, but I did visit her—she's here in Kansas City, and she's pretty upbeat about it. I even asked her what she believed about heaven. She said she really didn't know. She hopes she goes there if she dies, but she really has no sense that it's assured. I told her about you, our talks, and she said, I quote: 'Find out what he says and tell me. If I get interested, maybe I'll come to one of your little meetings.'"

I raised my eyebrows slightly, with a sense of hope. "It looks like we're getting a little Bible study going here. I wonder if Jesse will be back."

"Oh, I gave him my card the other day. I stopped here for a latte, and he sat by me with his computer. We talked. He said he really liked you, thought you were real down to earth. But he said he had a road trip this week. I think we'll see him again."

"I wonder what he's all about."

Doug smiled, a big toothy grin. "He told me a little. He's going through a divorce and might lose the right to see his kids. He says he has a violence problem. So I promised I'd mention it to you, so you could pray that you don't say something that makes him decide to beat us up."

I chuckled.

"He also said if God does something about his custody situation, he'll believe once and for all."

"I'll definitely pray about it."

Doug appeared meditative. "The really big thing is I took my son Gabriel out to lunch last week. He was kind of amazed I even cared. I didn't talk about you or religion, just him. I'm a little less concerned about him. He told me he knows college is the way to go, but he just needs to figure out what he really wants to study. He doesn't want to waste my money hanging out at college with no sense of direction. So that kind of encouraged me."

"Wow! That's great!"

"Yeah, well, he also said he was afraid his girl might be pregnant."

"Oh, man."

"Yeah. So I told him to think about an abortion." He gazed at me, his eyes unflinching. "Do you think that's wrong?"

I was afraid something like this would come up. But I took a breath and said, "I will probably disagree about this with you. I think there are better ways to deal with an unwanted pregnancy.

We can discuss it more. But I don't think you're really ready for a big study on what God says about it. Especially since he doesn't say a whole lot."

"Really?"

"There are many implications in Scripture, but there are only a couple of verses that actually refer to killing an unborn child. But—" I eyed him directly. "Let's talk about this some more later. I think when you understand other things about the Bible and God and all that, you'll be ready to give more informed advice to your son. It is one of the most divisive issues in the church, let alone the whole country and world."

He shrugged. "I'm open to whatever you have to say."

"Okay. Good. Now let's get on with this problem of how evil came into our world. By the way, did you ask anyone about it?"

"That, and the decisions thing, about free will."

"Good. Go ahead."

He told me how he asked the same three people about it—his wife, his partner, and his secretary—and he admitted that might have been a mistake. His partner lectured him more about not getting into the religion thing, and even became more vehement, saying he could see Doug headed in a direction that wasn't good for their company. His secretary gave him the Scientology line about the mystical thetans. And his wife said she didn't know, but she thought it was part of the evolutionary process, that there would be good and evil variations throughout history.

"Interesting," I said. "No one mentioned Satan?"

"Not a one."

"And about your decision-making process?"

"Well, there was only one thing. I was on my computer and this e-mail came through from I-don't-know-who. When I opened it, it was a picture of some very buxom girl with everything hanging out."

"Yeah, I get them, too."

"Usually, I just ignore them. But something in my head went, 'Aren't you even curious? Wouldn't you like to be able to say what these things are about and how bad they are, instead of just assuming they're bad?' I don't know where it came from. But it kind of made me mad, like I was less of a person because I shut it off. So I went to the Web site. Boy, did I get an eyeful! I flicked it off and then looked over my shoulder to make sure my wife hadn't seen what I did. I also deleted the history from my computer so no one could look up what Web sites I'd been to. My wife has sneaked up on me about such things before."

"Wow! It was that direct, huh?"

"Yeah. I was amazed. But listen. Afterward, I was thinking about that, and this other thing in my head goes, 'Have you learned your lesson?' I just sat there, wondering where that was from. Nothing more than that. It was kind of eerie. Like I became aware of two different voices out there that weren't my own. Or were they?"

"Believe me, they're there. We'll look at that in a moment, and after we look at this subject, I think you'll be even surer of where at least one of those voices was from."

"It sort of whacked me out for a while. But now—"

I waited. He seemed unsure of what he wanted to say. Then: "It just kind of freaked me. I've never really thought about such a thing before."

"Most of us don't. It tells me you're becoming more sensitive to spiritual issues."

"Honest?"

"Sure."

He sighed. "It really rattled me. But let's go on. I want to hear this."

"Good."

From there we embarked on one of the Bible's most powerful and fascinating stories—the rise of evil after God's initial creative act, not in Genesis 1, but before that.

I said, "Think for a second about the first time you ever encountered real evil in your life. Got it?"

Doug nodded, his eyes wide.

"Can you tell me about it?"

"Sure." He closed his eyes a second and appeared to reach way back. "I was about five years old. I was in kindergarten. We were on the playground. These two older kids argued, and none of the teachers was watching. The bigger kid started hitting the other and knocked him down. Then the older kid goes, 'Let's get him!' And all the kids jumped the smaller guy. I stood there with the little kids, just staring, until a teacher stopped it. But I remember the terror that bigger kid inspired in me, and I wondered why all those others piled on. I didn't really see a reason for it. It wasn't like the other kid was a bad guy or something, at least that I knew about. But I kind of saw how a crowd could get out of control. It's stuck with me ever since."

"Interesting. Amazing how those things can happen. Now let me tell you about one of my defining moments.

"One Christmas, when I was five years old, I received a little piggy bank as a present. I didn't think much about it until my grandfather asked me if I'd like him to put a nickel in it for me to save. I knew enough about money to know that it was well worth having, and in those days, 1955, a nickel could buy a candy bar, little toys from Japan, and numerous other things. So I held out the bank.

"Grandpop plopped the coin into it and I rattled it around in the metal bank, delighting in the melodic tinkling inside.

"Then Grandpop did something that was to have long-term consequences for my life. He said, 'Now, do you want to know how to get that nickel back out?'

"Did I ever. He sent me to the kitchen to retrieve a knife and soon he showed me how to stick the tip of the knife in the slot, shake the bank around, and eventually the nickel dropped out.

"While not a monumental moment, I later began my life of crime stealing money from various banks in my house—from my mother's to my sister's and brother's banks—without them ever knowing it. I had a problem for many years with stealing, really until I became a Christian at the age of twenty-one."

"Wow! You *were* a sinner," Doug beamed, as if this revelation made his day.

"Okay, big guy, tell me about all the sordid things in your life, too. Then we can be equals."

He grinned. "Believe me, I have far worse. But I'm not ready to go into details. When I walk the aisle, I'll make a big confession at the altar. It'll take several hours, but I'll invite you along."

I shook my head and rolled my eyes. "Great. But what I'm trying to point out, Doug, is how easy it is for evil to get a handhold in your life. It could have come subtly—it often does—but you know very well, that became a defining moment, and perhaps one that led to much anguish in your life. Every addiction began with one episode. Every life run down the toilet probably started with stars in the victim's eyes.

"That's how evil operates. It usually starts small, then moves you on to the bigger and better until you're safely entrapped in destructive behaviors that, if not stopped, will lead to your death.

"Why is this kind of evil so real to us, and so early in life? How does it get its start in our lives? It all goes back to an important cherub angel in Scripture named Lucifer."

"Satan," Doug said, his eyes fixed on mine again.

"Right. Though Scripture is not clear when God created the supernatural world of angels—cherubim, seraphim, and other supernatural beings—it's plain they were one of God's first creations. The book of Job provides a significant insight when God first appears on the scene and begins responding to Job's complaints. He asks Job,

> Where were you when I laid the earth's foundation?
> Tell Me, if you understand,
> Who marked off its dimensions. Surely you know!
> Who stretched a measuring line across it?
> On what were its footings set,
> Or who laid its cornerstone—
> While the morning stars sang together,
> And all the angels shouted for joy? (38:4–7)

"This passage speaks of God's original creative work. But look at the last two lines. The 'morning stars' and 'angels' apparently already existed as God put together our world and universe. They also seemed to be in some semblance of harmony and friendship with God. They were happy. They sang. They lifted their voices in praise to God for his actions.

"Who are they?" I looked at Doug and encouraged him to answer.

"I'd guess they're some kind of angelic beings. But I don't really know for sure."

"Good guess. In the Bible, these are names associated with angels. From this text, we can assume that angels such as Lucifer lived and performed before the creation of the universe. They witnessed that creation and perhaps were even part of it."

A Powerful Passage

It's in this context that we look at an easily overlooked Scripture passage in Ezekiel 28." I opened my Bible, and Doug opened his.

"Look in verse 2. There, God tells the prophet Ezekiel to address a certain leader who rules over the city of Tyre, one of the powerful Phoenician cities on the coast of Asia north of Israel during the Jewish monarchy and Israel's later exile in Babylon. This leader speaks arrogantly, calling himself a god and one who sits 'on the throne of a god.' The true God through Ezekiel warns this person his destruction is imminent (vv. 7, 8).

"Following that, the prophet addresses a second personage: the 'king of Tyre'" (v. 12). I pointed to the verse. "Who is this?"

Doug frowned. "Another king?"

"Good thought. But as you study the passage, remarkable things are revealed. This person had been the 'model of perfection.' What human could possibly claim that? He also visited 'Eden, the garden of God' (v. 13). Whoever this is is very ancient. What then can Ezekiel be referring to?"

"I have a feeling this guy is Lucifer," Doug said with narrowed eyes.

"Many scholars believe this passage offers us an illuminating portrait of the spiritual power behind the leader of Tyre. That person is none other than Lucifer, as you said, the most prominent and powerful being God ever created. His name means 'Day Star' or 'Morning Star' or 'lightbearer.' Who exactly was this person?"

"I bet you're going to show me," Doug said.

I laughed—I had to like his style. "Look, if you're going to treat me like a Sunday school teacher or a pastor, you can just go to church about this."

"No way," Doug said. "They don't have lattes there."

I laughed again.

A Look in Lucifer's Wardrobe

Let's look at what Ezekiel says in the passage:

"First, Lucifer had been the model of perfection (Ezekiel 28:12).

"That perfection refers to completeness. Not one of his faculties or parts was defective. Like the inspector of meat in the supermarket, God had pronounced him 'Grade A, number one choice, prime cut.' There wasn't a flaw in him. It doesn't mean, however, that he was perfect in the sense of all-powerful, all-knowing, holy, and so on, like God."

"Interesting," Doug said.

"Good. It says next he was full of wisdom (v. 12). At his creation, God infused Lucifer with knowledge and the skill to use that knowledge effectively and productively. He didn't start off like a child who must gradually learn to crawl, walk, speak, and play through trial and error. Rather, he began life with a level and measure of wisdom that exceeded Solomon's. That didn't mean, though, that he couldn't or wouldn't learn. He wasn't omniscient like God. We can assume that though he'd gotten a head start, there was still a long distance to go.

"He also was perfect in beauty (v. 12). That doesn't make him feminine—or even masculine. It appears from other Scripture passages that angelic beings are neutral (not neuter). The word means his appearance was excellent. All who looked upon him instantly recognized the superiority of his face and demeanor. He had 'the look.'"

"Ah," Doug said. "Wasn't that a song by Roxette?"

"You know your rock history for sure," I said. "But do you know your Satan history?"

"Only as it refers to bands like Led Zeppelin and Black Sabbath."

"Ah, a man after my true heathen heart. Although I was never much of a Black Sabbath fan."

"Yeah, I listened to a lot of their stuff in college."

"Then I'd venture you know a bit about drugs."

"For sure."

I grinned. "I'm learning what a sinner *you* are, too. It's a two-way street, you know."

"Pretty soon I'll be telling you about my escapades as a member of al-Qaeda. But let's not go into that yet."

I loved Doug's sense of humor.

"Good. Now it says his cloak was made of every precious substance God had created (v. 13). Lucifer was given a special covering that set him off from all other creatures. It was a unique robe of honor. Because God is light, Lucifer's jeweled cloak would fire up and sparkle as he stood before his Lord. He turned into a walking 'light show.' He was a reflector of God's magnificence, a little picture of what God himself was like."

"Maybe he should have worked for a modern rock group," Doug said. "Go on tour with, say, U2?"

"Definitely. But let's move on. It says next that he was anointed (v. 14). The word *anointed* is the same one used of Jesus when he is called the *Messiah*. Anointing denoted at least three ideas. First, Lucifer was specially selected and separated for God's personal service. Second, his authority derived from God. He led, commanded, and gave instruction under the auspices and power of God himself. Third, God empowered him to perform his duties. He had from God everything he needed to do his job."

Doug looked pensive.

"What are you thinking?" I finally asked.

"This guy was pretty awesome, more than I ever knew."

"Just listen. The next statement is that he was a guardian cherub (v. 14). Scripture describes cherubim as winged creatures with marvelous power and wisdom. They had special access to God and guarded his glory. The ark of the covenant, which was the centerpiece of the temple worship from the days of Moses on—*Raiders of the Lost Ark* pictured it accurately in terms of its outward features, though that last bit at the end of the movie was pure fantasy if you remember it—"

Doug chuckled. "Of course. Who doesn't?"

"The ark symbolized God's presence in Israel. Those two winged creatures on top were the two cherubs over 'the mercy seat,' which was the place where God dwelled on earth. Their wings spread out over the open area of the ark just above the seat, as if protecting God's presence.

"What is most startling is that the cherubim are pictured as shielding all others from God and God from all others. In effect, the cherubim gazed on God's face continually. But all others could see nothing but what the cherubim themselves reflected of God's presence. Thus, the cherubim became, in effect, the insiders from whom all others would receive information about God's nature. They were his personal interpreters and ambassadors."

Doug's hands were flexed, as if these thoughts tensed him up. "It's really incredible. Lucifer had the best spot in the universe."

"Yeah, but look at what else. Next, it says he was on the holy mountain with God (v. 14). That mountain was the home of God. Lucifer had access to God that few, if any, others had. Lucifer possessed absolute intimacy with God. He knew every trait, every attribute. He gazed on God's face and understood details of God's being that no other angel could comprehend.

"After that, we find he walked among the fiery stones (v. 14), as in diamonds or other jewels. It pictured intimacy with God. Perhaps God even instructed Lucifer in the secret things of creation. If this symbolized some sort of divine altar, then Lucifer would have been privy to the mysteries of God. He, in effect, was like the conductor of the divine symphony. He orchestrated the music of heaven."

"Then how did he turn into such an enemy?"

"We'll get to that." I was glad for Doug's questions. I worried this might be boring him. Sometimes straight teaching from the

Bible left listeners quite tired and rather disinterested. But he clearly was taking it all in.

"We see next that he was blameless (v. 15). It means 'complete, sound, innocent, without blemish.' Lucifer was God's highest creation. None equaled him. He could think higher, feel deeper, and do better than any other person in existence, except God himself.

"If someone asked Michelangelo what his greatest work of art was, he might reply, *The Pieta*, or, 'The ceiling of the Sistine Chapel.' If Edison were interviewed about his most far-reaching invention, he might say, 'The lightbulb.' When God was asked what his most marvelous act of creation was, he pointed to Lucifer."

"Really?"

"Definitely."

"But what about Jesus?"

"Jesus wasn't a creation. He was part of the Godhead, God incarnate, the human flesh picture of God."

Doug nodded and looked reflective again. "So you're saying Lucifer had every privilege, he had complete access to God in ways no one else ever possessed, and he knew more about God than anyone. I don't get it. Why would he decide to turn against him?"

"Just listen."

Four Steps to Infamy

I looked back at the Ezekiel passage. "Something clearly went wrong. Even though God had given Lucifer everything a creature could need or want, something inside the cherub began to twist and rend. Maybe he noticed that though all the creatures respected and admired him, they still worshipped God. While Lucifer was number one creature, God took the Creator slot and that was a trillion miles higher and more important. Though Lucifer's opinions were respected, though his leadership was revered, God still possessed ultimate authority.

"It's like a senator next to the president of the United States. When senators step into the assembly room, some may notice them, shake hands, and smile. But when the president strides in, famous music plays. Everyone stands. Many greet him warmly and embrace. There's an excitement over the whole gathering.

"That was Lucifer, the senator, next to God, the president. It must have irked Lucifer to no end that all he got was some tepid applause when God received standing ovation after standing ovation.

"So deep down, Lucifer desired that place. He wanted to call the shots. He craved the position of king of the mountain."

"But what happened?" Doug almost exploded. "I just don't see how, if he really knew who and what God was, Lucifer could risk everything like that!"

"Let's keep going." I grinned at Doug. "Didn't know this was in here, did you?"

"I bet I've read it before and never made the connection." Doug scratched his temple. "I mean, I've actually read the whole Bible. But every time we open it together, it's like it's completely new to me. I'm thinking I missed everything."

"Don't credit me. The Spirit of God is opening your eyes."

"You're kidding?" He regarded me so intensely, I wondered if I'd said too much.

"Look, Doug. For most people, the Bible is a closed book. In the New Testament, it says a veil lies over the eyes and minds of people. They're blind. But when someone starts to take the Bible seriously, it's because the Spirit is working in them. I think he must be working in you, or you wouldn't be this interested."

"He's not going to zap me, is he?"

I laughed. "What do you mean?"

"I'm not going to go home and be holy all of a sudden, am I?"

"Be holy?"

He grimaced. "You know. No more beer. No more movies. No more dancing, smoking, drinking, or chewing?"

I had to laugh. "Doug, that's an image of holiness that is so off target it's almost hysterical. We'll talk about real holiness in the days ahead. But for now, let's just say that when the Spirit starts working on you to make you holy, it won't be cosmetic surgery. He'll go right for the heart. A total transplant."

"Sheesh."

"Don't worry, it's not so bad. You'll find you actually enjoy it when it happens."

He rubbed his scalp. "I come home someday a Holy Roller, my wife will keel over."

"Don't be so sure. She might kneel and say, 'Thank you, God. Thank you. Thank you. Thank you.'"

He grinned and pointed his finger. "Okay, this is getting too personal. Let's get back to Satan."

"Sure." I pointed to the next verse in Ezekiel. "Here, the prophet outlines four steps Lucifer took that led to destruction."

Lucifer's Steps to Sin

Step 1: Unrighteousness

"First, Ezekiel says, 'Wickedness was found in you' (v. 15). The word for 'wickedness' means to do something not in line with God's will. For Lucifer to do something wrong, God must have already made clear the difference between right and wrong. Lucifer was a moral creature. He made real choices about right and wrong. God established laws his creatures had to live by. Perhaps he gave them their own Ten Commandments, or something akin to the Law in the Old Testament. Whatever they had and knew to be 'God's rules to live by,' Lucifer decided to reject them and violate them. He became 'unrighteous.'"

"So it's a lot more than just asking questions?"

"Of course. We're beyond the thought stage at this point. Lucifer might have considered several fleeting ideas of rebellion before he reached this point. Maybe God even warned him—several times—that the path he was on invited grave danger. But Lucifer hadn't sinned yet. He'd only 'thought' these things.

"It's the same for us. Thinking of doing evil, just having it pass through your mind, is not necessarily sin. It's when we dwell on it, savor it, and lust after it that it becomes real sin in God's eyes. That is undoubtedly what happened in Lucifer's mind.

"Thus, this unrighteousness signifies the fact Lucifer meditated on an evil course of action, enjoying it, and imagining himself destroying God. That's where Lucifer's mind was. He had begun to plot, to enjoy the idea of overthrowing God."

Step 2: Internal Violence

"We find the second step in Ezekiel's words, 'Through your widespread trade you were filled with violence, and you sinned' (v. 16). 'Trade' means 'traffic in merchandise,' and possibly 'gossip.' Lucifer's heart became violent, and he sinned; that is, he moved from mere thoughts to actions. What, then, was Lucifer doing?"

Doug narrowed his eyes. "I think I kind of see him beginning to lay out plans, possibly talking to several friends and confidants about what he wanted to do, enlisting them in his service."

"Precisely. My suspicion is that Lucifer used his position of intimacy with God to offer tidbits of information about God to others. He posed as an intermediary between God and the rest of the angels.

"At the same time, something within Lucifer twisted. As he talked about the intimacies of God, it says he was filled with violence. Undoubtedly, the other angels and beings began asking questions about the Creator. They wanted to know about this and that, and they reveled in learning the little details of God's life and interests. Lucifer realized how they revered, loved, and worshipped God. Instead of merely relaying information and leading others in worship, he wished others would ask about *him*, *his* power, and *his* position.

"It's like those columnists and paparazzi who write about and follow celebrities to get pictures and particulars about them. Have you ever wondered if such people wish they were the celebrities themselves? How many followed Princess Diana not only because they made money off what they told about her, but because they vicariously lived through her life? I'd be willing to bet many longed to be her, to have what she had, to be the great person she was in the eyes of the world.

"That was what I think happened to Lucifer. He couldn't stand to see God get all this adulation. He felt he deserved some, too. Eventually, he wanted all of it. He longed for the angels to worship him in place of God."

Step 3: Pride

I looked at Ezekiel again. "We find the third step in the words, 'Your heart became proud on account of your beauty' (v. 17). Instead of looking at himself as God's magnificent creation, Lucifer began to think of himself as better than God or any other because of his appearance. His pride made him tell himself he had a right to the same position as God. His pride told him he might just be able to pull off this coup. His pride said he deserved to take it away from God, because God was a virtual paper tiger."

"But . . ." Doug appeared mystified. "How could he do this? He must have known God really was greater than him. How could he think—" He shook his head. "It makes no sense."

Step 4: Corruption

"Just listen. We find the last step here: Lucifer 'corrupted [his] wisdom because of [his] splendor' (v. 17). That's how he could think he could actually pull this off. He ignored, rejected, and obliterated his wisdom. Instead of letting the truth be his guide in dealing with this turmoil in his heart, he pushed away his reason and turned against God. He jettisoned what he knew was right and good and decided to go for God's jugular. This is where we have to look at another passage."

I turned to Isaiah 14:13, 14 and pointed to it: "Here we get some insight into the nature of Lucifer's violence. Again, there are arguments among scholars about what this really means, but many, like me, believe this was Satan's battle cry. He said—really boasted—'I will ascend to heaven; I will raise my throne above the stars of God; I will sit enthroned on the mount of assembly, on the utmost heights of the sacred mountain. I will ascend above the tops of the clouds; I will make myself like the Most High.'"

"What on earth does that mean?" Doug asked, grimacing with disgust and amazement.

"Roughly interpreted, Lucifer was vowing, 'I will breach God's most holy place ("heaven"); I will set up a throne over all God's creatures ("stars of God"); I will stand before them when they're assembled and become their leader; I will penetrate God's most intimate place where no creature has been ("the tops of the clouds"); and I will take the position God has and cast him out ("make myself like the Most High").

"Lucifer's plot was nothing less than a coup d'état, the boldest stroke in all history. He planned to overthrow God."

Doug shook his head. "I mean, it sounds like some political thing in some foreign country. But this is the biggest one in history."

"You got it. And at the same time, he persuaded others to join him—about one-third of all God's creatures, according to Revelation 12:4—and soon a full-scale rebellion surged through heaven. We see the carnage of this war going on even today. Satan's out there trying to get humans on his side, and God works in the midst of it all to get *his* plans done.

"But this was the sordid beginning of every evil deed both men and angels have committed and will commit in history. This was the source of evil in our world today."

Doug's jaw hung a bit. "It's like the greatest movie in history. I mean, what if Spielberg or someone could have filmed this?"

"Maybe one day they will. If they ever begin to take evil seriously."

Doug sighed heavily. "I don't get it. Why don't more people know about this?"

"Think about it, Doug. Why wouldn't they? Who would keep it from them?"

He thought about it a second, then snapped his fingers. "Satan! That's it, isn't it?"

I nodded.

"Right now," he said, "Satan is trying to keep anyone from knowing this stuff. He doesn't want anyone to know the truth about him, so he gives us all kinds of lies about ways evil might have come—from evolutionary theory to other religions to whatever."

"You've nailed it. But there's another question we need to ask."

How Do We Know for Sure?

Sure, it makes good fiction, but this is preposterous. A rebel angel? A war in heaven? Come on! Isn't that what many people say?"

Doug's eyes were wide and expectant. "Right on."

"But think about it. What is evil—a force? No, a force is inanimate. It has no morality. Evil deals with right and wrong. A force merely acts on the basis of scientific laws. Gravity, magnetism, horsepower—these are all forces. But evil has a persona. It's real, and it has to inhabit a person.

"So is evil an idea? No, again. Evil pertains to conduct, action, behavior. Something has to be done that affects others for the worse.

"So what *is* evil?" Doug stared at me. "Go on. I'm here."

"Put in simple terms, evil is action taken by moral beings that is contrary to what is known to be right and good.

"Here we have a moral being—Lucifer—choosing to take action against what had already been established as what was right and good."

Doug shook his head. "And he's trying to get everyone to do the same?"

"Correct."

"What a waste."

"To be sure. But let's ask another question."

How Do We Know God
Isn't the Bad Guy?

How do we know the real bad guy here isn't God himself? After all, God could appear to be the proud tyrant, demanding that everyone worship him. Why didn't he let Lucifer receive worship?"

"Good question." Doug's eyes were alight with interest.

"Consider the nature of worship for a moment. Would you worship a flea? Or a tick? Or a blade of grass? No, we worship someone (or something) superior to us, worthy of our respect, love, and obedience. We worship that person we see as great, powerful, royal, even magnanimous."

"Right. I can see that."

"Good. Worship is also free and voluntary. You can't command it. In effect, God gave all those mighty intimacies to Lucifer so Lucifer could worship God with greater abandon and joy than any other creature. The purpose was that Lucifer would see and know all the great secrets of God's nature so he could lead all of heaven in ebullient, intoxicating worship of the Deity. That's what Lucifer was designed to do. That was his whole purpose for being. He would find fulfillment and joy only in living out that reality.

"But Lucifer chose not to. He rebelled. He wanted to be worshipped himself."

"Wait a second," Doug said. "You still haven't shown me why God isn't the bad guy in this scenario. How do we know he isn't, and that Satan isn't more like George Washington and the Americans fighting for independence?"

"Good," I said. "And the fact is, to some degree you don't know. But that's why God gave us the Bible. In it, he shows us who he is, what he's done in history, and what principles he lives by. He's also pointed out Satan's history and *lack of* principles. After laying it all out, he says to each of us, 'Choose whom you will serve—me, or Satan?'"

Doug gulped. "What an awful situation. I mean, what if I just say, 'You two have at it, and I'll go with whoever wins'?"

"It doesn't work that way. You have to choose now. Before you die. That's the way it is. But really, isn't that always the way it is? If we all knew how everything would turn out, we would win every time. But those who make the hard choices, take the greatest risks, are the ones who really show their character, their courage, and everything else. Who wants people on his side who sat around and waited till it was all finished? Those are the losers. The ones who really count are the ones who get into the fight and do all they can to help the one they believe in and trust to win. That's really what it's all about. Whom do you choose?"

Doug's eyes almost popped. "Man, I hate this."

I smiled. "But there is something you're missing here. God has told us how it all ends. He's shown us the future in the Bible. If we pay attention to it, we know that he wins, we know Satan is the bad guy, and we know God is not only good, but wise, loving, compassionate, and holy. We can see it all in his Word."

"So it's like we can know the future if we want. It's just that most of us don't care."

I nodded sadly. "I think that's it. And I'm not saying you have to make that choice this moment, but that's the issue. Satan will try hard to convince you God is a loser, God is a deceiver, he will cheat you, he will leave you high and dry. Whereas, he, Satan, will give you what you really want—pleasure, power, money, popularity. Whatever it is that matters to you, Satan will offer it to you if you'll follow him. Of course, you may not even realize it's he you're following. You're just spending all your efforts and lifeblood trying to make that first million. Or maybe it's some girl you want to bed. It could be anything. But Satan gets you to buy into it, and then suddenly you're stuck. You can't go back. It's too late. He's got you."

Doug seemed to stop breathing. "It's that bad, huh?"

"Why not? On the other hand, God assures you that with him you will gain salvation, an eternal home in heaven, life—real, joyful, peace-loving life—security, hope, loyal friends, and all the good things of this world as well as the next. But you have to trust him. You have to throw your lot in with him, no holds barred, and you have to be willing to obey his laws and principles."

"Sheesh."

"It's a tough decision. I believe every person in history will face such a choice sooner or later. It may not be defined as faith in Christ, since they may not have heard of him, but the Bible reveals that God deals with everyone in the same way. Either you believe in, trust, and commit to his kingdom and purpose, or you decide to go with the things of this world and your lusts, or the Devil himself."

"You're scaring the heck out of me."

"Good."

We sat there for a moment. "I just don't get it, though," stated Doug. "Why is Satan so hungry for worship? People bowing down to him? All that? Who cares?"

I nodded. "Let me give you an example."

An Example

Ask yourself: What really matters to me? What would I give my life for? What person, place, thing, or condition would I wish for that if I could have it, I'd know I had it made forever?"

Doug sat very still. "Well, when I was in high school, it was being better than my brother at something. In college, it was winning my wife. In business, it turned into making a pile of money, having a great home, being successful, being looked up to by my friends, all that. Now—I'm not sure. I know all those things were paramount at one time. But now, they all look a little thin."

"Why is that?"

Doug shrugged. "In the scope of things, they really don't amount to much. How much money is enough? How much sex is enough? After you've gotten some basic satisfaction there, those things suddenly don't look like the be-all and end-all of existence."

"But could you say at one time you worshipped those things? You bowed down to them? Did everything you could to get what they offered?"

"Sure. Yeah. I suppose."

"And then after you got them, you realized they weren't really what you were looking for?"

Doug sighed. "I think I get your point. What we want, what we give our lives to, that's what we worship. For some people, it's cocaine. For others, it's sex. For many, it's possessions. But like I said, those are all a little thin."

"Take it a step further," I said. "My daughter at one time was into a rock band called Hanson. These three cute boys wrote some songs, and they were all over the media. She plastered her room with their posters. But she outgrew them, and when I last asked her what she thought of that phase of her life, she told me she was just a stupid teenybopper. It was all stupid. But how such a thing can capture a person's attention and their life!

"So ultimately, worship is giving adulation, respect, devotion, and your resources—time, money, abilities—to those persons or things. God created us like that. It's in our human nature to worship something. But ultimately, anything less than God himself is a cop-out. God doesn't want or need our money, our houses, our cars, any of those things. But he will not allow us to worship inferior things, those people or articles inferior to himself, forever. Ultimately, he will call us all to account for what we worshipped and why, and why we thought he was little more than a problem."

"I think I'm getting it," Doug said. "But . . ."

"Okay, let me give you another example. Suppose the coach of a little league team works up his roster. Each player has an assigned job. Imagine he has made the selection on the basis of perfect knowledge and wisdom, so there's no mistake. John, who plays shortstop, is truly great at that position. Bill, who's the catcher, wouldn't function better elsewhere.

"But then there's Charley. He's the pitcher. He was designed to pitch. Everyone knows the whole game revolves around him. But Charley has this problem: He notices that the coach gives the orders and directs everything. Charley resents it. Even with all the power and adoration he gets on the mound, he's dissatisfied. He wishes he could be the coach.

"So what does he do? Instead of pitching to the batter, he starts throwing balls at the coach. Maybe he even persuades other players that the coach is a fool and they also start hurling balls at the coach.

"What would be the result? War!

"That, I believe, is what happened in heaven. Lucifer refused to find his joy and fulfillment in his God-given position. He wanted to take over. That meant active war against the Creator. He couldn't create his own worshippers, so he'd have to steal some from God. In fact, he'd have to get rid of God altogether."

"Okay, I think I see it," Doug sputtered. "But it doesn't make sense. Surely Satan knew he couldn't pull it off."

"Did he?"

It Doesn't Make Sense!

That's why we have to ask an important question: How could this happen? God had made Lucifer perfect, the greatest creature ever put together. So how could Lucifer choose the way of sin, degradation, and evil?"

Doug shook his head as I looked at my watch. We'd been at it more than two hours. He said, "This is absurd. This would be like me sneaking into the White House, trying to assassinate the president, imagining it happening, and then also imagining the whole United States suddenly clapping and saying they wanted me to take his place. No one would do that, except crazy people. Instead, they'd put me into prison and probably execute me five minutes later."

"Right," I said. "But that's the source of evil in all the universe. Lucifer became proud and murderous and then made some futile but far-reaching decisions about what to do. He started a movement to overthrow God. And he's been doing the same thing all over planet Earth ever since. His primary goal is to get enough angels and people on his side so he can ultimately deal God the mortal blow."

Doug shook his head. "Amazing. Really amazing."

I gazed at him evenly. "That leads to the next question: So why did he do it? How could he make such a stupid decision?"

Doug looked at his watch. "Man, I wish we had two more hours."

"We do. Next Monday. So here's . . ."

"My assignment." He grinned.

"Right. But frankly, I'm not sure what to tell you to do."

"I know what it is," Doug said with a mischievous light in his eyes.

"What?"

"I need to think what was inadequate about Lucifer's perfection, or what it was that led him into sin."

I just stared at him. "I can't believe you said that."

"I know. I'm a genius. But you did it to me. So you can blame yourself."

"Okay, let's not get cocky." I stood. "You go out now and get in your car. I don't want to see it again. If I do, I'll really be sinning."

"Oh, come on. You convert me, my family will probably buy you one as a gift."

"No way."

"Well—" He cocked his head and shrugged. "Maybe a watch with 'your Lexus' written on the back."

"I hope it's not a Timex."

"Come on, I'll spring for anything at Wal-Mart. They have some good stuff."

"Thanks a lot."

He clapped me on the back. "Stick with me, Mark. I'll help you find the good things in life."

I nodded. He left and I sat there thinking. Was I really up to this? Doug caught on quickly. Would he soon begin asking me rather big questions I would have no idea about the answers to, or where to find them? Then I realized, that was the fun of this. And the excitement. I was learning as much as he was.

As I left, I prayed for Doug and his family, and then the new things I had learned about Jesse. I really hoped he would be there next week.

CHAPTER 8

The Ultimate Problem of Evil Is Not Knowing Enough, or Feeling the Wrong Desires and Choosing to Do the Wrong Things Regardless

The Story Continues

When Doug arrived the next Monday, Jesse stepped in a moment later. It gratified me that they stuck with me on this. So when they sat down, I said, "God must be doing miracles these days because I really wasn't sure you'd both show up."

"Why not?" Doug said. "You have me hooked."

Jesse nodded. "Plus, if you get borin', I can always order another latte."

"Thanks a lot."

After the usual preliminaries I asked them how things were going. Doug gave a report that he and Gabriel talked more and he felt the relationship was building. "I even took a ride with him on his motorcycle. That really blew his mind."

"Scared?" Jesse asked.

"You bet. I haven't been on a bike since college. And then I was driving."

We all chuckled. Doug continued, "That's about it. My mom is hanging in there, and I visited her again, told her all about the evil stuff we talked about last time."

"What did she say?"

"She said, 'It explains a lot.' I agree," Doug said. "I really think it does. For instance, I'm starting to see all the multitude of ways the Enemy, the Demon, or whoever, is trying to mess me up. The other day my wife broke one of my kissing dolls."

"Kissing dolls?" Jesse and I said in unison.

Doug rolled his eyes. "Okay, fine, I have to tell you. I collect these little figurines that are a girl and boy and they're kissing. They're collector's items. I'm building a collection. Hey, I have to do something with my spare time!"

"It's okay," Jesse said. "I do salt- and pepper shakers. My wife and I used to go all over to antique malls and stuff. Course now she won't go nowhere with me." He looked down at the table.

I put my hand on his shoulder. "Doug told me what was going on, Jesse. I've been praying."

"It'll take a miracle," he said, looking up. "We been together since high school. But now she's all against me."

"Have any idea why?" Doug asked, appearing just as concerned.

"I think she may be hung up on some guy she met at this bar she works at. It's happened before, but this time—"

"I hate that stuff," Doug said stiffly.

"Let's take a second and pray," I said, and we all bowed heads. I quickly prayed about Doug, Gabriel, and Doug's mom, and then Jesse's situation. When I finished, Jesse smiled and gave me a quick nod.

"I never had no one ever say nothin' like that for me before."

"It'll keep happening, my friend, as long as I know you need it."

He nodded. "Okay, enough about me. I'm sicka me. What're we doin' today?"

I decided to plunge in, no preliminaries. "Last time we talked about how Lucifer started this rebellion against God in heaven. We ended with the question of how could Lucifer, a supposedly perfect being, more magnificent than any other in creation, make such a stupid mistake? How could he, knowing all he did about God, just go against all reason, wisdom, and everything else to try something utterly impossible?"

Jesse chuckled. "You guys don't talk about stuff like the best oil for a bike or nothin' like that, huh?"

Doug and I laughed. "We can talk about that, too, if you want," Doug said. "I recommend Quaker State."

We all laughed again, but I said, "Seriously, that question proposes an immense dichotomy. If Lucifer was created with absolute perfection, then how could he have made such a bad choice to rebel against God and try to kill him?" I turned to Doug. "So did you work on your assignment?"

"I've thought about it," Doug answered.

"Well, spit it out," Jesse said.

"Okay, I guess it's kind of like what I see happening in so many places—business, sports, entertainment—you read about it all the time. Like this Michael Vick thing that happened—the Falcons' quarterback who got caught in this dog-fighting issue?"

Jesse and I nodded.

"You get out there like that—you're rich, you're important, you have some power, I think you can get to the point where you think you're invulnerable. Nobody can touch you. You can do anything and no one will say a thing about it. That's what I think might have happened with Lucifer. He got too big for his britches and he forgot who he really was and who God was and he just started thinking he wanted to be God, and then he got so full of himself he thought he could pull it off."

"Wow!" I chortled.

Jesse said, "I've seen it happen too many times to think it's not real."

"Good. But let's look a little deeper," I said.

More Explanations

Some would say, 'No, God didn't make Lucifer perfect. He still had some flaws and fell into sin because of them.' You see anything wrong with that?"

Doug squinted, and then said, "It means the Bible is wrong in saying he was perfect. And it also means God couldn't make anything but a messed-up creature. So then God's flawed, too."

"Excellent! And it ultimately means God is the cause of evil in the universe. He made a faulty creature. But could God—who, according to the Bible, is holy, wise, all-knowing, all-powerful, and perfect himself—create a faulty creature? That suggests that God is so weak and fallible that he can't fashion his subjects properly. And if that is so, perhaps he shouldn't have made one at all, since he knew what would happen with such creatures."

"Yeah, I think that one has to be wrong," Doug said.

A Developmental Problem

I moved on. "But then someone else will say that evil is a necessary step in the development of a creature. In order to reach perfection, God had to start off with imperfection. Gradually, through trial and error, he'd arrive at the right result."

Doug said, "Isn't that the ultimate idea behind evolution? We're all heading toward perfection step-by-step?"

Jesse laughed loud this time. "If that's so, how do you explain me?"

"Or me?" Doug said.

"Or any of us?" I added.

"Let's hear it for big, fat, dumb guys!" Jesse said, lifting his latte.

We all clinked, but then Doug said, "Hey, you may not be some silver-tongued speaker, Jesse, but you're not dumb. Give yourself some credit. I don't hang out with idiots."

Jesse smiled. "Thanks for sayin' that. I been called dumb all my life. My nickname in high school was 'Bonehead.' But I'll take what you said and put it in my pocket."

"Put it on a plaque on your wall," Doug said. "Anyone who tackles questions like these can't be anything less than a true thinker in my book."

I looked at both in amazement, sensing we'd be talking a lot more about things like this in the days ahead and noting to myself to pray about Jesse's self-esteem problems. Then I continued. "Actually, the point is quite good. If we really are moving toward perfection in an evolutionary sense, how then is it that the twentieth century brought on more wars, genocides, and murders than any other century?"

"Cause there're more idiots out there than ever before!" Jesse said.

I chuckled. "Good answer, but I still don't think it covers it. The idea of God starting with imperfection and working toward perfection comes down to the same thing: God is the author of evil. He may be doing what needs to be done to create a perfect creature, but he's still the ultimate cause of evil, and perhaps the blamable cause. How could any of us ally ourselves with such a God?"

I looked from Jesse to Doug and realized they didn't respond because the idea began to take hold in their minds. Doug said, "What then is the answer? If Lucifer was really perfect, how could he make such an imperfect choice and plunge the whole universe into evil?"

The Nature of Lucifer's Perfection

I said, "The first step in answering is to determine in what sense Lucifer was perfect. A lot of what I'm about to say is not specifically spelled out in the Bible. But it's based on the whole picture of God you find in the Bible, and the same kind of snapshot of Satan. So take some of this as my own opinion. But as Paul once wrote, I think I have the Spirit of God on this issue."

"So now you're gonna start throwin' opinions around?" Jesse said. "I'm outta here!"

We all laughed again, and I continued, "If what we mean by perfection is that he could never under any circumstances disobey God, we obviously are posing the wrong question. Scripture says he was 'the model of perfection' and he still disobeyed. So obviously that kind of perfection doesn't rule out evil thoughts, ideas, and ultimate rebellion. What exactly was Lucifer's perfection?"

Both stared at me, silent.

"Consider several facts about Lucifer."

The Information Gap

Lucifer possessed tremendous intelligence and wisdom, but he wasn't omniscient—all-knowing. He didn't know every detail of the past, present, and future. He only knew what God had put into him, and he certainly could not predict or 'see' the future in some prophetic sense. He didn't know every detail down to the number of hairs on a person's head. Lucifer had to gain that kind of knowledge through study, research, experience.'

"His ability to learn was flawless. He could reason properly, without mistake. His wisdom gave him the ability to use his knowledge efficiently and effectively. In a sense, God had given him perfect tools to work with. But—and it's a big 'but'—Lucifer didn't know everything. It's like the difference between possessing an encyclopedia and actually having memorized, digested, and understood everything in that encyclopedia. God gave Lucifer the tools, but didn't give him all information everywhere. Lucifer had to gain that over time. God created Lucifer and all the angels so they might relate to him (God), learn of him, talk with him. His purpose was that through such learning they would desire to know him and worship him even more. In doing this, Lucifer would become the kind of worshipper he was intended to be."

"So Lucifer's perfection wasn't like God's perfection?" Doug said.

"Correct," I answered. "It was a matter of choice."

A Matter of Choice

Lucifer had to choose to do that research, learn about those issues and subjects, and in general, be a student. So you can see that presents a problem. Such learning is a matter of choice. Bio-chemists have to mix their chemical solutions, record their results, and pore over documents. They sweat it out in the laboratory. Similarly, Bible scholars memorize languages, scrutinize grammar, study texts, engage in archaeology. They choose to sacrifice their time and talents to learn.'

"Lucifer also would have had to choose to ask God questions, to relate to him, to trek with him up the mountain of discovery. It's here we can see the possibility of a problem. If Lucifer didn't choose to learn of God and to work with him in the growing process, he could easily come to wrong conclusions when he encountered a problem."

"Like whether he should take God on in a big fight," Jesse said.

"Exactly. Undoubtedly, at some point Lucifer began to pose questions to himself: 'Why does God get all the worship? What about me? Why shouldn't I get some of those things?'

"Eventually, he arrived at another question: 'What if I refuse? What if I depose God? What if I rebel?'"

"And he couldn't know the answers to those questions because he wasn't omniscient," Doug said. "He couldn't see into the future."

"Right," I said. "We've all seen the process in our own lives. I wrestled through such things about drugs, sex, drinking, the Bible, everything in my life in different ways, and I'm sure you did. You just don't know the answers until you either ask someone who does know, or you try it out to see what happens. What Satan asked himself was never seen before in angelic history. He probably debated those questions in the quiet recesses of his mind. But he couldn't have gained definitive answers. He could get answers if he wished. Where do you think he could have gone?"

"Maybe there was a guy like some general who wrote a book about it," Jesse said with a grin.

"I'm sure," Doug said. "He simply had to ask God. Sort of like, 'Lord, if I stage a rebellion, would I have a chance of winning?' Or, 'Father, you're all-powerful. Am I? Could I defeat you in battle?' Or, 'God, you made me beautiful, perfect in wisdom, and power-ful. Then why don't the angels worship *me*, too?'"

"You're really getting down to it there," I said. "That's it exactly. Of course, for obvious reasons, he probably didn't go to God with such questions. So there was only one other way to find out what might happen: actually doing what his mind and research suggested."

"Wow!" Jesse said. "He was really tied up."

"Definitely." I took a breath. "But that wasn't Lucifer's only problem."

Lucifer's Job

Whenever God creates subjects, we know he also gives everyone plenty to do. The moment he created Adam, according to Genesis 2, he gave him a job: Name the animals.

"Similarly, Lucifer and the angels also had a multitude of tasks God had planned long before they came into being. Lucifer proclaimed God's holiness. He taught the angels about God's nature. Perhaps he even orchestrated the symphonic music of heaven.

"Undoubtedly, Lucifer noticed that all this activity was for one purpose: to glorify God. To give him pleasure. To meet his requirements. To please him. To worship him.

"Sooner or later, Lucifer also must have asked, 'Why should I do this? Just because God said so? What about me? Shouldn't somebody be doing something for me?'"

"I ask that all the time with my partner," Doug said with a grin.

"Yeah, 'n' I'm askin' it right now about my wife," Jesse added.

"It's a natural question to ask," I said. "Probably none of this was verbalized. Perhaps it all reverberated only in Lucifer's head. But sooner or later, these things must have occurred to him. He was God's highest achievement, his greatest creation. His intelligence and wisdom were unequaled. His ability to perform his duties nonpareil. His position lofty. Certainly he had the time to consider these things. Where could he get answers? Only from one person: God.

"At that point, Lucifer again had to make a choice: Should I go to him or not? The answer was obvious. Of course he should go to God. God undoubtedly invited him to ask anything he desired.

There's no reason to think God would shut him out for a simple question. We see God like this all through the Bible. In fact, there's a verse in Jeremiah that says, 'Call to me and I will answer you and tell you great and unsearchable things you do not know' (33:3). We see in the portrait of Jesus in the Gospels that he invited anyone and everyone to ask him anything they wanted. God has never told people, 'No, you can't ask that.' Or, 'Get out of my face. I'm not telling you that!' He's not afraid of anything we can throw at him. So it's inconceivable to me that God would have shut Lucifer out."

"But what if Lucifer decided not to go to God? What if he tried to figure out answers on his own?"

When You Don't Understand,
to Whom Do You Go?

Frankly, we often experience the same problem. Suppose your boss says to you, 'I want you to chop up this pile of wood. But you can't use the blade of the axe; I want you to use the blunt side.' You're out there trying to break those logs up and getting more and more frustrated by the minute. 'How can anyone chop wood this way? Why is he doing this to me?'

"Now at that point you have a choice. You could think up all sorts of good reasons your boss may be doing this, and talk yourself into it. Eventually, though, you wouldn't be able to cajole yourself to complete the task. It's just too maddening. Meanwhile, you're building a bonfire of resentment. In the end you explode, march into your boss's office and quit. Or accuse him of some dastardly mean streak. Or tell him he's an idiot."

"Been there. Done that," Jesse said.

Doug and I laughed.

"But there's another possibility," I said. "You could go to your boss and say, 'Why are we doing it this way? It's totally unreasonable.' Then that boss might offer a perfectly valid and even good explanation. 'I wanted to teach you that when I ask you to do something you don't understand, I want you to feel free to come to me and talk about it.'"

Both men nodded. "I can see that," Jesse said. "When I get frustrated, I start thinkin' up all kinds of horrible motives for why someone's doin' something. Like my wife. I'm thinkin' she hates me, she thinks I'm ugly, she's fed up. And I might be wrong on all counts."

"Absolutely," I agreed. "It's often when we refuse to talk out something reasonably that we get into the most trouble. Look at it on the political scene, how liberals think conservatives don't care about anyone but themselves, and how conservatives think liberals are all bleeding hearts."

"I see it all the time where I live," Doug said.

I said, "So you see it makes sense that a boss might ask you to do something he's really using to help you grow as a person and understand the reasoning behind such tasks. "However, every step of that process requires something. Can you think of what?"

Doug nodded. "He has to choose to go to him and talk it through."

"He has to wanna, as my priest used to say," Jesse added.

"Right. It's a matter of choice," I agreed. Millions of people in our world have quit jobs, broken off relationships, and terminated friendships because they assumed sinister motives on the part of others, or because they refused to verbalize their inner thoughts and get some answers.

"For instance, recently my son Gardner came home in a snit. I could tell he was angry by the way he snarled at his little sister, slumped onto the couch with blazing eyes, and protested at every little thing I asked of him. I finally said, 'What's the matter? Why are you so angry?' I honestly thought I must have done something to him, but being an adult I reasoned that was not necessarily it.

"He answered, 'Jerry asked me if I'm a gardener today, because of my name.'

"I'd always wondered when that might happen. So I said, 'You know, you're named after your grandfather, and your mother, whose last names were Gardner. It's a very great thing to be named after people your parents love and respect.'

"'But it makes me mad,' he retorted. So I asked him what part made him mad.

"'Because I feel stupid. I wish you named me another name.'

"'Like what?' I asked.

"'I don't know. Something else.'

"I cleared my throat, then told him, 'So what you're really saying is you're mad at me and Mommy for naming you Gardner.'

"He looked away and answered, 'I guess.'

"So I explained to him more about why we'd named him that, and what other names we'd considered. He was quite relieved we hadn't chosen Harold (after my father) or Thurman Leroy (after my wife's father). As he began to understand, he realized it wasn't so bad that his name sounded like a horticultural term. In the end, he said, 'I'll just tell Jerry I have a cool name that isn't like his.'"

I grinned at the memory. "Haven't you done this a million times? When we don't understand the reasoning or history behind some event, we can lose our cool, accuse others of nasty motives, and assume all kinds of wrong things about them. But when we really do comprehend those things, when we find out the truth, we not only are relieved, but perhaps even inspired.

"So God might have explained to Lucifer, 'Your rebellion won't work because you can never be as strong as me. But really, you have to understand what I made you to be. You're the leader, the orchestral conductor, the guiding light of the angelic millions. They will listen to you and follow you because that's the way I made them, and that's what I made you for. But worship is an altogether different thing. I reserve that only for myself, not because I mean to withhold something worthwhile from you, but because you and the angels can only worship Someone truly greater than yourselves. To worship you, or one of my creations, is to sacrifice the essence of worship, which is to say, 'God, you are worthy of my love and my adoration because of who you are, and all you've done.' Worshipping anyone of lower stature would be a prostitution of truth, integrity, and holiness.'

"As a result, Lucifer could have learned the truth and discarded his irrational thoughts of glory and power. But like his refusal to learn of God, Lucifer's ability to make right choices and judgments was also dependent on his willingness to go to God with his questions and concerns. So what happened? Undoubtedly, at some point Lucifer chose not to go to God about any of the real issues boiling inside him. Instead, he began working things out on his own. His plot began to form. He began to think in terms of overthrowing God."

"It makes a lot of sense," Doug said, "if you buy the whole idea of Satan to begin with."

"Of course. But think about it. What makes more sense in our world today—that good and evil can never defeat one another, or that some person is responsible for inserting it into our world? That the same person does all he can to conceal that fact while at the same time doing all he can to mess the whole world up because of his hatred for God?"

Doug nodded. "Much as I hate to say it, it really does make more sense than those other explanations we talked about. But my question is, If Lucifer had perfect reasoning ability, how could he come to such conclusions?"

"Great question," I said. "But remember, Lucifer wasn't omniscient. That meant that ultimately to get information he had to go to God. He had to relate to him, to trust his answers, to believe the truth. All those things are responses. Choices. Moral choices. That's the essence of what it means to be in God's image. We can make real, free, moral choices. And Lucifer was the first to begin to test out the wrong side of them."

"It really is incredible," Jesse said. "I mean, I hardly ever think about some of the choices I make. I just think, *Who cares?* Or, *No one will find out.* But it just ain't true."

"Those are Lucifer's first lies, the ones he told himself," I said, giving Doug and Jesse a knowing look. "So as Lucifer chose not to relate to God the way he was supposed to, he came to wrong conclusions about God. And he began formulating a plot to start a rebellion. Let me give you an example."

An Example: Garbage In, Garbage Out!

I work regularly with computers. I'm amazed at how precise these machines are. They never make a mistake. Their logic is flawless.

One day our office manager asked me to program the computer to perform a function. I showed her how, ran the program, and immediately discovered we made a big mistake. After checking the program, I saw my error.

"But according to the data it had, the computer had 'reasoned' perfectly. It did exactly as its limited knowledge had told it. But it came to the wrong conclusion because it had the wrong data.

"Similarly, though Lucifer's logic was perfect, he had the wrong data. He didn't know all the facts about God because he hadn't been around long enough. Therefore, he came to a wrong conclusion."

"It really is true," Doug said. "I've assumed all kinds of bad things about Gabriel because I refused to talk to him. Though his answers haven't encouraged me, at least I'm not living in fantasyland anymore."

"Maybe I oughta try that with my wife," Jesse said. "Just go to her and lay it all on the table."

"It can help," I said. "So as for Lucifer, we see the process. Lucifer didn't simply wake up one morning, stretch his wings, and say, 'I think I'll overthrow God today.' It was a lengthy process of making wrong choices. First, he chose not to go to God with his questions. Next, he chose not to be what he was created to be."

The Power to Choose

And this brings us to the third and critical truth about Lucifer. God would let him make those choices freely. He wouldn't interfere. When God created Lucifer and all the other angels, he gave them the ability to make moral decisions. Not just choices between eating an apple or a banana, or between taking High Street or Low Street to get to the same place. No, Lucifer made 'moral' choices. He could choose between doing what was right and what was wrong. He could choose to worship or not worship, love or not love.

"This is the very issue that separates angels and humans from all other creatures, such as dogs, cats, lions, and amoebas. As I said before, it's what being made 'in the image of God' means. We are like God in that we can make free moral choices. We can choose evil or good, right or might, truth or falsehood. When God made the angels, he endowed them with the freedom to obey him or not. He was taking an incredible risk, for there was nothing to guarantee that his creations would love and worship him. But God took the risk of making a creature who could defy him, because he saw something great and magnificent in such a being. In essence, he built a creature who had much higher powers than any of the lower creatures: the ability to love, sacrifice, and give himself to others. The power not only to admire beauty and wondrous things, but to fashion and build and invent our own beautiful creations. All of it was for one purpose: to glorify the God who had given them those abilities.

"But would each of those creatures do those things for the right reasons? Would they invent, fashion, form, and produce such things for God's glory, or for something less—their own fame, fortune, and popularity?

"For each one of God's creatures, such a choice could go either way. That was their birthright, their privilege, and ultimately their towering joy or dismal despair. For just as God risked creating beings who could defy him, so those creatures risked their destiny on the basis of that choice. For them, it was hell or heaven. Let me give you another example."

Love without the Right to Choose

One of the most gratifying moments of my day is to come home and have my daughter screech, 'Daddy' and then rush up to hug my leg. An even more incredible moment sometimes comes at night when I tuck her into bed. Ever since she was a small baby, I told her I loved her. But there came a day when she returned the favor. As I fluffed her pillow and tightened the sheets, she suddenly said, 'Daddy, I love you.'

"It was a deeply moving moment. I looked at her and said, 'What?' She repeated it. Then I picked her up and hugged her. 'I love you, too.'

"'I know,' she answered. 'Good night.'

"There's something precious about such moments that makes whatever pain or suffering you might also have at their hands all worth it. It's the most valued thing we know.

"On the other hand, another great joy of mine is programming my computer to do various tasks. Recently, on a lark, I made that computer print out 'I love you' five hundred times in a nanosecond. It didn't do a thing for my emotional life."

Both men laughed.

"Why?" I asked as I looked from Jesse to Doug. "Because there's a vast difference between that and what my daughter says."

Both men nodded. "The day my little one said that to me, I went in the bathroom and cried," Jesse said. "It just melted me."

"Yeah," Doug said. "I remember Gabriel saying that as a little kid. Not anymore, though."

"The time will come again, my friend," I said, and he nodded as his eyes glimmered.

The Great Risk

That's the rub, isn't it?" I asked. "Having a child is a great risk. Elizabeth could grow up and defy me, hate me, rebel, even try to destroy me. You only need look through one day of news to see how many children have turned against their parents, shamed them, hated them, even murdered them. I knew that such things could happen before Jeanette and I ever decided to have a child. In fact, Jeanette asked me several times, 'Are you sure? What if this child turns out to be a prodigal? A wastrel? A druggie?'

"I had no answers to such questions, but I do know one thing: I would still love that child no matter what she did with her life.

"So we took the risk. Why? Because even though the risk is great for misfortune, there's also great blessing in raising, loving, and knowing your own flesh and blood. There's great joy and happiness in seeing a child grow into a solid, God-fearing adult. There's tremendous exhilaration in simply being part of each stage of that child's life and knowing you had some influence in making them great.

"So God also took the risk of creating autonomous creatures because he saw the value of it. He knew that those creatures could turn against him. But he also saw that they could become the crown of creation, too, his greatest art and achievement.

"I'm sure God longed for Lucifer and all his angels to grow and learn and choose the right things because they were right, not because they were forced to choose those things. He wanted them to love him freely, not because he ordered them to."

"It must've been tough for God to see him go the way he did," Jesse suddenly interjected.

"I bet it was. So now we see how Lucifer made the choice he made."

Lucifer's Choice

So we come back to the question of why Lucifer rebelled. We can see all along the line that at each and every juncture he had to exercise his will. He could choose to learn of God and grow, or he could choose to strike out on his own. He could depend on God, or he could find another way. He could choose to function as a cherub, or he could rebel against the place God gave him. We see that he rebelled not because his perfect wisdom told him to do so. Nor did he rebel because God had done him wrong. No, he rebelled because he chose to think the wrong thoughts, feel the wrong emotions, and make the wrong decisions.

"How often have you chosen to do things that you know are stupid, wrong, even harmful? In my life, I recall many such decisions. Why do we make such wrong choices? I think there's one reason: because we want to. We don't care about the facts. We don't care what we've been told. We want to find out for ourselves. We don't care what's right. We're convinced that we won't suffer any consequences. We think we can 'beat the odds.'"

I suddenly remembered an old joke. "Like the lady who made a bad investment and went to the Better Business Bureau for help. 'But this man is a cheat,' they told her. 'Why didn't you come to us first?'

"She replied, 'Because I thought you'd tell me not to do it.'"

Jesse and Doug cracked up. "Now that's a good one," Doug said.

"But isn't it so true?" I asked. "She thought if she didn't ask for the answer, it would all work out in her favor. Similarly, we may choose to ignore the truth because we think it will foul up our grand plans. Or we may just gather enough facts to support our side and then 'jump the gun' and make an uninformed decision. Or even worse, someone may tell us that our plan can't work, but we try it anyway. Because we just 'want to.'"

"I'm beginnin' to think I'm Lucifer," Jesse said, and we all laughed.

"Isn't that the ultimate confirmation for you?" I asked. "That it's so in line with real life? That's the Bible. We read it and cry, 'That's me!' That's one way I know it's true."

Both Doug and Jesse agreed.

I said, "I recall the pressure I felt as a teenager to have sex. I knew the facts about STDs from movies shown in health class in high school. I knew I could get a girl pregnant and mess up her life and mine. I had friends in high school who did that very thing, and the results were dismal. My father also had told me numerous times about how I should marry a girl I could love and trust, and who proved it to me by keeping herself pure till the wedding night. I had heard it all.

"But in my heart (I wasn't a Christian at the time), I didn't care. I burned to lose my virginity and become a 'real man,' as so many of my friends put it. I even remember how ashamed I was of being a virgin in college. When one of the psych students in my fraternity passed out a questionnaire about sex experiences for a research project, I was so ashamed of my lack of experience that I answered the questions as if I were Casanova himself.

"Finally, a girl came along who was willing to oblige me. We consummated the act several times over a weekend. At first, I thought I'd conquered the world.

"But then reality set in. What if she got pregnant? This idea terrorized me for a month as I waited for her to tell me her period had come. I also worried constantly I might have picked up a disease. Instead of feeling elated and happy, I was miserable and fearful for weeks afterward. There was nothing of the joy of first sex on a honeymoon with someone I deeply loved. Just a dirty deed in the dark.

"Of course, it all wore off eventually, and I moved on to the next conquest.

"When I became a Christian, though, I greatly lamented giving away something precious—the intimacy and joy of a first experience together in marriage with someone I truly loved. Instead, I gave it away to a girl who didn't even go out with me again and probably never cared much about me to begin with.

"Why was I so obsessed with this? Certainly my friends and peers made me think I had to experience it. The pressure that way was overwhelming. But there was something more: I didn't really care about what God said, or the Bible, or my advisers, or even my father. I just 'wanted' it, and it didn't matter who tried to warn me of the dangers.

"That was precisely Lucifer's situation. His reason told him no. Undoubtedly, even God warned him no. But he kept looking at God and wishing he had what God had. His emotions responded. And finally his will said yes. He honestly thought he could win, that he'd beat the odds and take the place of God."

"It's so like a million things I done wrong," Jesse said, "I'm beginning to think this is my story."

"Me, too," Doug said. "Why is that?"

"Because deep down we're all very much alike," I responded. "We're all made in the image of God. Satan knows what works, and he tempts us on that basis. He uses the same things on us that got him messed up. But there's one last question we need to consider."

One Final Problem

That brings us to one last thought. Could Lucifer have gotten all the facts and learned his plan was folly?"

Both men stared at me like I'd just dropped down from Jupiter. It made me smile inside.

"How? By asking God. As I said earlier, all Lucifer needed to say was, 'Lord, I'm troubled about some things and I need your advice. I'm getting this incredibly strong desire to overthrow you. I'm even starting to think it's possible. I know I don't know all there is to know about you. So would you please inform me whether such a coup has any hope of success?'

"Of course, Lucifer wasn't about to approach God with such a request. But way back in the process, when he first started to feel those twinges of jealousy and that desire to be Number One, he could have discussed it with his master and friend, Jehovah. He could have confessed his feelings before they became sin and cleared the air. He could have asked God to help him deal with them.

"Always in Scripture we see that God warned people in danger of judgment for their wrong choices, their sins. It's inconceivable God wouldn't have warned Lucifer when he saw this line of reasoning in Lucifer's mind. But Lucifer must have even rejected that. Instead, he chose not only to let those feelings and thoughts remain, but he let them grow into the monstrous rebellion that followed. He chose to sin, knowing he was sinning, and probably even knowing, deep down, that he couldn't succeed.

"For God, it was all part of the risk of creating creatures with real wills."

Doug shook his head. "But if that's true, why did God create Lucifer in the first place? Why didn't he pass over him, and make all the other good ones, who worked out?"

Not a Total Loss

That could be one of the mysteries you'll get to ask God when you get there. But the truth is it wasn't a total loss. Two-thirds of all the angels stuck with God. They freely chose to be loyal to him. Clearly, it's possible for a creature (an angel or otherwise) to choose to go God's way as well. If all the angels had rebelled, we could accuse God of making faulty creatures. But since most stayed loyal to God, it's easy to see that Lucifer's act was bred of ill will and hatred, not faulty abilities.

"In the end, for whatever reasons, Lucifer chose to go the way of rebellion. That wrong choice became the origin of all evil in the universe. One magnificent creation of God exercised his freedom of choice to go the wrong way. And multitudes followed him.

"And that leads us to another question: What was God to do now that he had a rebellion on his hands? Squash them all? Cast them into hell?"

I looked from Doug to Jesse. "I feel an assignment coming on," Doug said.

"Lay it on me," Jesse said. "I want to get into it."

"Then think about that. What could/would/should God have done now that he had a full-scale rebellion on his hands? The answer will show us how God deals with evil, and I think you'll find it's a lot different from the way most of his creatures deal with it."

"I'm tingling," Doug said.

We all laughed as we left the shop again. Outside, Doug said, "Look, I know this is presumptive, but I'd like to bring someone with me next time."

"Really?" I said. "Do you think they'll have missed too much?"

"No, I've been telling her all along."

"Then who?"

"You'll see."

"Great. Suspense. Just what I love."

We headed to our vehicles. On the way home, I once again prayed about these two men I now felt real love for.

CHAPTER 9

The Ultimate Truth about Our World

We Are Smack-Dab in the Middle of a Do-or-Die War

Julie Arrives

When I stepped into Starbucks the next Monday, Doug and Jesse were already sipping their coffees. A striking woman sat with them at the table and I felt immediately intimidated. As I walked over, I sent a heavenly telegram asking God to give me both grace and wisdom for whatever this lady brought to the table.

Doug immediately introduced her. "This is one of my clients, Julie Hendricks." I shook hands with her, looked her in the eye, and noted a sardonic smile tugging at the edges of her lips. I sensed she would be formidable. "She was one of my first sales," Doug said. "And we've been friends for years. When I told her about our little study here, she asked if she could stop by. So here she is."

"Welcome," I said. "It'll be nice to have a woman's point of view on all this."

Jesse said, "I ordered you a regular coffee, if that's okay."

"Fine with me."

"It should be ready. Be back in a sec." Jesse walked to the counter and I asked Doug how things were with his mom.

"The doc has ordered radiation treatments and then chemo," he said. "She's afraid about losing her hair. But that's a little thing, in my mind."

"Not for a woman," Julie said. We all smiled knowingly.

"I'll keep praying," I said. "And Gabriel?"

Doug took a deep breath. "His girlfriend's definitely pregnant. He's talking about marrying her. I can't believe it."

"They're in love," Julie said. "It's a very normal response."

"He's eighteen years old. He knows nothing about responsibility, let alone being married and having a kid. If he marries her, I give 'em six months after the baby arrives."

"Don't be such a pessimist, Doug," Julie said. "Give them a chance."

"It really frosts me," Doug said. "There's a simple way out here, and no one will listen to me. Not even my wife. Although she wants him to encourage the girl to give the baby up."

Doug gazed at me through slit eyes. "What do you say, O great wise one?"

I detected the sarcasm and I wondered if Julie had curdled some of Doug's enthusiasm for the Bible material. "We've been talking about how important our decisions are, all of them, and how a single decision of a single angelic personage plunged the whole world into the problems we have today, and have had throughout history. I think Gabriel's situation is the kind of decision that has to be approached with caution, counsel, an openness to hearing everyone out, and prayer, if you believe in that."

Doug sighed. "I guess I could have predicted that answer."

I gazed at him evenly, realizing something had changed in his attitude toward me, perhaps toward everything. "What do you suggest I say? I can tell you what I believe the Bible would say to do. I can give my opinion about what to do. But ultimately I think it's your son's decision, a decision he'll have to live with for the rest of his life. I think calm heads are what are needed, not quick decisions designed to find an easy way out, an escape clause, or anything like that. We're dealing with human lives—Gabriel's, the girl's, and the child's."

"Fetus," Doug said tightly.

Jesse rejoined us and put my coffee in front of me. He dropped several half-and-half shots and two yellow packets of sugar substitute. "Thanks, Jesse. Next time it's on me."

"No," Jesse said. "You teach. We pay." He glanced at Doug, whose eyes looked dark and ready for battle.

"Who am I to argue with grace?" I asked, trying to crack a joke. No one got it. I turned to Jesse. "How's the situation with your wife?"

Jesse gave us this big grin. "Well, I did some of what you said. I took her out to dinner—Applebee's, her favorite—and I just laid my cards on the table. We haven't never talked like that for years. She cried a coupla times and I felt a lot better. She said she wanted it to work—our marriage, that is—but she was fed up with me always off someplace, either truckin' or with my Harley guys, or bowling, or just out drinkin'. So I'm workin' on being a good boy."

"How's that going?" I asked, feeling worried about how Doug kept sighing and looking out the window as if he was bored.

"Like I said, I'm workin' on it. You don't teach an old dog new tricks in a day or two."

I smiled. "It sounds like things are looking up then."

"A little. I got somethin' else, too."

Everyone turned to Jesse. "I was out on the road the other day, listenin' to my tunes and havin' a fairly decent time, feelin' better about the wife and all. And suddenly, I notice the gas gauge. It's like below empty. My heart starts poundin' and I'm lookin' all around for the next service station with diesel."

"That can be tight," I said.

"Yeah. Anyway, I just said, 'Okay, God, you and me. If Mark is right about you, you can help out with stuff like this. So just let me get someplace to fill 'er up. That was it. Thirty-five minutes later—I was way out in the middle of Nebraska—I haul in and fill up. The tank is exactly a hundred gallons, and it took a hundred-point-one. I stood there and just said, 'Okay, God, you're all right.' Made me smile for the rest of the trip."

"You think he really did that?" Doug said, the contempt in his voice unmistakable.

Jesse shrugged. "I don't know. All I know is I prayed and it worked out. Maybe if I hadn't prayed, I woulda been stuck out there. Maybe not. But it's the first time since I was a little kid that I even prayed. So I'm not about to write it up and do a book or somethin', but I thought it was pretty cool. Honest."

Doug shook his head and then Julie jumped in. "For every prayer like that, I bet there are a million others that aren't answered. So what do those people do—just say, 'Guess it doesn't work for me'?"

I glanced around. Jesse grinned like he'd just caught the Lotto Jackpot. But Doug and Julie looked grim. I had to go on, though, regardless. "I think the test is how many times such things happen in your life. If you pray and consistently see answers of all sorts—not just for gas, but other things, both big and little—you begin to see a pattern. I don't think God always bails us out of tight situations. And I also believe many things could be explained just as well by coincidence or chance. But when you see things like that happen over and over, you start to realize God may really be there, listening, working behind the scenes."

Julie eyed me with skeptical large blue eyes. "Tell me one, just one that really worked."

I looked from her to Doug, whose fingers drummed on the table with exasperation, and Jesse, who appeared all ears. "I'll give you one that just happened this week. My daughter just went away to college. We planned to let her take a car we inherited from my father-in-law, but it's a giant Crown Victoria, and my wife was a little nervous about Alisha taking it. For a long time, I wanted to give her a nice little rig for her high school graduation, but I just couldn't swing it financially. In the last few years, though, my mom, whom my father left fairly well-heeled, offered to help us buy Alisha some nice wheels. I don't like going to my mom for money, though, and she's very forgetful these days. So I didn't put much hope in her helping out with this.

So I prayed about it and said, 'God, if you can make a way, I'd appreciate it.' The next thing I know, I get a call from my mom. We talked about all the usual things. Then she suddenly said, 'Honey, I know Alisha needs a car, and I really would like to buy her one. What should I do to help?'

"I was floored. So I said, 'Whatever you want to do is fine with me, Mom. I think she could drive the Crown Vic for a while until we can see if that's the right car for her.'

"We talked about other things, and then she said, 'You know I forget everything these days, but this is something I want to do for Alisha. So don't be afraid to remind me that I promised to help you with this. Okay?'

"'That's fine, Mom.'

"I hung up and that was the end of it. I prepared to ask my sister to cut me a check—she handles my mom's finances—but then one night a few days later we talked about it at dinner. Without me saying anything about my mom's offer, Alisha just said, 'I think I'll just go down to school without a car for now. I have four friends there now who all have cars. So I'll be okay.' I just stared at her. For several years, all she had talked about was having her own car. Now . . . ?"

I looked around at the group. "It's not the kind of thing that smacks of the miraculous or anything. But for me, I knew God was behind it. He's working in my mom, he's working in Alisha, and me and Jeanette. I've seen things come together like this multitudes of times, but ultimately I take it by faith. But that's how I see it. Other times, from always finding and buying new houses that were perfect whenever we had to move, to my insurance company paying me off far better than I hoped after I totaled my car, to meeting my wife at a distant writer's conference and later marrying her, to turning around my daughter when she got in with the wrong kinds of kids. That's to say nothing of all kinds of other small things, like finding our hamster in the house when it escaped from its cage, to locating my keys when I misplaced them, to being able to get U2 tickets against all odds when they came to Kansas City."

Julie's brow wrinkled and she said, "But how do you know it's really God? All kinds of people misplace their keys and then remember where they left them. I've gotten great deals on a couple of houses I've bought. And I found ways to get to an Elton John concert when it was sold out. I didn't pray about any of those things."

I nodded knowingly. "The element of faith is never going to be left out of the equation for me, that's all I can say. I can't prove God did any of those things, just as you can't prove that God didn't do those things for you because he cares about you regardless of your lack of prayer. Like Jesse just said, all he knows is that he prayed and he reached the truck stop safely. There's a similar kind of statement in John 9 about a blind man Jesus healed. All the skeptics started firing questions at this guy afterward: 'How do you know Jesus is the Messiah?' 'How did he do this to you?' 'How can you believe he's a good man when he violates the Sabbath?' This guy just said, 'One thing I do know. I was blind but now I see!'

"There are many things about faith in God and Christ that no one can really explain. How do I know God exists, that he's involved in my life? Because by faith—it's like a sixth sense—I have seen him, felt him, tasted his goodness, experienced his love and presence. You can say, 'But how do you know it's real?' I can't answer that one. I haven't heard voices except the 'still, small voice' of God in my heart. I haven't seen anyone appear. I haven't even really experienced a bona fide, verifiable miracle, like those in the Gospels. But I know what I've experienced, and I could never deny that it's he."

"Can we move on to the subject of the day?" Doug said with irritation.

I stared at him a moment. "I sense something's eating at you, Doug. Perhaps now's the time to tell us what it is."

His lips puffed with exasperation, then he said, "Things aren't going well at the moment. I'll leave it at that. I really don't want to talk about it."

I studied him a moment, then decided to go on. "That's fair. So why don't we just move into the study I had prepared for today?"

"Good by me," Jesse said.

"I'd like to hear it," Julie said.

Doug just shrugged.

"Okay, what we've learned is that Lucifer, who became Satan, which means 'the adversary,' decided to oppose and overthrow God. He wanted to take God's place and he enlisted the allegiance of millions, possibly billions, of angels like himself, though not as powerful, to join him in the battle. According to Revelation 12:4, a 'third of the stars out of the sky' followed him into action.

"At the same time, presumably two-thirds—the remaining angels—stayed loyal to God. The question is, What action was God to take now that he had a full-scale insurrection on his hands? If you've ever read much of John Milton's *Paradise Lost* you can imagine the battle lines drawn. He pictures Jesus and the loyal angels firing giant cannons at Satan and blowing him to smithereens. God, all-powerful, all-knowing, infinite, and eternal, could never be defeated by such forces. But Milton's imagination or not, we don't know precisely what happened in terms of the actual battle. At some point, though, God made a decision about what to do with these rebels without resorting to swords clashing, angels lying bloody and dead on the fields of war, and carnage throughout heaven.

"So what was he to do? Frankly, if I had been in God's situation, I think I would have wiped Satan and his cohorts out. On the spot. Even executed each one publicly. He could have stopped them with a single word."

"I woulda smacked Satan upside the head and knocked the thing clean off," Jesse said.

Julie just sat still, her lips tight. Doug appeared to be lightening up a bit.

I kept on with the argument. "The problem is that killing Satan, imprisoning him, or whatever, could have adverse results. What if after all the rebel angels were executed, another rebel rose up later from the remaining loyalists and led more astray? They might see

God now as the tyrant Satan undoubtedly said he was, and decide he really wasn't worthy of their love and fealty. In that respect, God could have endless rebellions on his hands, as he whittled the masses through each series of executions down to nothing. How would any of that show his wisdom, his justice, his kindness?"

Everyone appeared interested now, and I inwardly breathed a sigh of relief.

"That's the real issue," I continued. "Whatever God did, he would have to be true to character. He claims to act always with holiness, righteousness, and love. But killing off every rebel would not demonstrate that at all. He'd merely show himself to be a bully and a murderous potentate who tolerated not even the least dissent. Ultimately, to be fair, each rebel would require a trial and a proper punishment."

I watched the eyes of each of my listeners closely, and everyone seemed to be following me intently.

"On the other hand, one could argue for mercy. 'Let them all come back with open arms. Just forgive them and go back to normal.' But could God do that? These beings were entrenched in their rebellion, Satan most of all. They believed they could win and would not recant. Any sign of weakness would be taken as an indication God was a wimp, and ultimately powerless. How many times have you seen in your life that unrepentant people, who, given mercy and forgiveness, just come back and attack a second time?"

"Been there, done that," Jesse muttered.

Doug nodded slightly. Julie's eyes, though, looked hard and skeptical. I wondered where she stood in the faith spectrum—atheist, agnostic, cynic, what?

I just plowed on. "The fact is that God couldn't simply declare amnesty, either. Harm had been done, sins committed. He had to exact real justice for any crimes committed, or he would be compromising a most important facet of his nature. He could not simply free them from all responsibility. 'Let bygones be bygones' was impossible. Why? Because they didn't want to be bygones. They wanted God to be gone so they could get by."

Jesse grinned. "Good one, teach. What do they call that?"

"A pun," I said when no one answered.

"It was punny," Jesse said, and everyone smiled this time.

"And there's also the problem of the other angels who had done nothing wrong. How would they take a so-called 'amnesty' in light of God's declarations of his perfect justice and righteousness? They'd immediately perceive him as weak, compromising, and possibly hypocritical, a virtual liar about all those grand promises. Don't we do the same when we see court judges who let off hardened criminals with slap-on-the-hand sentences, presidents who back down on promises they campaigned on, and the people in our lives who make loud boasts and vows, then go off and do the opposite? We call those people frauds, charlatans, and worse.

"No, these murderers chose to rebel. They should bear the consequences."

"Hear, hear," Jesse said.

Is Evil Inevitable?

So let's take this apart," I said. "Some would say that evil is inevitable, there's no use trying to prevent it, and it's the natural way of things. You just have to learn to live with it. God should just realize no matter how hard he tried, his beloved citizens would do wrong, turn against him and others, and do dastardly things. It's human and angelic nature!"

"The Devil made me do it!" Jesse said with a chortle.

"Or, God made me that way!" I said. "But is that true? Can a God who claims to be holy, righteous, and always good tolerate evil? Can he simply let it persist? Shouldn't he, of all persons, deal with it, effectively and finally?

"Some might even suggest he should have created for Satan and his subjects their own universe where they could wreak whatever havoc they wanted. It would be their own special playground. But could God do that to those who were weaker? Would that be fair? Could God just let them go to their own ends, one stomping the other to oblivion? It's inconceivable that a God who is loving could allow beings with differing gifts, powers, and motives to inflict themselves on one another for all eternity. Imagine you having to live in the same house as Hannibal Lecter. Even if you didn't much like God to begin with, how would you feel about that happening to you?"

"Hey, I been in prison," Jesse said suddenly. "I know what those guys are like. It's hell!"

"Exactly," I said. "And this doesn't solve the problem of the initial rebellion. Other loyal angels could still rebel after God gave Satan his own universe. Such an action could in fact be an inducement to rebellion. Ultimately, if God is God—holy, righteous, loving, wise, all-powerful—he should be able to find a course of action suitable—no, admirable and laudable—to all. The question is, could God find a way to deal justly with the rebels, convince the loyal angels he was worthy of their love and obedience, and end up with a pure, clean, and happy universe?"

"He does that, I'm on his side in a flash," Jesse said.

Julie commented, "So, if we take this fable about Satan and everything to be the true story of all that happened way back when, you're saying you think God has solved this problem and revealed it in the Bible?"

"Absolutely," I said without hesitation.

"I've got to hear this one," Julie said with a smirk.

I knew I was suddenly up to my belt in alligators.

Some Important Facts

I took a long breath, then hurried on. "Okay, obviously, evil is no simple issue any way you look at it. But let's consider several facts the Bible asserts.

"First, God is all-powerful. 'I am the LORD, and there is no other. I form the light and create darkness, I bring prosperity and create disaster; I, the LORD, do all these things' (Isaiah 45:6, 7). We can't eliminate this truth just because evil exists and appears to continue to go on without hindrance. God could stop evil at any moment.

"Second, God is perfectly loving. 'God is love' (1 John 4:8, 16). Whatever action he would take, it had to proceed from a heart of love.

"Third, God is just. 'He is the Rock, his works are perfect, and all his ways are just' (Deuteronomy 32:4). Therefore, he ultimately has to bring all evil to justice and deal with it fairly and finally.

"Fourth, God is omniscient. He knows the end from the beginning (Revelation 22:13). He knew from the very start who would do what, even before he created them. Therefore, this rebellion did not catch him by surprise. Nor is he sitting up in heaven wondering how to get out of this problem.

"Fifth, God is wise (1 Corinthians 3:18ff.). He knows how to take circumstances and turn them for the best. He can even make all things, even evil things, work for the good of those who love him (Romans 8:28). He knows precisely what he is doing, even if we don't understand it.

"Thus, the questions persist. If God is all-powerful and loving, why didn't he stop evil, or at least destroy it when it arose? How could he in love let it affect so many millions? If he's omniscient, why didn't he see it coming and prevent it? If he's just, how can he let it go on and on? And what wisdom is there in letting evil persist? Take any scriptural attribute of God and evil makes a mockery of it. We all want to know how evil can persist, let alone exist, when you realize this is the God in charge of a universe that has gone off its hinges.

"These questions pose terrific difficulties for any thinking person. Yet, let's not forget another basic fact revealed in Scripture. Sixth, God can give us wisdom. "If any of you lacks wisdom, he should ask God, who gives generously to all without finding fault, and it will be given to him" (James 1:5). If we don't understand why he has acted as he has, we can ask him to give us insight. That provides an approach to an answer, and it's not so difficult.

"So this is what we know: There is a being called Satan who led a rebellion against God, and who the Bible says is the ruler of the whole world today. We also have humanity, whom we know came after the angels and their problems. Another fact is that evil

exists in our world, all over the place. So clearly God didn't execute all those angels, snuff them out, put them in prison, or carry
out any of those other options.

"So these are some things we can start with: Since God is all-
powerful, he could have wiped evil out immediately, but he chose
to let it survive—for a while. Since he is loving, he could stop evil
wherever it touches a life, but he chose to let evil touch all of us—
for reasons we'll look at in a moment. Since he is just, he could
have justly executed all the rebels the moment they turned against
him. But he chose to defer his justice in order to accomplish something even more important.

"In other words, though God could have stopped, annihilated,
and terminated evil, he chose to take an alternate route, one that
would allow evil to go its wicked way for many years. What then
could God do?"

Two Major Problems for God

In this respect, I see that God had two problems: One, convincing the loyal angels to remain loyal to him. Two, dealing with
Lucifer and the rebels. How could he do both, perfectly, justly, to
his own glory, and for the good of all concerned?

"Very simply, this is what I believe he did, based on my reading of the Scriptures: God began to execute an ultimate and final
plan that would achieve both those ends. On the one hand, this
plan would convince the loyal angels he was worthy of their love
and allegiance. Once that was accomplished, then he could deal
with Lucifer justly and properly. But not until then.

"Do you see the situation? God couldn't just kill Lucifer. That
would lead to further problems with the remaining angels. They
wouldn't love him freely because they'd feel coerced on pain of
death. As a result, God chose to begin working out an incredible
plan that would lead to the good of all those who love and follow
him. That plan would involve the revelation of all that God is—in
character, power, and holiness. That plan is the one that involves
all supernatural and natural history. At the end, once all the loyal-

ists and rebels have been winnowed out, he can judge Lucifer and his cohorts and still have the support of everyone concerned.

"This plan involves not only the creation of our universe, but also the coming of Jesus Christ, his death and resurrection, and everything else that happened before and since. Through understanding some elements of that plan, as it is revealed in the Bible, we can begin to understand why things have happened as they have."

Jesse swore. "You got me on pins and needles here. What is it?"

I couldn't help but grin. "I'm not trying to make you all sweat. But I do think what I'm about to tell you is totally awesome and astonishing."

"Then git to it," Jesse said.

What God Did

So what did God do? Scripture reveals several facts. The first thing he chose to do was to let evil run its course. In effect, he said, 'All right, Satan, you think you have a better way? Then let's see your plan, your ideas, your actions. We'll give you a chance to prove your way is better. Do your best. (Or your worst.) Once you've shown us all your methods and tactics, we'll take a look and decide.'"

I could see skepticism return to Doug's and Julie's eyes, but they didn't stop me. "God has always taken this course. He has nothing to fear. If someone thinks he has a better plan, he will consider it. He doesn't flatten us with derision, argument, judgment, or punishment. He doesn't call us names or shout us down. Rather, he gives us an opportunity to show what we can do.

"A few examples from Scripture help confirm this. For one, there's the situation of Job (Job 1). When all the angels came in for a meeting, God asked Satan if he'd noticed Job, a person who was loyal, blameless, upright, and believing. Satan replied he had, but if God would simply strike Job down, Job would turn against him. What did God decide to do? Smack Satan across the cheek for being impudent? No, he put Job into Satan's hands. He said, 'Very well, then, everything he has is in your hands, but on the man himself do not lay a finger' (v. 12).

"Satan took that opportunity to decimate Job materially, hoping to get Job to screech that God was a fraud and that Job wouldn't believe anymore. In the process, he destroyed all Job's possessions and even killed off his sons and daughters. Yet, Job only fell to the ground and worshipped God, saying, 'Naked I came from my mother's womb, and naked I will depart. The LORD gave and the LORD has taken away; may the name of the LORD be praised'" (v. 21).

"Wow!" Jesse said. "That must've shook Satan up."

"Sure it did. But that's not the end of the story. Later, when Satan scoffed at even this, God allowed him to attack Job personally. Job was afflicted with boils so severe he wanted to die. But when his own wife counseled him to 'curse God and die' (2:9)— the very thing Satan wanted him to do—Job refused. He said, 'You are talking like a foolish woman. Shall we accept good from God, and not trouble?'" (2:10).

"This is in the Bible?" Julie said, her plucked eyebrows knitting skeptically.

"All in the book of Job, chapters 1 and 2."

Doug quickly found the spot and moved his Bible over to her side of the table.

I said, "Clearly, God was not afraid of what Satan might prove. In fact, all Satan ended up doing was affirming that God's way was the right way. Evil had a chance to show its stuff, but it came up empty-handed."

"I see it," Julie said, her head bowed over the book. "It's right here, just like you said."

"I'm not making these things up."

She looked up at me, something new in her eyes. Respect?

I went on, feeling bolstered. "Another example comes from Psalm 2. Here the writer speaks of the nations 'conspir[ing] and the peoples plot[ting] in vain' (v. 1). All the world's rulers gathered together to rebel against God. Did God reach down and squash them? No, he let them have their councils, plan their wars, offer their boasts and toasts. But ultimately he said he would speak to them 'in his anger' (v. 5). But not until later—after their so-called 'better plan' was examined in the light of day.

"Thus, God has chosen, not to squash evil, but to allow it to show us all it can do—its theories, its boasts, its plans, its activities. Throughout human history God has allowed every sort of evil to start, do its bit, and die. I'm convinced human history (and angelic history) will unearth every possible kind and combination of evil. Think of all the governments our world has seen—monarchies, democracies, dictatorships, and all sorts of combinations thereof. Think of the plethora of sins—murder, strife, gossip, adultery, genocide, torture, you name it. Think of ways that people have been treated. It's as though God has given Satan free rein to prove his point. But so far, Satan has not been able to produce a single empire that subsists on harmony, love, freedom, and dignity.

"At the end, everything evil has done will be open to the scrutiny of all concerned. Then we'll all be able to see who's right, God or Satan. God is not afraid to stand in the light. He has nothing to hide. So he'll, in a sense, let us all see, study, and dissect both his way and Satan's way and then determine who is truthful, faithful, just, right, holy, and worthy of allegiance."

"But why would God do that?" Julie asked, her brows knitted again.

"Because he's absolutely wise. He knows the best, most expedient way to solve any problem. And this was the biggest problem ever. So it would take a long-term, drawn-out, very detailed solution."

"It's pretty amazin', if you ask me," Jesse said.

"It nearly blows my mind every day thinking about it," I said. "But there's more. The second step is that God reserves the right to limit and govern evil. Even though he has allowed evil to flourish and appear to be in charge for the time being, he remains sovereign. Nothing can happen that he doesn't allow to happen. Evil cannot overstep the bounds God has set.

"For instance, in the case of Job, even though God allowed Satan to strike him financially and personally, God still decreed

Satan could not kill him. Satan even complained God had put a 'hedge' around Job to protect him from evil influences (1:10).

"In another situation, Satan had to ask God for permission to test Peter, Jesus' foremost disciple, as mentioned in Luke 22:31–34. There, Jesus told Peter that Satan wanted 'to sift [him] as wheat' (v. 31). God gave him permission, and that was when Peter three times denied he knew Jesus. But in the end, Jesus made sure Peter found the courage to repent and go on in the knowledge he was forgiven. God gave him grace. The reality is that Satan couldn't touch Peter and can't touch any other person unless God allows it.

"In other passages we see God speaking to indicate he has power over evil. 'He spoke, and it came to be; he commanded, and it stood firm. The LORD foils the plans of the nations; he thwarts the purposes of the peoples' (Psalm 33:9, 10). When the nations met in counsel to try to overthrow God, God 'scoff[ed] at them' (Psalm 2:4). No one can do anything apart from his permission. Jesus himself said, 'All authority in heaven and on earth has been given to me' (Matthew 28:18). That authority refers to the right and power to rule.

"So we see that God is not passive before this onslaught of evil. He works in and behind the scenes making sure the result he aims at is accomplished."

"So it's like God gave Satan the opportunity to strut his stuff," Jesse said, "but he won't let him get downright awful all the time."

"Right. In fact, at the end of the world, for seven years before Jesus comes back, God will let Satan pull out all the stops. But let's not go there yet."

Jesse looked thoughtful, his lips pooched up inside the giant beard. "So it's like God's givin' Satan a chance to try and do it better than him. It's like Satan could, if he wanted to, set up a better world than anythin' God could do, if he wanted."

"In a sense. But he can't do that."

"Why not?"

"Because there's no better world than God's. So Satan has to lie, deceive, and spread falsehood about God and his world, trying to convince us his way is the best."

"Sex, drugs, and rock 'n' roll," Jesse commented.

"In a way. Satan counters all God's good things with twists, variations, and outright deceptions. God tells us that knowing him and living in his will give us joy. But Satan says, 'No, it's sex and drugs, drunkenness, and driving fast that will get you what you really want.'"

Jesse nodded. Doug and Julie looked startled. "So for every good thing out there," Jesse said, "Satan tries to figure out a way to screw it up and make his way sound better."

"Exactly it," I said. "God says eat with moderation. Satan says, no, eat till you bust every day. God says don't lie to people. Satan says, you'd better lie about this or you'll get in worse trouble. It goes on and on."

"Amazin'," Jesse said.

God Can Do Even More Amazing Things

I glanced around and said, "Yet, even more than all this is a third principle: God reserves the right not only to overrule evil in many cases, but to turn its disasters into good for those who love him. Paul wrote, 'We know that in all things God works for the good of those who love him, who have been called according to his purpose' (Romans 8:28). In other words, God is personally involved in the struggle to right the wrongs of our world. He assures us that anyone who believes in him and loves him need not fear the destructive power of evil; he will turn it all for good."

I looked from face to face. Everyone appeared relaxed now, just drinking it all in. Maybe this session hadn't gone as wrong as I had thought it might.

"Please note," I continued. "Paul is not saying evil is good. Nor is he suggesting that God uses evil to produce good. God cannot look on or affirm evil in any way. He hates it, defies it, and will ultimately remove it from creation. But he does work around it. Evil does its deeds and then God comes in and creates an alternate situation that leads to good, but only for those who love him. He offers no such obligation to his enemies.

"A good illustration of this is one I read years ago from a teacher named Dr. Donald Barnhouse. He tells the story of a king who owned a beautiful forest with many prized trees. However, he also had an enemy who tried to ruin everything the king owned. One day the enemy learned of a certain tree the king favored. He stole into the forest and proceeded to cut the tree down. But as he was cutting it and it began to fall, he tripped, and the tree fell on him. As he lay there dying, the king rode up with his entourage and saw his enemy. The enemy wheezed, 'Maybe I'm dying, but I have hurt you. I have cut down your favorite tree.'

"The king gazed on his enemy's face and said, 'So you have. But I should inform you that just today we had decided to cut down this tree for a certain purpose. So even though you meant to do me evil, you have actually helped us. And also eliminated yourself in the process.'

"The enemy's face clouded with fury and as he wrenched to free himself from the tree, he tore his heart and died."

"Very cool," Jesse said.

I smiled. "You can see the point. While evil beings devise plans that seek to hurt God and his people, God's greater plan and knowledge make it possible for him to turn those ends for good. In fact, I have seen this happen repeatedly in my own life. One small example is the many rejections I, as a writer, have received in seeking to publish a variety of books. But in each case those rejections have led me to rethink and rewrite so as to produce a much finer work. This kind of thing has happened even in the midst of some personal disasters in which I could see no good when they happened. But once I got beyond them and saw the results they brought into my life, I could see how God turned such circumstances for good.

"Always trials, suffering, and evils in my life have led to greater character and a closer walk with God. In fact, James tells us, 'Consider it pure joy, my brothers, whenever you face trials of many kinds, because you know that the testing of your faith develops perseverance. Perseverance must finish its work so that you may be mature and complete, not lacking anything' (1:2–4). Consider bad things and trials a joy? Yes, but only in a world where you know

God rules and leads and engineers circumstances for your benefit. Otherwise, without such faith, all you see is that bad things have happened, you're a victim of bad luck, and there's nothing to do but live with it."

A Fourth Truth: Final Judgment

The fourth truth is that God will ultimately judge evil. The author of Hebrews, chapter 9 wrote, 'Man is destined to die once, and after that to face judgment' (9:27). And John wrote in the book of Revelation, 'And I saw the dead, great and small, standing before the throne, and books were opened' (20:12). Though evil will have a heyday for a long time in human and angelic history, it will also reach its payday. Once it's clear that God is right and all his ways are perfect, then he will execute judgment on all who have defied him unfairly and without cause.

"This is an important issue, for it means that evil, though it has rampaged for centuries in our world, will have to face up to its errors, every one. It cannot escape its crimes."

An Example

On January 23, 1989, the most notorious serial murderer in history, Ted Bundy, was executed in Florida. For more than ten years his punishment had been held up in the courts because of various appeals. Some people came to the conclusion our justice system doesn't work at all when such a killer's penalty can be detained so long. Up until the last few days before he would face the electric chair, Bundy maintained his innocence in the killings. But when the governor of Florida signed the final death warrant, Bundy made a dramatic turn and confessed to more than twenty of the murders.

"Lawmen say they can tie Bundy to thirty-six in total. But Bundy himself said the numbers might be in 'three digits'—over a hundred. And in the end, he was executed in the electric chair. One man remarked that his death was so much less painful than the deaths he inflicted on others, that it all seemed grossly unfair.

"But is it? One day Ted Bundy (and everyone else) will face God. If he truly accepted Christ, as some have claimed, then he will find complete forgiveness in Christ. But if it was just another ploy, he will not only answer for his crimes, but every piece of truth will be known and shown to all creation. Then God himself—perfectly just, all-knowing, and holy—will render the punishment, one that all creation will agree was fair and righteous.

"Everyone who rejects Christ, God's Truth and the True Way, will pay for his or her crimes. Completely. And eternally.

"We'll never see true justice in this world. But one day, because of God's plan, we will."

I could see now that all three of my new friends appeared on edge, so I knew I had to give them some good news on top of all this.

Evil Hasn't Gotten Away with a Thing

So let me encourage you. For those who believe in God and love him, this is great assurance. For one thing it means evil really isn't getting away with anything. Only that its punishment has been temporarily postponed.

"It also assures us every sin will be paid for. Every single evil act in history will be dealt with—justly and finally.

"It also means that in the end God himself will right every wrong. We will all be satisfied he has acted with justice, equity, fairness, and accuracy. Nothing will be overlooked, overturned, or overpunished. All accounts will be settled once and forever."

Another Way

But there's a fifth point here that is most essential: What about all of us who have committed evil deeds? Is there still a way out, a way back for us?

"YES! God has done something to deal with evil so all people who have committed sins may find a way back, a way, in fact, not only to start over, but to become perfectly righteous in God's eyes.

Through allowing evil to take its course, God has put together a plan that will make it possible for all believers to live forever, in perfection, unity, and love. In other words, God has done something to solve the problem of evil for all those who will trust him about it.

"What is that 'something'? The life, death, and resurrection of Jesus. What he did accomplishes something far greater than merely the extermination of evil. God made a way for anyone, anywhere, no matter what they've done, no matter how badly they've let evil control their lives, to come to him and find mercy, grace, forgiveness, and a whole new outlook on life. Through faith in Christ, anyone can find salvation, redemption, freedom from whatever evil they've been gripped by, and be completely cleansed and made new inside. That's the gospel—the good news."

A Joyous Note

So let me conclude this section on a joyous note. What I'm trying to say is that evil has not won, it cannot win, and it will not win. Ultimately, God's righteousness will be shown and all will agree that God indeed is worthy of our love, trust, and commitment. His plan is in effect, and he will carry it to its final conclusion. God is not uncaring, or powerless, or uninvolved. Rather, he has done everything possible to make it all work for glory—in the end. Samuel F. B. Morse, in the first long-distance use of his newly invented telegraph, asked, 'What hath God wrought?'

"What? The perfect plan toward dissolving evil, creating harmony, and establishing a kingdom of righteousness and love forever.

"That's the plan. That's the power of Christianity. That's what he's doing now in every place and every person. Those who accept his offer of forgiveness and new life will live on eternally in a new universe where truth and righteousness are the only way to live. Those who reject him will also be given a place, where they can no longer hurt anyone ever again. They will also live for eternity, but without any of the blessings God gave them in this life. They will have to live only with the realization they rejected all God offered and now they must make their own way, alone, without light, food, air, or water. That's what I believe hell will be."

I suddenly stopped, took a breath, and glanced around. Everyone looked too stunned to say anything, but then Julie said, "So the old atheistic foolproof dilemma about evil no longer works?"

I nodded. "Right. The old dilemma is, If God is all-powerful and loving, evil couldn't exist. So either he is all-powerful, but because he hasn't destroyed evil, he mustn't be loving. Or he loves us, but can't stop evil, and thus he can't be all-powerful. Either way, God cannot be both, all-powerful *and* perfectly loving, as the Bible says, or evil could not exist."

"Right. I've heard it several different ways," Julie said. "But that's basically it. But you're saying something different."

"Correct," I said. "My reading of the Bible says God is both all-powerful and perfectly loving, as well as just, righteous, holy, gracious, eternal, and many other things. With all those characteristics, the argument goes, God certainly couldn't allow evil to exist like it does in our world. But like I already said, God is all those things and he has decided to take a third road—not eliminate evil now, but let it have a chance to make its case to the angels and to us. Satan is out there saying, 'Worship me. I'm better than God. I'll give you a better world. I'll make things more fun. I'll give you what you really want.'

"So God has given him the chance throughout human history to prove his point. As a result, Satan has just gone crazy tempting people to do every kind of evil there is. At the same time, God is working in the midst of the world teaching his truth, giving us the Bible and Jesus and all that, and transforming those who trust and believe in him. He's raising up a race of righteous and good people who truly want to follow him and obey his Word. They're not perfect yet. Not in this world. But one day he will do a final rescue out of this world, bring all evil to justice, and create a new world where his truth and principles will be lived out perfectly, every day."

"Sounds like pie in the sky to me," Julie said tautly.

I gazed into her deep blue eyes. She seemed sincere, but I detected a softening I hadn't expected. "Then what is your answer?

How do you explain both good and evil in the world today? How do *you* think it will be resolved?"

She shook her head. "I don't really know. I only know I can't believe the one you just laid out for me here. Think about it. It's preposterous. You're telling me that this person Satan goes around tricking all of us into doing bad things? I really don't think he, if he did exist, could be that powerful."

I nodded. "Right. I don't think Satan personally works on all of us. Maybe he just has a president here and there, and a few others. But remember, there are millions if not billions of rebel angels who turned into demons, according to the Bible. I believe every one of us probably has one or more of those tempters assigned to trip us up. First, to prevent us from becoming Christians. Then from living a godly life. Then from becoming committed Christians who go out into the world, live a God-honoring life, and try to tell others about the good news. Those demons are out there everywhere. Just think about the number of times you've heard a little voice in your mind telling you to do something you know is wrong, or to make a bad decision. That could be your own experience or lusts speaking. I have found it can also be demonic influence and pressure.

"All that's to say nothing of our basic human capacity for evil, too. Probably many of us have been tempted to do wrong by some resident demon on our block. But at the same time, we all have enough imagination to dream up plenty of bad things on our own. I'm sure there are demons who have worked on me when I've gone off in some other direction and they're scratching their heads, saying, 'Why didn't I think of that?'"

She gazed at me, and suddenly blurted, "You think you have an answer for everything, don't you?"

I swallowed, a little taken aback. "Julie, I don't pretend to be any smarter or more educated than anyone else. All I know better than many, but not all, is what the Bible teaches on these and other subjects. You are completely free to reject the Bible, Jesus, God, all of them. You're free to live your life entirely without the influence of Christians, the church, or anyone else who preaches God's truth. Not I, not Billy Graham, not even God can 'make' you accept any of this. While I believe God has to draw a person spiritually, and has to 'open' his or her heart, it's a process. God woos a person, they respond.

"I believe God has spoken to every person who has ever lived. He gives everyone many chances to listen to him and heed his truth. But if someone pushes him away, tells him to 'get out of my life,' God won't force himself on that person. God himself speaks in Isaiah 1:18–20: '"Come now, let us reason together," says the LORD. "Though your sins are like scarlet, they shall be as white as snow; though they are red as crimson, they shall be like wool. If you are willing and obedient, you will eat the best from the land; but if you resist and rebel, you will be devoured by the sword."'

"God is very open and willing to dialogue with anyone who comes to him—skeptic, cynic, atheist, or holy man. But he always couches his invitations with a warning such as the one above. You are free to come, but if you reject him and his truth, you are in grave danger."

Julie stared at me, incredulity in her eyes. "Are you threatening me?"

I shook my head. "Not at all. But just think for a second that if this is the truth, if there really is a God who cares about us and wants us to come into his family, do you think it would be fair if he said something like, 'Hey, take it or leave it. Either way, you'll be okay.' That would be a lie. In fact, that is one of the lies of Satan. He tells people all the time, 'You can believe whatever you want. It's all right. Do your own thing. It'll all work out.' But God offers us both the truth and the reality: Listen to him, trust him, and you will be blessed. But if you go your own way, you do so at your peril."

"It sounds like a threat to me," Julie said, her eyes narrowing.

"Look at it this way: You have a five-year-old. You tell her, 'don't go out in the street. Stay in the yard, and you will be blessed. But if you go out in the street, you could get hit by a car and die.' Isn't it the warning that often motivates us? If we said, 'Sure, go out in the street. Chances are you'll survive. And it'll be fun. You'll find coins in the gutter, and dead bugs, and all sorts of cool stuff.

So go ahead. It's completely up to you.' Would such a parent be honest, let alone a decent parent? If there is danger, we should be told of it. So God tells us there is danger: 'Go Satan's way, and you could end up in hellfire.' That's the reality of the Bible. Of course, right now you can take it or leave it. But what if it really is true? You're taking a tremendous risk under those conditions."

She glanced away, and I sensed I'd struck a nerve. Which one, I didn't know. So I just continued, "My purpose here was to show Doug what the Bible said in reference to a number of questions he had. We sat and talked and then Jesse overheard us one day and he joined the table. Today, Doug brought you. I'm willing to listen to anything you have to say. But what I can never say is that I think the Bible is wrong, or that Jesus didn't really die for the sins of the world, or that God doesn't exist. With all my heart, I believe the Bible to be God's truth. If there are dangers out there, if the world is going off to hell in a handbasket and I know it, what kind of person would I be to go blithely through life and pretend everything's fine, whatever you want to believe is okay with me and with God? That would be the ultimate abuse, if you ask me.

"Perhaps I can put it this way. The Bible is an old book. It's influenced billions of people through history and even today. Many great things have been done because of various people's beliefs in the Bible. Of course, there have been some aberrations, like the Inquisition, where some people went off on a wrong course and brought shame on the church. But really, how often does that happen? For the most part, I have found many people influenced for good through the Bible. I'm one of them. For that reason, I think for someone like you, it's worth spending a little time to find out what it says. You are free to take that or leave it. But you are not free to escape the consequences, if it proves to be true."

She glanced away, then centered in on Doug. "Do you believe this baloney?"

Doug stiffened. "I don't know, to be honest. For some reason, it fascinates me. I really want to find out what the Bible says about these things. But at this point, I haven't committed to anything. Why does it matter?"

"Because you're a sensible person," Julie sputtered. "This is simply preposterous. Anyone who doesn't see that has to be a complete idiot."

Doug cleared his throat. "Mark has a bachelor's from a reputable university in math, chemistry, and physics. He has a master's in theology from a conservative, but highly regarded, seminary. I don't think he's an idiot."

Julie rolled her eyes. I touched her hand and she flinched. I reeled back slightly, then said, "Julie, I don't expect Doug or Jesse or you for that matter to just keel over and cry, 'Hallelujah, I believe,' because I say these things. It's a choice on your part. It's a choice to hear more. It's a choice to jump ship and say you're outta here. I don't want to see you leave, but I sense your frustration and concern. Could it be that right now, one of the reasons you find it so preposterous and difficult to accept is because that's precisely what God said it would be like for all of us? Peter said Satan goes through the world like a roaring lion 'looking for someone to devour' (1 Peter 5:8). Other places it says he deceives the whole world. He says, 'The Bible is bunk,' to quote something Doug said to me. When someone opens it, Satan laughs and whispers, 'You're going to believe that horse manure? Come on. Get a life!' He uses the unbelievers around us to pressure us into agreeing with them, that the Bible is just a bunch of myths and stupid stories.

"Repeatedly, the Bible tells us we'll face opposition and persecution if we speak up for God, Jesus, the Bible, or any of that. Jesus himself said, 'Be on your guard against men; they will hand you over to the local councils and flog you in their synagogues. On my account you will be brought before governors and kings as witnesses to them and to the Gentiles . . . Brother will betray brother to death, and a father his child; children will rebel against their parents and have them put to death. All men will hate you because of me, but he who stands firm to the end will be saved.' That's in Matthew 10, verses 17, 18, 21, and 22.

"So you see, God has made it clear this isn't an easy ride. To top it all off, God also says he rarely seeks out people who think they have it all together, who have no needs, who believe they have the world by the tail. Jesus himself said, 'It is easier for a camel to go through the eye of a needle than for a rich man to enter the kingdom of God' (Matthew 19:24). But he followed that up with the words, 'With man this is impossible, but with God all things are possible' (v. 26).

"And listen to this. In 1 Corinthians 1:26–29, Paul writes,

'Brothers, think of what you were when you were called. Not many of you were wise by human standards; not many were influential; not many were of noble birth. But God chose the foolish things of the world to shame the wise; God chose the weak things of the world to shame the strong. He chose the lowly things of this world and the despised things—and the things that are not—to nullify the things that are, so that no one may boast before him.

"The fact is that the best I can say about myself is that I'm a fool for Christ. I'm a lowly nobody. I don't have money, position, popularity. In high school, I could never get elected to anything. So why did God pull me up out of the dirt? Why didn't he go after all the winners, all the big shots, all the people who could have a real influence? Because perhaps they're all just too proud to admit the need. Too stuck on themselves to think they're sinners. Too cocky to think they can't make it on their own in this world. Too deep into their sin and addictions and lusts to turn away from them. And that's their downfall. Jesus said if you want to enter his kingdom, you have to become like a little child. What did he mean? I think it's a picture of someone who is dependent, willing to admit they need help, and totally trusting of the adult who gives that message to them. That's what needs to happen in a person's heart before they'll ever accept any of these things."

Julie shook her head. "I don't mean to put you down. That's not me at all. But how can you expect me to believe the world is run by a guy with horns in a red suit carrying a pitchfork?"

"Actually," Doug suddenly said, "that's not at all the portrait Mark gave us of Satan. In—what was it?"

"Ezekiel 28," I said.

"Right. That passage paints a picture of a very powerful, formidable, amazing, wise, and beguiling person who, if we saw him in person, we'd probably think he was God. In fact, the red-suited dude is probably one of his deceptions to make us think he's really no one, when in reality he has us by the you-know-whats, excuse my French."

Julie sighed. "It's a lot to bite off."

"Sure," I said again. "That's why we've been meeting. I didn't accept all these things the first time I heard about Jesus and the Bible. It took a good fifteen or so years of searching before it all began to make sense. I'm willing to keep meeting as long as you all wish. But I will say that my goal is that each of you will one day come to know Christ like I have. I make no apologies for that. I'd like to see you all become believers. But I also know in most cases that doesn't happen overnight."

A long silence ensued.

Finally, Julie said, "Okay, I'd like to hear more. But I'm not going to suddenly fall to my knees and start confessing all my—er—problems."

I smiled and so did Doug and Jesse. Jesse said, "Hey, if that's what I gotta do to get my life back, I'll do it. But for now, I'm bidin' my time. I need to hear more. Although I have to admit, this is gettin' kinda exciting. I'm thinkin' of bringin' my wife herself next time."

Doug nodded. "I was in a real bad mood when I got here today. But I've thought about it, and it's not really that big a deal. So I'm hanging in there."

"Good," I said. "Thanks for the vote of confidence. How about an assignment?"

Doug and Jesse groaned in a friendly way. Julie just looked a bit shocked.

"You learned today that God has this plan he's working out in human history. I'd like you to take a hard look at your life and see if there are any times you see that God might have been working in your life. On any level. In any way. Even something you think is a stretch. Think it through. Then come next week, and we'll discuss that."

"But what will we be lookin' at next time?" Jesse wanted to know.

"Ah." I stopped to think. "I'm leaning in the direction of talking about God's overall plan. What he did in history and where he's taking it. And how that plan is the greatest thing any of us can plug into."

"The book of Revelation?" Jesse asked with light in his eyes.

"Maybe a little. I don't think we'll have time to cover every detail. But I want you to get what I call the 'long view,' which is the best way of looking at life in general and your own in particular."

I stopped and we all gathered our things. When we stood, Julie offered me her hand again. "I'll try to be here. Can't guarantee it. But I think at least you're reasonable. So I'll give you another shot."

"That's all I can ask."

We filed out and as I climbed into my van, I wondered where this was all headed, and when Starbucks would kick us all out.

CHAPTER 10

Discovering the Plan of God That Commandeers History Is One of the Greatest Encouragements That Can Come into Your Life

The Story Continues

I sat down with the same group the next Monday, gratified they stuck with me. Even Julie seemed in a better mood. Before I started in, Jesse raised his hand to say something.

"I gotta tell ya," he said, "I got another answer to prayer."

Everyone turned to him.

"After our meeting last week, I went to the terminal where I drive. The big boss told me I needed to get ready cause I'd be drivin' from Thursday till Tuesday every week for the next coupla months. A coupla guys quit and they needed to shift around my schedule. As you can imagine, I was heartbroken."

Everyone chuckled.

"No, really. I don't wanna miss any more of our meetings."

I jumped in and said, "Jesse, we don't have to meet on Monday afternoons. We could change the schedule to accommodate you if we needed to."

He stared at me. "Well, okay, but I never thought of that. Anyway, I just bowed my head in the truck and said, 'God, I think you want me to hear what Mark's tellin' us. So if you can, I'd like you to switch things so I can be there.' That's all. Then I added, 'And if you do it, I promise I'll go to Mark's church and listen to his preacher guy.'"

Jesse looked around at us, his eyes twinkling. "So next thing I know, I come in on Thursday and my boss tells me, the two guys who quit came back, said they didn't like the new situation, and could they still drive. So my boss said, 'Back to the old schedule.' I said, 'So I have Mondays off?' 'And Sunday,' he said. 'You drive from Tuesday till Saturday.' So I just walked away, looked up at the sky and said, 'God, was that you doin' that?' So now I guess I gotta go to your church, Mark."

I laughed. Julie and Doug just looked flummoxed. But then Doug said, "I guess something's happening with me, too. My mom hasn't lost a hair despite the radiation, and Gabriel is coming around about the pregnancy. He seems to think giving the baby up for adoption is the way to go at this point, even though he says he loves the girl and wants to marry her someday. So I don't know whether it's God working, or coincidence, but you said you've been praying about it. And so, I'm starting to think God may really be out there."

Everyone smiled, but then Julie indicated she had something, too. "Okay, I know I was pretty tough last time we met, but I'm here again, though I'm not sure why. But I actually did say something to God. I'm not sure I'd call it praying, but something."

"What happened?" I asked.

"After we met last Monday, I couldn't get all these things about the Bible out of my mind. So I just stopped one afternoon, took a few seconds and said in my head—not out loud—'Okay, God, if you're there and you really think you can convince me the Bible is the truth, I'm willing to listen. But you better make it real convincing.'"

We all laughed.

She shrugged. "That was it. No remarkable answers to anything else, though I have been concerned about Doug's situations. Anyway, I almost didn't make it here today. Some problems at the office. But they all cleared up about a half hour ago, and I just thought, 'What the heck? I'll go again.' So was that God working, Mark? Is he rearranging *my* schedule, too?"

We all laughed again. But I said, "I think when you begin to understand God's plan for planet Earth, you will get rather excited about the idea of God being intimately involved with everything in your life. So why don't we begin?"

Doug shook his head. "Julie and I talked this past week and she asked me what kinds of things you have asked for prayer about. I told her you hadn't yet. So I think since each of us is speaking up about our problems, we need to hear about yours, too. So we can pray. Or at least show some concern."

Surprised, I smiled. "Fine. Here are several things. I'm working on a book now that I'm really engrossed in but it takes a lot out of me, and it's due in a month. My wife Jeanette and I run a writer's conference we're gearing up for. Last year, we got killed on it financially. So please pray—or show concern—"

Everyone laughed again.

"—that God will bless our efforts. My son Gardner has been doing some bad things of late—stealing money, lying—and I really need to work on him about this. And my little one, Elizabeth, needs to go to preschool. We haven't found one we like yet."

"Oh, I know a good one," Julie said right away. "I'll give you the number later."

"Great, thanks. So that's the main stuff right now. Think you can handle it?"

Everyone nodded. But then Jesse said, "But if I ain't a real believer yet, will God really answer me?"

I reflected a moment. "Take a look for yourself. You already think you've gotten answers. So why wouldn't he? He knows about your prayers, certainly. There's such a thing as 'common grace,' which is God's largesse and blessing on people regardless of whether they have faith. God is good, and he will never refuse to be good to someone just because they haven't crossed the faith line. In fact, that is one way he draws people to himself. By blessing them, and showing them he cares, even before there's any kind of commitment."

Julie looked interested suddenly and said, "You talk a lot about this thing of God 'drawing' people. What do you mean by that?"

"It's from John 6:44. After feeding five thousand (or more) people, Jesus said, 'No one can come to me unless the Father who sent me draws him; and I will raise him up at the last day.' The Bible tells us over and over that no one would ever come to God and believe unless God works in that person, wooing, coaxing, encouraging, warning, and so on. That's the work of the third person of the Trinity, the Holy Spirit. Since Jesus is no longer here in bodily form, God sends the Spirit to touch the lives of millions.

"When a person becomes a believer, the Spirit actually comes and 'lives' in that person's heart in some supernatural sense. That's how we begin to experience God talking to us. That's how he assures us he loves us and that we belong to him. The Spirit is the one who speaks to us to warn us of danger, or to compliment us on a job well done. Remember, God wants a relationship with you. He's not this giant person on some throne out there, and we go and bow down before him. No, he's right inside us and when any of you becomes a believer, you'll find out about that reality rather quickly."

Julie narrowed her eyes. "So do you think God is 'drawing' me right now? And Doug? And Jesse here?"

"Sure. I mean, how do you think he would work such a thing? Write it in the sky? Have Jesus come to your door? No, he works mainly through people, even bad ones."

"Like you?" Doug said.

We all laughed.

"Right. And the fact is, God usually works so subtly, you hardly know he's there until one day you walk an aisle, pray in a restaurant, or just cry out to him for help in the midst of trouble. And then he comes firing into your life in a way that will be convincing and meaningful to you."

Julie just sat very still. "So you think God could be working in me right now to get me to one day take the step of becoming a real Christian?"

I laughed. "Definitely. Are you scared?"

"Terrified."

We all laughed.

"Hebrews 10:31 does say it's a 'dreadful thing to fall into the hands of the living God.' But believe me, after the initial shock, most of us discover it's the greatest thing that can ever happen to anyone. It was, is, and will be for me. I can say that without hesitation."

Julie shook her head. "So I won't be able to cuss, drink, smoke, or hang around with all my atheist friends anymore?"

I laughed. "Look, it's very true that when God takes a believer on, he's not going to let them run off and do all the nasty things they've always done. God transforms us. The Bible speaks of the Spirit remaking us in the 'image of Christ.' That's not a physical thing, but spiritual. God intends to retool every one of us to have the character, holiness, goodness, and perfection of Jesus himself. That doesn't mean he'll destroy our personalities, our senses of humor, our abilities, or anything like that. But he will—gradually in most cases—start to eliminate the bad stuff from our lives and replace it with good things. Instead of having a huge anger or violence problem, like Jesse mentioned he has, God will give him the power to overcome those negatives and replace them with kindness, gentleness, self-control. He can help an alcoholic shed his thirst for the drink. That doesn't mean that person won't struggle at times with those temptations. It doesn't mean he'll stop drinking one second after he asks Jesus into his life. But it does mean God is in this with each of us for the long haul. Starting at point A, he plans to get us to point Z, where we arrive safely in heaven, perfect and utterly good and holy people."

"Holy?" Julie said with a quaver.

"Absolutely. But don't think of holiness as the caricature Satan has given it. Holiness isn't becoming a monk, thrashing yourself daily with a whip, spending every second in church, and telling yourself what a total creep you are. It's also not looking around at everyone else and thinking how great you are because you wake up every morning and pray for ten minutes before you start your day, like the Pharisees in the time of Jesus.

"No, holiness simply means you have committed yourself to serve God in any and every capacity and in any and every way he desires. I mean, sure, holiness involves shucking a lot of bad things and habits you may have, especially big ones like using drugs, committing sexual sin, stealing from your boss, and so on. But the real thrill of it is when God starts using you in ways that fulfill you.

"Like for me, one of the gifts God gave me—and he gives such gifts to all believers—is to teach others about the Bible. Right now, telling you about the Bible is not only a responsibility, but fun, exhilarating, challenging, even thrilling. Such things will be different for each person. Jesse might have a real gift for reaching bikers and truckers with the gospel. You, Doug, might find you have a knack for making money so you can contribute it to people and organizations who seek to spread the good news all over the world. And Julie, who knows, you may find God gives you something special in your work, your church, or your home life. You just never know what God will do with each of us.

"The guarantee is that if we flow with it, if we let him develop that gift in us, we will receive a tremendous sense of purpose in life. We'll see that our existence is not just surviving, but that he will use us to have an impact on the world, on our friends and relatives, on all sorts of people. That impact, we will soon realize, will be the whole reason we were put on this earth. We'll see that God uses us, tiny little us, for mighty things in our world. Isn't that what we all wish for, to have a legacy, to leave the world better off than we found it, to influence and be a source of good for others?"

I looked from face to face. Everyone appeared transfixed. Then Jesse said, "I'd give everything I have to get that kinda feeling about myself."

Doug nodded. "I have to admit, that's probably the most enticing thing about this whole gospel deal."

Even Julie looked intrigued. "Why haven't I ever heard this before? I went to church till I got into college. Why didn't they tell me these things?"

I said, "Sadly, not all pastors, not all churches are aligned with God the way they should be. Many don't teach the basic truths of the Bible like God calls them to. It's the sad state of our world that Satan has infiltrated the church all over the place. In fact, that's probably the main thing he tries to do—keep churches from preaching and teaching the truth. When he accomplishes that in a church, every one of those people in it may be affected in a way that keeps them from learning the gospel and becoming true members of God's family."

Julie shook her head. "If all this is true, I have to ask, how have I missed it all these years? I'm forty-six years old, a mother of two, a divorcée, a businessperson. I've known a lot of people, even people who go to church regularly. But no one has ever told me the things you have."

I cleared my throat. "That's another sad truth about God's people. I've read a statistic that 95 percent of people who commit their lives to Christ never tell anyone—not one person—about their faith, at least not outsiders, the people who really need to hear it."

"You're kidding! I would think people would be screaming these things from the mountaintops! If I had heard these supposed truths years ago, I think my life would have been very different."

I stared at Julie a second, wondering what pain and horrors had struck her life over the years that might have been prevented had she connected with God in her early years. If just one person had told her the truth before this.

Sighing, I said, "Don't blame all of them, Julie. But remember, what I'm going to show you about God's plan is that he knows exactly the right time to talk to you about his kingdom. For some reason, he must have seen that for all the previous forty-six years you wouldn't have been open to his message. So maybe now is the time he sees that you will be most willing to hear what he has to say.

"The wonderful thing about the gospel is that no matter where you start—two years old, or a hundred and two—God will take you from there and get working to make your life all it can be. The great truth is that you can begin wherever you are now. Like that old song, 'Just as I Am,' God starts with us where we are, just *as* we are, not where he might wish we were, or where we might have hoped to be. You just have to trust that God truly does know the best for each of us. And therefore, his plan was that you wouldn't really hear, understand, and perhaps embrace the truth until now. I was twenty-one when it happened to me. And the first question I asked was like yours, 'How did I get through twenty-one years without knowing this stuff?' And, 'How did I ever make it through those years without God at my side?' The truth is that God was there every step of the way, watching, preparing, working. I just didn't know it, until then."

I detected a tear in Julie's eye. "I want it. I want him," she suddenly said. "I know I started out as a hard case last week. But all that was a façade. I've been looking for this all my life. What do I do?"

I gazed at her, absolutely floored. I had expected her to be the last one to take such a step, if she ever took it. I said gently, "Then just tell him. Admit you've messed up your life. Tell him you want to start over with him. Tell him you believe in Jesus, that he died for your sins, that he rose again to assure you he's really God incarnate and will get you safely to his heaven. Just speak your heart. It's not real complicated."

She returned my stare, a tenuous smile flickering on the edge of her lips. "Right now? Right here?"

"Why not?"

"Okay," she said. "Do I bow my head and just say it?"

"Sure. We all will."

We all bowed, and Julie started in. "Okay, God, I'm kind of nervous about this, but here goes. I've been pretty hard about this all my life, and I've done a lot of bad things. I can admit that up front. So I'm laying it all out right now. I believe what Mark has told us, what the Bible says about Jesus, you, everything. I want to be in your family. I want to know you, like Mark—"

She stopped suddenly and sobbed for a moment. I said nothing; we all remained quiet.

"Okay. I'm all right. I just have to get this done. If nothing happens, at least you'll know I tried. I believe in you now. And I want to follow Jesus. Whatever he says. If it means giving up Dave—he's my boyfriend—I'll do it. Whatever you say. I've got to get my life together, and I'm hoping this is the way. So, there it is, God. I'm ready and willing and here, and I guess now it's up to you."

She stopped and I said, "Amen."

We all opened our eyes.

Jesse blurted, "That was the coolest prayer I ever heard."

Doug regarded her with what looked like respect and awe as Julie wiped her eyes with a Kleenex. "I'm sorry for getting emotional," she said. "I just . . . well . . . this has been a long time coming. And I'm amazed I've taken this step so quickly, but I really believe it's right. All I kind of feel is very nervous. But I guess that's natural. But I better get some peace and joy soon, or I'll be very disappointed."

I laughed. "Believe me, those things will come. Tell me, don't you feel relief or anything like that?"

She nodded. "Very much so. And something else. Like this giant heaviness is gone. My depression. All the guilt I've piled up for years that I rationalized away and told myself it was just stupid. I guess it really wasn't."

"You'll be finding out a lot more," I said. "Let me give you your first verse to memorize and think about. It's Philippians 1:6. It says, Paul writing, 'Being confident of this, that he who began a good work in you will carry it on to completion until the day of Christ Jesus.'"

Julie smiled in a way I had not seen from her. "That's really there?"

"Of course. Look it up." I repeated the Scripture reference. "It's a tremendous promise. It means—"

Julie held up her hand. "I think I get it. It means what started in my life just a few minutes ago is just the beginning. God's going to do amazing things starting now until the day I get up there in heaven with Jesus and I'm that perfect person I always thought I was but now know I wasn't."

We all laughed. It exhilarated me to see her sense of humor coming out.

"No, really," she said, "I think the first thing that's going to go in me is my pride. When I tell my mom what I just did. That will really be humbling, to hear her talk about what a little idiot I am. She's even more of an atheist than I was."

"Maybe she'll be the first one you get to tell about Jesus, then."

"That will be a major miracle." She smiled. "Anyway, I am feeling something. Lighter, I guess. Like life doesn't have to be that serious, or something. It's kind of fun."

"That's one of the first things God does in us," I said. "Jesus said, 'I have come that they may have life, and have it to the full.' What is that fullness but the ability to laugh and enjoy God's world?"

"Where's that one?" Julie said. "I want to memorize that one, too."

"John 10:10."

She typed it into her iPhone. "Okay," she said, "I think we need to get on to the subject of the day. I have to hear more about this, now that I'm actually part of it."

Doug stared at her and touched her hand. "I'm happy for you, Jules."

She smiled at him. "You've got to do it, too, Doug. I won't let you get out of this without taking that step."

He nodded. "I'm working on it."

Julie glanced up at Jesse. "You too, big boy."

Jesse nodded. "Workin' on it, too."

Julie turned to me. "Okay, hit it. I need to hear everything the Bible says about everything."

I chuckled and started in.

The Plan of God

I began laying out the bricks of God's plan in order, as I understand them.

"First, God created a universe of angelic beings. These beings were designed to worship, serve, and know God. Their purpose was to make the music of heaven. All that went well, until one day . . .

"Second, Lucifer began thinking his murderous thoughts against God. As he meditated on how he might overthrow God, undoubtedly he began enlisting the aid and support of various angels he knew and trusted. He somehow persuaded a third of them to follow him in a war meant to take over heaven, depose God, and run things the way they desired.

"Third, God stopped the insurrection, drew a line in the sand, and had every angel make his choice—to follow and trust God, or to ally himself with Lucifer, now Satan, the "adversary."

"Fourth, in order to deal with the problem of the evil that infected his universe, God decided not to destroy the rebels, or incarcerate them. Instead, he created a place where he and Satan could test their theories and principles: Earth, and the universe we know as our home. Of course, there were many other reasons God took this step, as we see in Genesis 1 and 2. He wanted to create a race of people who would glorify him and show off and experience what he was really like in ways even the angels weren't capable of. God gave Satan a lot of freedom in this environment. At the same time, God placed limits on what Satan could do so he wouldn't do things such as just step in and start murdering everyone who didn't follow him. God also reserved the right to work in the midst of these people to show his real nature and program.

"Fifth, Satan talked the first couple into rejecting God as their leader and into becoming like him, people who wanted to be their own gods and run their own lives as they pleased.

"Sixth, God reacted to this development by cursing the whole thing. At the same time, he set into motion his plan to redeem the mess and make it possible for humans to return to him and find out the truth.

"This led to God's more intricate plan for planet Earth. In effect, he would allow humanity to do whatever they wanted. He would at times set limits, offer guidance, and enact principles and judgments that would prevent the evil part of it from completely destroying everything. He would also make a way for humans any-where to come back to him, know him, and trust that he would bring them to another creation where God's truth would rule and stand."

God's Plan for Humanity

Thus, God started a program to educate, lead, and transform human beings. What he would do was give humans a chance to try all the possible ways of ruling their lives. In the end, God would show unequivocally which methods worked and which didn't.

"So, the seventh step was to kick Adam and Eve out of the Gar-den of Eden and set them on a course that would make them long for what they originally had, or even for something better. Through this process, God hopefully would lead them back into a faith rela-tionship that would prepare them for that new world.

"However, since Adam and Eve had rejected God's way of doing things, God allowed them to live in a state where there were no rules. God made no demands. Presumably, the only restrictions were what he imprinted on their hearts, the basic laws of morality and conscience.

"So what happened? A world situation arose in which every-one did their own thing. Whatever anyone wanted or needed or desired, they pursued it with a vengeance. People violated the moral code written on their hearts and turned the world into a cesspool of sin and degradation. At the same time, a few followed God and loved him, people like Enoch, who the Bible says "walked with God." Undoubtedly there were others. But the vast majority com-mitted the foulest deeds imaginable, and in time, their conduct so sickened God that he realized he would have to wipe the slate nearly clean.

"He found one man whose family still revered God: Noah, his wife, and their three sons and their wives. God commanded Noah to build an ark because in a hundred years he would cause the world to undergo a monstrous flood. This would eliminate all the bad guys and girls and hopefully give planet Earth a new start.

"After the flood, Noah and his family were told to go throughout the world and populate it. God gave them a few new rules, among them the law that if someone murdered anyone, that criminal would pay with his life. The people, though, as their numbers increased, went east to a place called Babel. There, in defiance of God, they erected a tower. No one knows precisely what the purpose was. Genesis 11:4 says they wanted to reach the heavens—perhaps to protect them from another flood—and make a name for themselves. The verse also says they specifically didn't want to be scattered throughout the earth.

"As you will see throughout biblical history, God would give some directive. People would fail to obey. God would judge them. This happened with Adam and Eve after they ate the forbidden fruit, Cain after he killed Abel, and the people in the time of the Flood. Each time, God was saying, "Okay, you couldn't make that system work. In fact, you violated every principle, so now I will have to do something to right things." A judgment. In the case of the Tower of Babel, God judged that generation by "confus[ing] their language" (Genesis 11:9).

"What happened, I believe, was until then everyone spoke the same language. But God separated all these groups, and gave each a special language. When they found they could no longer communicate, the people began to do what God had told them to do—spread all throughout the earth.

"It was after this time that God began to move more intentionally into the peoples of the world. As a result, he selected one man, Abraham, and his family, and decided to use them as the means of spreading his truth throughout the world. Abraham was the "father of the Jews," God's "chosen people." They were chosen in effect to be the vehicle by which God would give the world his Word, the Bible, and his Son, Jesus.

"So God called Abraham, and a new period in history started. All the rest of the world continued as before, building nations, making laws, and trying to create societies that could function with some efficiency. But with Abraham God did something totally new and unseen: He started a personal relationship with Abraham, talked to him, led him, gave him promises, and taught him his truth. He also gave Abraham a "promise," or "covenant" (agreement), whereby God promised to bless him and his descendants if he and they would be faithful to God.

"Abraham, still called Abram at this point, concurred and Genesis 15:6 says that "Abram believed the LORD, and he credited it to him as righteousness." It meant that Abraham gained God's perfection, not through doing good deeds and obeying God, but through believing in God and trusting him. It was a totally new concept, even though God had attempted to teach it from the beginning.

"Through a miracle, Abraham, at the age of one hundred, and his wife, Sarah, at the age of ninety, had a son, Isaac. Over the next few generations, God raised up a people who knew of him, believed in him, and, to some degree, obeyed him. When a famine arose in the land, Jacob, the grandson of Abraham, took his family down to Egypt, where God allowed the Hebrew people to incubate into a specific race and nation. God did this because Abraham's descendants had begun to marry the Canaanites, who were idol-worshippers. To preserve the purity of his people and to get them off to a strong start, God moved them temporarily to Egypt, where the Egyptians, who despised sheepherders, had nothing to do with the Hebrews. As a result, the Hebrew people came together as a single nation and race unlike all those on the face of the earth.

"In time, the Egyptians enslaved them and God raised up another man, Moses, who would lead them back to Canaan, freedom, and safety. However, since the time of Abraham, the people of Israel had failed to live on the basis of God's covenants and promises. So God once again saw a change of gears was necessary. Until then, God conducted business and gave his truth personally to those who followed him—Abraham, Isaac, Jacob, Joseph, and many others. But now he had a whole nation—some say more than three million strong—and God decided to initiate a new system. This system would teach the Hebrews his rules and laws, show them how to worship him, and ultimately make them understand his holiness and what kind of perfection he required of them.

"God gave Moses the history of the world in Genesis, the continuing history of the Hebrews, or Israelites, as they came to be known, in Exodus, and numerous laws and guides for living in the next three books: Leviticus, Numbers, and Deuteronomy. There were 613 specific laws regulating Israelite life.

"But what happened? Over the next 1,400 years, the Israelites messed up so many times, left God and became idol-worshippers, violators of the Ten Commandments, and so on, they proved themselves completely incapable of following God's numerous rules. Strangely, this was exactly what God wanted them to find out. They needed to discover that keeping a bunch of rules wasn't what life and God's kingdom were all about. Instead, he wanted to use the law of Moses as a "tutor" to teach them about faith.

"How did that work? When an Israelite realized he couldn't keep all the rules and follow all the temple regulations to deal with his mistakes, he was either driven to despair or back to God. 'What do I do, Lord?' he should have asked. 'How can I please you?'

"God revealed to many of his followers—Joshua, Gideon, Samuel, King David, and many others—that the real issue was faith. 'The righteous will live by his faith,' he told them through Habakkuk (2:4). And that Abraham was justified by faith (Romans 4).

"But the children of Israel weren't getting it. They only hyped the legalism and rule-following to monstrous levels so that by the time Jesus appeared in Israel, the Jews (the tribe of Judah) were divided between the common people just trying to survive, the Pharisees who made all the demands about the rules, the Sadducees who turned worship into a business, and others like the Essenes, who fled into the desert and would have nothing to do with anybody.

"Once again, God showed the people that rule-keeping didn't work. So he next instituted another step: the age of grace. Here, God would extend grace (as he always did before but no one except a few seemed to get it) to every person. All they had to do was believe in Jesus, who paid the penalty for their sins and lapses, and trust him about everything in life and the future.

"As a result, Jesus lived a perfect life, taught amazing truths never heard before, performed all kinds of supernatural wonders, confirmed with his life and deeds all kinds of prophecies given centuries before in the Old Testament, and did miracles to prove he really was God incarnate. As might be expected, Jesus ran into intense conflict with the Pharisees, who didn't like Jesus' rejection of all their little man-made laws and regulations. And with the Sadducees, who made fortunes off the temple worship rules, which they used to manipulate the people of faith. At the end, the leading Jews and Romans lied and cheated and bent rules so they could crucify Jesus and get rid of this nuisance.

"But God had this planned all along. When they killed Jesus, what actually happened was a tremendous sacrifice of himself for the sins of the world. God had told Israel over and over in the Old Testament this would happen. Jesus paid the penalty for every sin that was ever committed. Then, three days later, he rose from the dead and, over the next forty days, appeared to more than five hundred people, to show he'd conquered death and to prove in a final sense he truly was God.

"The moment he died, the veil that hid the 'holy of holies'— the place God lived in the temple in the form of the Spirit—was torn open. This represented the fact that anyone anywhere could come into personal contact with God through faith and live.

"After Jesus' death and resurrection, a whole new period in human history began in which God invited every person to put their faith in him and allow him to fill their lives with good things. God instituted the church at that time, which would be the way the 'good news' (gospel) would spread throughout the world, those who converted would be nurtured, and all his truth would be taught.

"Once again, God raised up men to write all these things down in sacred books inspired by the Holy Spirit. These books were collected into the New Testament. Jesus gave all his followers in his last days after his resurrection something called 'The Great Commission.' Through this, God would send out into every corner of the world missionaries who would tell everyone the gospel.

"This is the part of God's plan that we're in right now.

"Nonetheless, in the end the church will also fail in their mission. Satan will continue to deceive and trick and tempt people the world over, and the problem of evil, though defeated by Jesus on the cross, will continue down to the last blows.

"What happens next? I believe an event known as 'the Rapture' will whisk all believers out of the world sometime in the future, perhaps the near future. At that time, Satan will be given his final chance to make his point to the world. It's like God will say, "Okay, Satan, let it rip. Here's your time to show whether you can really run things better than I can."

"Of course, Satan has been doing this all along. But God limited his power all those years so he could build his own kingdom and keep Satan from simply murdering off every vestige of faith wherever he found it. Now, in what is known as the seven-year Great Tribulation, Satan will have a final say. This will be God's judgment on the world for not believing through the efforts of the church.

"Of course, you must understand there is much controversy in the church and among scholars about how all these events will happen. So I'm only offering my opinion here, and I know there are many who would dispute it. But I believe that once the church is removed through the Rapture, in God's plan evil beings will take the opportunity to do all they can to prove they're better and wiser than God.

"During that time, a world leader will arise, known in Scripture as 'the Beast,' or 'the Antichrist.' This person will be Satan's version of Jesus. He will do miracles, be a tremendous public speaker, create a coalition of nations never before seen in history, and, for a while, bring in world peace.

"At the same time, God will raise up 144,000 Jews who will become evangelists along the lines of Billy Graham. Imagine 144,000 of him going throughout the world. As a result, a great revival will happen for God's kingdom. Many people will turn to God, trust him, and seek to spread his truth.

"Naturally, Satan will not be able to abide such a thing. So he, through the Antichrist, will initiate a murderous campaign to kill off anyone not allied with him.

"One of the most amazing aspects of this period will be the book of Revelation in the Bible. For centuries, people have complained that God doesn't do miracles or signs as in the Bible in olden times. For millennia, people have boasted that if God just 'proved himself' in some convincing way in the here and now, they would believe.

"This time will be God's answer to such statements. People will literally read the events in the book of Revelation and see them happening the world over. The earthquakes, the judgments, the strange whirring insects like scorpions, all the events predicted in that book will begin happening throughout the world at precisely the times predicted, and in that order. As a result, multitudes will be converted because they will see clearly that God is real and his Word is the truth.

"On the other hand, billions of others, because of the judgments and the agonies they will suffer, will become bitter, will hate God all the more, and will join with the Antichrist in his battle against God.

"It all comes to a slam-bang conclusion in the Battle of Armageddon on the plain of Megiddo in what is Israel today. There, the forces of Satan and Jesus himself will do battle. Jesus will wipe them out with one word, though. There will never be a moment or a sense that the Antichrist could possibly win this one.

"After that battle, Jesus will rid the world of every unbeliever and cast Satan and all the demons into hell. There they will be kept for a thousand years, perhaps to give them a chance to consider their evil ways and repent as well.

"At the same time, Jesus will set up a thousand-year reign called 'the Millennium.' In this time, he will actually reign in Jerusalem physically. It will be then that people will 'beat their swords into plowshares and their spears into pruning hooks' (Isaiah 2:4; Micah 4:3). The 'lion will lie down with the lamb.' Universal peace will ensue. All crimes will be punished immediately. And anyone who wants to talk to Jesus personally, hear him speak, or spend time with him, will have the opportunity. Presumably, all the people raptured before this time—all the Old Testament saints, all the church saints, and all those killed in the Tribulation—will have new spiritual bodies and will be able to travel between heaven and earth, see what Jesus is doing, and glorify God because of it. All during this time, no demon will ever be able to deceive any human. Any sins committed will be done because the perpetrators simply refused to obey God's laws. At this time, God will show that even with Satan and his cohorts removed, people remain sinful and stubborn.

"Thus, by the end of the Millennium, God will have shown that even Jesus' presence doesn't get people to truly love and follow him. For that reason, he will once again release Satan for a 'short time,' according to Revelation 20, verses 3 and 7 through 9, to show that some people still don't 'get it' about faith, trust, and obedience.

"That final revolution will end in disaster for Satan once again and those who ally themselves with him. And thus, God will have proved, by this grand plan, that there's only one way righteousness, goodness, truth, love, and peace can work: through every person believing in, knowing, and trusting God personally through Christ.

"To make it all stick, the 'Great White Throne Judgment' will occur, in which all the unbelievers from every time of the world will be raised to live again. They will all stand before God and answer for everything they've ever done wrong. After each case is heard—all the rest of believing creation is watching and probably participating (see 1 Corinthians 6:2, 3).

"Every person who rejected God and refused to believe will be shown to have done so not because of anything God did to them, but because of their own rebellious will and resentment. All creation will see God's perfect justice carried out as a sentence is rendered and each person is sent off to a place where he can't hurt, slander, violate, abuse, accuse, ridicule, or torment any other soul again. It will be the ultimate 'solitary confinement.' In total darkness, those people will be given not a single blessing that God gave them in the real world—light, water, food, friends, sex, community, self-worth, meaning, purpose, or anything else worth having. They will be utterly bereft of everything good in life and will experience eternal death—separation from God and all his creation forever.

"At the same time, eternity will begin for all those who loved God and believed in him. We will have incredible powers, bodies, positions, activities, feasts, and everything else we can't even begin to imagine. God will pull out all the stops and bless us like never before. It will be so amazing that the Bible actually says little about it except that we will see God's face, shed no more tears of pain or hurt, and be comforted completely about anything we suffered while on planet Earth. At the same time, I personally believe we will begin a whole new education plan by which we will learn everything there is to know about God and his creation. It will take eternity to even get close to comprehending it all.

"So that's the plan," I said to the three astonished faces staring at me when I finished. "That's what God is doing in human history. And that's why he has changed course at times, made stern judgments on humanity, and done all he could to get us to sit up and pay attention. All of it was designed to lead us back to him and move us to express our faith in him, our trust in his wisdom, and our love for him personally."

Reactions

Jesse looked like he'd swallowed a hamster, but then he said, "It's just totally amazin'. I never heard any of this, either, like Julie said, when I went to church as a kid. It was all 'do this, do that, don't do this or you'll die.' I mean they should be shoutin' this on every street corner. This is incredible. This is the best news I ever heard. Now I see why it's called the good news. That's what 'gospel' means, right?"

"Right. I remember hearing a missionary tell about how he went to this tribe in Africa and told the story of Jesus and the chief jumped up and said, 'When did this happen? Last week? Last month?' The missionary had to say, 'No, almost two thousand years ago.' The chief was aghast. 'But my father, my people, have longed to hear this news. They have died without it.' But despite his horror, that chief became the first Christian in that tribe, and today Africa has one of the fastest-growing Christian communities in the world."

Julie sighed. "It's so beautiful, like the greatest story you could ever hear."

I nodded.

"I wish we were taping these sessions," Doug suddenly said. "I'd like to listen to them again."

I smiled. "Don't worry. I'm writing a book about it. With every word written down."

"Really?" Julie said. "That is so cool."

Doug narrowed his eyes, though. "But how do we fit into this plan? I can see all these things happening on a grand scale. But what about little us? We're not just pawns on the chess board, are we?"

I quickly opened my Bible to one of the most treasured passages of Scripture, Jeremiah's assuring words to Israel in captivity. "It's here in Jeremiah 29, verses 11 through 13. Let me read it. '"For I know the plans I have for you," declares the LORD, "plans to prosper you and not to harm you, plans to give you hope and a future. Then you will call upon me and come and pray to me, and I will listen to you. You will seek me and find me when you seek me with all your heart.'

"That's the basic truth. God has a plan for every one of his children. It includes everything that will ever happen to us, the good and the bad. It includes the mistakes we will make. It also includes all the ways God will get us to where he wants us to go.

"You find the same idea in numerous places in the New Testament. I guess my favorite passage would be Jesus' words in Matthew 11, verses 28 through 30: 'Come to me, all you who are weary and burdened, and I will give you rest. Take my yoke upon you and learn from me, for I am gentle and humble in heart, and you will find rest for your souls. For my yoke is easy and my burden is light.' What do you see there?"

"That Jesus will personally be with us like in a yoke," Julie said. "That he'll be there every step of the way with us."

"Excellent," I said. "And listen to this one: Jesus says to his disciples after his resurrection: 'All authority in heaven and on earth has been given to me. Therefore go and make disciples of all nations, baptizing them in the name of the Father and of the Son and of the Holy Spirit, and teaching them to obey everything I have commanded you. And surely I am with you always, to the very end of the age' (Matthew 28:18–20). What do you see there?"

"It's like the boss givin' a command," Jesse offered. "Go out and tell everyone, he says, because he has absolute authority. He's in charge, and that's what he wants all of us to do."

"The thing that struck me is the last part," Julie said. "He says he'll be with us always. Again, that's a great promise. I've always felt so alone in the world. But already I'm beginning to feel like I have the best friend I could ever have on my side, looking out for me and ready to step in anytime I need help."

"That's exactly it," I said. "You're already beginning to get true biblical insight, Julie. Keep with it. Let God speak to you through his Word."

When Bad Stuff Happens

Okay," Julie said, "but about the really bad things that happen to good people? I know some people, even those who are Christians, who have gone through terrible things."

Everyone looked serious and hanging on whatever answer I would give. I decided to offer them something truly atrocious. "I recently received some very bad news. My wife, Jeanette, stepped into my office in tears. She told me about an e-mail she'd just received from a friend. This friend's daughter had been taken out of college and put into a drug rehab program because of her problems with drug addiction. But the friend wrote that she had been 'kicked out of the program, because she wouldn't admit she had a problem.'

"I thought that was the end of it, but Jeanette said, 'While this girl was in counseling, though, she told the real story. As a freshman, she was raped in her dorm room by three football players. During the whole thing, they taunted her about her virginity, which apparently they knew about, as she had been a fervent witness for Jesus. These three beat her physically, raped her, sodomized her, and then left. She bled for four days, but told no one about it because of the shame, because of her belief that no one would support her. Later, these three football players were found out. They had done this to several other women. Two of them were kicked out of school. But one is playing in the NFL today.'

"I sat there in tears as I listened. Jeanette said her friend told her that 'her faith in humanity has been deeply shaken' as a result of this.

"To date, this young woman won't reveal who these men were, nor will she pick up a phone and seek counseling from her church or anyone else. The mother said she believes her daughter's faith has been 'rocked to its foundations,' maybe obliterated.

"In a later e-mail, the mother wrote me, after I corresponded with her several times trying to offer some comfort, that she 'wishes she could have her precious daughter back, where she had been before the rape.' But she believes now that she will never see that happy, charming, and loving person again."

I finished, my hands visibly shaking, my voice rasping. "Do you think this qualifies as 'terrible'?" I finally asked the group.

Everyone shook their heads, though I wasn't sure because the tears in my eyes blurred my vision. I went on, "This is the kind of situation that stuns me. How could God let something like that happen in this world? And to a Christian, to whom he has written over and over in the Bible that he will protect us, and deliver us from evil, and be present through any trial or trouble?"

Julie's voice came out hoarse. "That's exactly what I thought."

"It's what we all thought," I said. "That's the kind of evil that is so close to us, so personal, that we can't imagine that God has anything to say about it. Furthermore, it's the reason many people totally reject the idea of a loving God. Surely, if he is loving and all-powerful and all that, he would have stopped this. But clearly he didn't."

"It makes me want to beat on those guys," Jesse said. "With a tire iron."

I added, "And that the one guy ends up in the NFL? Making millions? It's so unfair, so unjust."

"I just can't grasp it," Julie said.

I waited, gathering my thoughts. "You know, I look at that and I weep. I can't imagine the horror of it. And yet, our world is filled with such things. So let's take a look at this. The first thing is that I would never try to help this young woman out of her darkness by preaching at her, hurling Bible verses in her face, or trying to explain why God let this happen. We may never know why, at least in this world, and certainly no one can speak for God.

"The thing to do, and this is what was done—her family rallied around her, they comforted her by being there, by listening, by letting her talk, complain, scream, yell, whatever. They didn't try to say that anything she said or did was a wrong response. Some people just sat and wept with her. In fact, I remember a vivid story about a little girl whose neighbor, an elderly woman, lost her husband. She decided she should visit this woman. When she returned, her mother asked her what she said to the bereaved lady. The little girl said, 'I didn't say anything. I just sat with her and we held hands and we wept.'

"In the Bible, you'll see in some places where God did exactly that with hurting people. When Jesus came to the tomb of Lazarus, planning to raise him from the dead, the first thing he did was weep with Mary, Lazarus' sister (John 11:33–35). God feels our pain and he lets us know that—by being with us, by weeping with us through godly, caring people, and by refusing to preach to us at a time when most of us could not hear his words anyway. He did the same thing with Elijah, with Jeremiah, who was known as the 'weeping prophet,' and with others. God never tries to force truth on us when we're not capable of hearing because of the incredible pain we may be in."

Julie looked transfixed. "It's so perfect, but we mostly miss it."

I nodded sadly. "Too many times we want to rush in and fix a bad situation with explanations or biblical truths, but most of the time the hurting person first needs time to heal, think, and recover.

"Eventually, though, my friend's daughter will get beyond the immediate horror and agony of the attack. She'll start to think, to go over things, and to ask questions. That's when I believe the Bible has much to say to her, and that's what I'll tell you next."

I paused and then mentioned several books by atheists Sam Harris and Richard Dawkins. "What do they say to people in situations like that? All I can really see is something like, 'Well, it was a matter of evolution taking its course, natural selection and all. These three guys were superior on the evolutionary scale, and they just dealt with the inferiors and showed that once again, evolution has triumphed.'"

I glanced around and everyone looked stunned and horrified. That, I thought, was good. They felt deeply about this, and that was what we needed in this discussion about evil.

"Of course," I continued, "I don't believe they would say anything of the sort. Perhaps they would weep as I have. But that's precisely what their view of the world, their philosophy, demands. They believe everything happens as a result of the progress of evolution. Natural selection. Survival of the fittest. So if they tried to apply those principles to this situation, or any like it, their beliefs would force them to such conclusions. Yet, in their hearts, I'm sure they realize they could never say such things. It would be callous, uncaring, brutal. And that's why their theories don't really work or speak the truth about our world. When it comes down to it, they don't have a satisfying answer for it.

"And what can they really offer such a person? A better world? No, to unbelievers this one is it. There's nothing else out there. A God who can dry her tears? No, according to them, there is no God. Supernatural comfort from the Spirit of God? Again, no, the Holy Spirit is a figment of our imagination. Comfort from others who truly care and love her? Like people in the church? No, atheists don't have churches. They might give her a hug and say, 'I'm really sorry,' but what can they offer by way of lasting comfort? In my mind, there's nothing."

I stopped and gathered my thoughts. "What does Islam say to that woman?"

"She was an unbeliever and was getting what she deserved for not believing in Allah," Julie said bitterly. "And then they'd take her out and stone her because of the shame she brought on her family."

"Could very well be what they would say and do," I answered, "at least those who adhere strictly to the Qur'an. Who else—the Buddhists? They'd tell her to meditate, get rid of all thoughts and desires, and eventually she will have forgotten the whole thing. Do enough good, die enough times—maybe a million or so—to reach nirvana and then she'll have peace. Or something like that. The Hindus? 'Ah, it was the law of Karma. You must have done some very bad things in a previous life and that accounts for it. You are being punished for all those bad things you did.'"

I gazed around at the anxious eyes staring back at me. This was something they wanted an answer to on much more than an intellectual level.

"Okay," I said, "I won't hold you in suspense. The truth is that Christianity offers that young woman and her family some very powerful truths they can embrace. Like what?

"Here are a few: First, I think God would assure her these men will not escape punishment from him. One day, each of them will stand before him and answer for their crimes. And then justice will be served. In this world, they merely get expelled from school or play in the NFL. In God's justice, they will pay dearly for their crimes, unless they repent and try to make right what they did.

"To me, that's great assurance. Beyond that, here's a verse I've always loved dearly. Jesus told the disciples this as he informed them of his impending death on the cross: 'Do not let your hearts be troubled. Trust in God; trust also in me. In my Father's house are many rooms; if it were not so, I would have told you. I am going there to prepare a place for you' (John 14:1, 2).

"For my friend's daughter, the hope of a heaven free of pain and fear would be a tremendous encouragement. She can be sure from verses like this that her pain, her fear, her horror is not the end. One day, she will be with Christ in heaven, and he will personally dry her tears. She will be comforted by him and ultimately experience complete emotional healing at his hands."

"I gotta admit, that's really encouraging," Jesse said. "Whenever I start to think this world is all there is, all I can think is how it totally stinks. But with that, at least there's something to look forward to."

"Right," I answered. "And think about the millions of people who have lived lives that ended in tragedy. What would that mean if that really was the end? What hope could they have? How could they face such demoralizing circumstances? There is only one way: When you know your end is not this world, but that your destination is heaven, you can get through some pretty rotten things."

I glanced around at the group, and they appeared to be brightening. Then I said, "But what about for the here and now? Here's another verse, again, Jesus speaking: 'I have told you these things, so that in me you may have peace. In this world you will have trouble. But take heart! I have overcome the world' (John 16:33). The truth is, God does not promise we will not have trouble in this life, even serious trouble, like being murdered, or tortured by persecutors, or anything else, like gang rape. But he does promise to give us peace in the midst of it, and after. That's supernatural peace, not just something to salve it all over. For my friend's daughter, that peace might not be felt immediately. But it will come.

"I remember the great book and movie, *The Hiding Place*, about the life of Corrie ten Boom, a Dutch woman who hid Jews from the Nazis during World War II. When she and her family were caught and sent to concentration camps, she and her sister Betsey stayed together. In their camp, they, being deeply committed Christians, started a Bible study for anyone who would come. In it, they often dealt with the horrors they faced at the hands of the Nazis.

"One day, as Corrie and Betsey met with their little study, a group walked over to question them. One woman raised her broken hands and said something like, 'I was first violinist of the Berlin Orchestra. I will never play the violin again. Did your God do this?'

"It's a question we all ask. Did God do this to me, whatever my horrible situation is at the moment? Did God send those football players to rape that young woman? The answer is, 'No, never. God cannot do evil, or even think it, wink at it, or let it get away with its deeds ultimately.' But the way Betsey answered this woman was to say that with God there was 'no pit so deep that God is not deeper still.'

"That meant to her that no matter how deep we may think the hell we have descended into is, God is still there, all the way, touching, comforting, speaking, assuring. This world is a hellhole, and we will surely experience some hell in it. But God promises to be there, to see us through it, to give us real, lasting peace in the midst of it, and to get us to heaven after it, where everything will be made right."

I looked around. No one appeared able to speak.

"Let me give you another one. This is from Paul as he discusses some of the agonies we all face in this life: 'I consider that our present sufferings are not worth comparing with the glory that will be revealed in us' (Romans 8:18).

"That one I find particularly encouraging, because of some of the things I've gone through—a harrowing clinical depression that lasted more than two years while I attended seminary, a terrible first marriage that ended in divorce and a custody battle that cost me nearly twenty-five thousand dollars, pastoral ministries that blew up in my face and made me determined never to be a pastor again, and a prodigal daughter who went off the deep end and hated us for nearly a year after she turned eighteen. When I look at those things and realize God's going to make it all up to me and more, I have to say, 'I can hang in there then, knowing that something great and wonderful is up ahead of me. I don't understand it all now, but one day I will, and I will see God's plan behind it all.'"

Once again, everyone was silent.

I wasn't sure what was getting through, but I continued, "And then there's this biggie, from the second-to-last chapter of the whole Bible: 'He will wipe every tear from their eyes. There will be no more death or mourning or crying or pain, for the old order of things has passed away' (Revelation 21:4).

"What greater promise could any of us ask for? God is saying, in effect, 'You live in a fallen world where evil roams around looking to devour everyone. Sometimes evil people have their way, even with my own children—look at Job and his sufferings, look at

Daniel. Look at Esther, and Peter, and Jesus himself. But there is a better day coming. Look forward to that, and you will be able to stay strong and courageous.'

"In fact, when you realize that God didn't even spare his Son the attacks of this world, you realize God knows what it's like to suffer. In Jesus, we see the ultimate torture and pain: The cross was perhaps the most evil, painful, and lengthy form of execution ever devised. Why do you think God let Jesus die that way? Why couldn't he have been hanged, or shot with arrows, or had his head cut off, something quicker, easier even? For one reason: because God wants us to know he didn't even spare himself when it came to the horrors of this world. He knows what it's like to be hated, vilified, rejected, laughed at, cursed, spit upon, beaten up, and everything else. If you look at Jesus in the Gospels, you will see he experienced every kind of punishment and torture this world offers. So he knows what it's like, and for that reason, as Hebrews 2:17 says, he can be 'merciful and faithful' to us in our times of trouble."

I looked around and Julie shook her head. "I had no idea," she said.

Doug and Jesse simply looked knocked over.

I said, "These are the kinds of truths I cling to when my life goes wrong. And yet, God keeps on telling us more. Like in Romans 8:28, where he says, 'We know that in all things God works for the good of those who love him, who have been called according to his purpose.' What do you think this is saying?"

No one spoke. Then Julie said, "I guess I would say that God will somehow work in this terrible situation and bring good out of it in some way. I imagine most people wouldn't know how that might happen, though."

"But it will happen," I assured her. "I've seen it a million times. God really does work in a bad circumstance and turn it around in some way. My depression came to an end, and I discovered a multitude of great things I had learned in the process, in addition to a much closer relationship with Christ. My divorce went through, but I got custody of my kids, and I reel with horror at the thought they might have been raised by a woman who was a schizophrenic.

My pastoral problems led me to a speaking and writing ministry that has flourished well beyond anything I could have done in a small church. And my prodigal daughter came back after about a year, got married to a decent guy who loves her, and seems very happy. Sometimes you just have to give God time to work.

Somehow, God will also help my friend's daughter through this time. I'm confident of it. It may take a lot of help, a lot of tears, a lot of screaming and kicking, but one day she'll emerge a stronger and better person with one more tool in her spiritual pocketbook: the ability to truly comfort other women who have gone through similar horrors."

Julie nodded with concern in her eyes. "I've seen that. It seems I'm always better able to help my kids or a friend when I've been through what they're going through."

"Isn't that true with all of us?" I asked. "I think the main thing is that our world is shot through with evil, because of our own rebellion. God could have left us to duke it out among ourselves and completely annihilate one another, but he stepped in, redeemed us through Jesus' sacrifice, and made a way for us to escape from this wretched place once and for all.

"As if that's not enough, he always promises to make everything right. Look at these words." I quickly turned to Psalm 34:15–19, a passage I have studied often:

> The eyes of the LORD are on the righteous and his ears are attentive to their cry; the face of the LORD is against those who do evil, to cut off the memory of them from the earth. The righteous cry out, and the LORD hears them; he delivers them from all their troubles. The LORD is close to the brokenhearted and saves those who are crushed in spirit. A righteous man may have many troubles, but the LORD delivers him from them all.

Julie looked particularly pensive. "What a powerful statement of hope! It says it all."

I nodded. "You will find yourselves turning to passages like this many times in your life, if it's anything like mine. We're in the middle right now. Evil is all around us. God promises to be there, to be close, to give us the power to never give up. But that doesn't mean we'll never face bad times."

Julie said, "So it's like, though our world is full of evil, and we will suffer at times, it's just a temporary thing. Ultimately, we will get far beyond this, and it won't have an effect on us in that new place."

"Exactly," I said. "And beyond all that, we have some powerful, real, and hopeful things to hold on to no matter how horrible this world gets: his Word, his presence, his assurances, and the power to help others who are going through the same things we went through. That's empowering. That gives you and me a real reason for hope in the midst of devastation. I honestly don't know how people who have none of those things survive."

"So what about that girl who was raped?" Julie asked. "It's so awful."

"Last I talked to her mother, she's not ready to hear or talk about God and his Word. So I would hope more than anything that her family and loved ones will continue to just be there, listen, offer comfort, friendship, and love. Being there is a tremendous part of it.

"In fact, that's the next thing."

Resolutions

That is why I'm doing this. I want people to know there is a God out there who cares about them personally, who can work in their lives and transform them, who can solve even the worst problems, and who will ultimately take them to a perfect place where they will never face evil again.

"My friend's daughter is in the middle of her struggle, and I imagine it will be a long one. Right now, as happens when bad things happen to Christian people, doubt, fear, and anguish have become the realities of her life. I've been there. And every Christian I've known has been there, too.

"But in God's world, none of those agonizing troubles is the end. Hard as my friend's situation is, the God I know is more than likely right now assuring her that even this horror she has gone through can be healed, forgiven, overcome, and used for some good in her life.

"That is the power and beauty of Jesus' message, life, and plan.

"What can an atheist or a Buddhist or a Hindu or a Muslim offer as a realistic, hopeful, and healing alternative?"

Everyone looked amazed and even relieved.

Julie said, "So once again the Bible has blown my mind. I just never knew any of these things was in there."

I smiled, somewhat grimly. "If you continue to read it and memorize verses and meditate on them when you have time, you'll find it speaking to you at all times and in all places. That's its amazing power. It's the Word of God, not the concoctions of demented men who had nothing better to do with their day than spew lies about their lives. So trust what it says and apply it to the situations of your life. You'll find that resident power working in amazing ways every day of your lives."

Making It Happen

Doug scratched his head, and I knew another heavy question would be forthcoming. "Okay, I'm willing to buy that this plan may be the one God's using to guide human history. But I just don't see how he can make it happen. Aren't we all free spirits? Don't we make free decisions and stuff? How could God make sure we go his way when he needs it? It seems to me that's the one thing none of us can do."

I smiled. "That's a tremendous insight. And that's probably what we should talk about next week. How God makes his plan happen and stay on course despite the stubbornness and freedom of the human soul. What do you say?"

"I'd like to hear it," Doug said.

"Yeah," Jesse added. "I'd like to know where God was when I made some of the really bad decisions of my life."

Julie nodded. "I guess I'm already beginning to think this God of ours is quite a bit bigger and greater and more magnificent than I'd ever imagined."

I laughed. "A great thought. In fact, that's a big problem with God's people today. They just don't see how powerful, wise, and loving God is. They imagine this sort of grandfatherly guy sitting on this throne with a big megaphone up to his ear, saying, 'What was that? What did you say?' Like some doddering old man with Alzheimer's. But God is far from that. In fact, what's most stunning about God is that the more you learn about him, the bigger and more amazing he becomes. You start to think you have this aspect of him nailed and then he shows you something that knocks it all to pieces and makes you realize you have a lo-o-o-ng way to go."

"I'm excited," Julie said. "I really am."

Doug let out a long huff. "Well, things have certainly taken a turn I never expected."

"Got a lot to think about," Jesse added.

"Assignment?" Doug asked.

"Think about how it's possible for God to be totally in charge of human history, and at the same time, how we can do things utterly without force or manipulation."

Doug sighed. "You never give us anything easy. Like who killed Goliath or something?"

"If that's the kind of thing I was pulling here, I don't think you'd be very interested."

"Yeah."

Everyone stood and Doug and Jesse moved toward the door and left. But Julie grabbed my hand. "Mark, can you talk with me for a second?"

"Sure."

I gazed into her deep blue eyes and for the first time I noticed the fear in them.

"I'm terrified," she said. "What's God going to do to me? How am I going to do all this—give an ultimatum to my boyfriend, stop other things—I occasionally use pot and I drink a lot in the evenings—and keep my head together? I'm scared God's going to tell me to pack up and head for Africa or something."

I laughed. "Julie, let me give you a couple more verses. Remember the one about Jesus' yoke in Matthew 11:29, 30?"

"The one about his yoke being easy and so on?"

"Right. Jesus is not going to blast you to pieces, believe me. He'll work with you step-by-step. He'll show you the way. He'll be there whenever you're scared or upset or things go wrong, or whatever. But here's another verse."

I opened my Bible to Philippians 4:6, 7 and read, "Do not be anxious about anything, but in everything, by prayer and petition, with thanksgiving, present your requests to God. And the peace of God, which transcends all understanding, will guard your hearts and your minds in Christ Jesus."

"Prayer," she said. "And thanks. And he'll give me peace?"

"Absolutely, though it may not come in the way you expect."

"I so need that. And what was the other one?"

"Okay, the Devil's going to be working you over big-time. He wants you to go back on your commitment to Christ. He wants to make you feel guilty. He wants to destroy you so you become totally immobilized as far as learning and walking with Jesus are concerned. So here's one for that situation." I turned to James 4:7, 8 and read it: "'Submit yourselves, then, to God. Resist the devil, and he will flee from you. Come near to God and he will come near to you.'"

Julie wrote furiously, then she looked up into my eyes. "These are so practical. I never knew the Bible could really help you with anything. But these are hitting me right where I am. It's like . . ."

"Like God wrote it just for you?"

She smiled and cocked her head slightly with recognition. "Yeah. Really. It's amazing. I read it a little, years ago. You know—some of the great stories. David and Goliath. Daniel in the lions' den. But this. This is right where I am, right now."

"Believe me, there're passages for just about any need you will ever have. That's why God wants you to read it, memorize verses, meditate on it, study it. You'll find it's the most amazing book ever written, beyond anything by Stephen King, Danielle Steel, or anyone else."

She laughed. "I think I'm finding that out even as we speak." She sighed and glanced to the door. "I'm so afraid I'll walk out that door and I'll instantly be back to where I was when I walked in, depressed, bitter, and ready for war with you."

I smiled. "Just relax, Julie. God's in charge now. Trust him. Tell him whatever's on your mind whenever you think of it. Listen for his voice in your heart. And devour the Bible. You might also want to attend a church this Sunday and get into some kind of support group. My church has one for new believers, if you're interested."

"I am."

I gave her the address and phone number as well as my own business card.

"Look, let's just pray for a second before you go. And if you have any questions between now and next Monday, don't hesitate to call me. No matter what time it is."

She nodded and I thought she was tearing up again. I prayed briefly and then walked her out to her car, a sleek Infiniti. As I watched her go, I prayed again and asked God to take special care of her this week.

As if he would do anything less!

CHAPTER 11

We Have True Freedom, and Yet, Miracle of Miracles, God Is Still Totally in Charge

Julie Doesn't Know What Hit Her

I got the call Monday morning about ten. I was preparing some notes and thoughts for meeting with Doug, Jesse, and Julie that afternoon. It was Julie, and she was crying.

"I have to talk to you. I have to," she blurted. "Can you get to Starbucks a few minutes early?"

"What's up? You sound pretty upset."

"I am. But I need you to show me stuff in the Bible. I need to see you in person. Please. Maybe a half hour early?"

"Can you get there at two? It's an hour early. I'm fine with that."

"That will be great."

"Will you be okay till then?"

"I'm trying."

"Okay, pray, and keep praying, and know that God is there." She said nothing. "I'll see you at two."

"I'll be there."

I worried, prayed, paced, and worried some more the next few hours. What had happened? How bad could it have gotten? When I first met Julie, she seemed like Woman Rock, the unshakeable person. And now it appeared she was an emotional wreck.

In the end, I gave it over to God and went back to my work. But I knew this might be a tough one. If only God would give me the words.

I got there about ten minutes early and Julie was already there. She sat stony-faced, staring out the window, not even a coffee in front of her. When I stepped over to the table, she looked up and smiled tentatively.

"Need a coffee?" I asked.

"Oh, I'm sorry. I'm just so frazzled. Please. Here's some money." She held out a ten-dollar bill.

I waved her off. "This one's on me."

Hurrying to the counter, I ordered a couple of strong coffees and returned to the table, praying the whole way. She took a sip, then hung her head. "I've blown it, Mark. I've done everything wrong, and I think God hates me."

I touched her hand. "Believe me, there is nothing you could ever do, last weekend or in the future, that could make him hate you."

She sighed and looked away. "You don't know what I've done."

"Okay, I'm here. If you want to tell me, I'm listening. I'm not going to condemn you, or judge you. And neither is God. Romans 8:1 says there is no condemnation for anyone in Christ Jesus, so—"

"What if I'm not in Christ anymore?"

"Sounds like the Devil's been frying you up good," I said. "Let's just talk it out. There's another verse that says it's good to confess our sins to one another so we can be healed. Let's do some healing."

She nodded. Then a sob struck and she bowed again, unable to speak. I decided to let her get some control rather than spew more verses at her. Meanwhile, I prayed silently that the Spirit would give her whatever words she needed.

Getting her composure back, she spoke to the tabletop. "It was going great. I read my Bible—a lot in those places where you gave us verses, to see what went before and after—"

"That's a great way to do that. Get the context so you make a correct interpretation."

"Right." She nodded vigorously. "It was so, like, energizing. And I was learning stuff, like about Jesus, how tough he was. I always thought he was kind of a milquetoast, but he didn't take no crap, to use the expression. And he really let the Pharisees have it. I was cheering. I even talked to my kids—John is twenty-three, and D.L. is twenty-one. Of course, they wrote it all off to one of 'Mom's new fads,' so I was just thinking I should lay low with them and let them see any changes. And then—"

She sobbed again, then wiped her eyes. "It's all so sordid."

I waited, praying silently.

"Okay, I called Dave last Monday after we met, told him what had happened to me—which he promptly told me was a load of you know what—and then I said no more sex or anything until he was properly divorced and we were properly married. He cursed me, screamed bloody murder, tried to talk me out of it, all that. I stood my ground. After he gave up and said, 'This isn't over by a long shot,' we hung up and I felt relief, real relief. I've lived with a lot of guilt about the whole thing. He's married, in a bad one according to him, and we were just plain committing adultery. I never felt right about it, but, well, you know how that goes. So—"

For the first time she looked up into my eyes, then flinched away. "I'm so ashamed."

"Nobody's going to judge you about this," I said again.

"I know, but—okay, this is it. He comes over Saturday night. A big box of Godiva chocolates. Twenty-four roses. And some friend. This guy is some kind of rank atheist, but he's like showing me all these problems in the Bible and trying to prove to me over and over it's just another book. A lot of the stuff he brought up I could kind of figure out. But a few things, like Jesus telling some woman she was a dog because she wasn't Jewish, and Paul writing about women having to wear these 'head-covering' things and that women couldn't talk in church and things like that really threw me. Anyway, after he left, with me totally not knowing what was going on, then Dave starts making the moves on me. I resisted—"

She took another deep breath. "But then, it was like it was just the easy way out or something. So we go upstairs, drink a few shots of tequila and a couple of beers, and I'm feeling really crazy and then—well, you know. We just got back into the sex stuff like nothing had ever happened to me.

"He slept over that night, but I didn't sleep a second. I lay there totally freaked, like I'd just slapped Jesus in the face. And it felt like every angel in heaven was staring down at me and calling me a whore. And—"

She stopped and shook her head. "And after Dave left I just felt like such a crumb. I wanted to go to your church, but it was like I thought everyone in the whole place would know what I'd done somehow. And I feel like God's done with me. And . . ."

Her eyes filled with tears, and she wiped at them ferociously. "I hate crying like this. But it's like after last Monday, I'm feeling so real for once. So in touch with everything, even my feelings. And then . . . this."

I started to flip through my Bible, but she held up her hand. "And the only reason I'm here is because this little voice kept saying I needed to talk to you. That was all it said. I have no idea where it came from."

"I don't think that was the Devil."

She smiled. "Yeah, I guess not." She gazed at me, blinked, and then shook her head. "So have I ruined everything?"

"Okay, you need to read about some of the great sinners of the Bible, first. David and Bathsheba. Peter denying Jesus three times. Paul hauling off Christians and having them put in prison and tortured and killed. Abraham lying about Sarah being his wife. Samson and Delilah. It goes on and on. Believe me, it takes a lot to really tick God off. You'd have to see his miracles over and over for years, listen to his words and think what stupidity they are—for years and years, and then decide, after seeing it all, God's a flake. Now that would make him mad. But believe me, not this."

She smiled for the first time.

"Let me just show you a couple of things. First, the thing you need to know is that all you need to do now is confess the sin and resolve not to do it again." I turned to the classic verse in 1 John 1:9 and read it: "'If we confess our sins, he is faithful and just and will forgive us our sins and purify us from all unrighteousness.' You've confessed it to me right now, and I can say with all the authority of Jesus, you're forgiven."

"I am? Really? Honest? You wouldn't kid me, would you?"

"Why would I kid about something like that? Look, just take it by faith: There is nothing you could do that would make God turn against you. Here's another verse from Hebrews 13:5, paraphrasing God from Joshua 1:5 in the Old Testament: 'Never will I leave you; never will I forsake you.' And right after, 'The Lord is my helper; I will not be afraid. What can man do to me? (v. 6). Like I told you last Monday, Satan's going to attack you big-time, and right where he knows you're most vulnerable. That's why it says in another verse, 'Flee from sexual immorality' (1 Corinthians 6:18). You have to run. If Dave comes over again, don't even let him in the house. If he wants to talk, step outside. If you need help talking to him, ask God for wisdom. If he keeps pushing, call the police. And feel free to call me anytime. I'll come over and help you deal with him, if you need that."

"You would?"

"Of course. That's what it means to be a Christian. You're family now. Family sticks up for family. The best thing about it is there's not just one or two of us, but millions, the world over."

"I knew I should have called you. But I just was caught so off guard."

"That's prime time for the Devil and his subordinates, when you're unprepared. They're very sneaky, and they study us. Watch us, learn what we do when we're down, worried, feeling stressed. They pick our weak moments especially to surprise us, but also our strong ones, when we're feeling on top of the world, like nothing can ever go wrong again. Believe me, demons are cagey and very shrewd. That's why you have to always be ready to duel."

"I had no idea."

I smiled. "Now, don't get the idea you're at his mercy, though. Here's a verse you should also memorize." I opened my little Bible to 1 John 4:4 and read, "'You, dear children, are from God and have overcome them, because the one who is in you is greater than the one who is in the world.'"

"Wow! That's a great one."

"Yeah. Now just remember this and here's another to memorize, from Romans 8, verses 38 and 39, 'For I am convinced that neither death nor life, neither angels nor demons, neither the present nor the future, nor any powers, neither height nor depth, nor anything else in all creation, will be able to separate us from the love of God that is in Christ Jesus our Lord.' Isn't that great assurance?"

"I just have so much to learn."

"And you learned a big one this weekend. You can mess up, flub up, sin, make a big mistake, whatever. But remember—God knew this would happen, and he has planned around it. He knows how to help you escape from it, if you're willing. In fact, that's another verse, 1 Corinthians 10:13. I'll let you look it up. It's another powerful one."

She gazed at me with real respect in her eyes. "How do you know all this? I mean you just, like, spout it all out at the drop of a hat."

"Over thirty years memorizing, thinking about Scripture, and studying. You'll get there, too, if you take it seriously."

"I will."

I leaned forward. "Okay, here's probably the best one of all." I opened my Bible to John 8, the story of the woman caught in adultery. Pointing to it, I asked her to read the passage. By the end, Julie was in tears again. "Wow! Just wow!" she said, looking up at me.

"It's amazing what Jesus was like," I said. "It must have been awesome to have walked with him back then, seen those things. But I believe one day, in heaven, we'll be able to actually see it all happen, like watching old movies. But let's not get into that. What is it about this story that hits home?"

"Everything. Just everything." She bent over her Bible and spoke again. "I mean, Jesus is so strong against the Pharisees who, I guess, wanted this woman stoned. He just like—whoosh—whacked them but good. Not a one left. And then, just amazing. He takes this poor soul who, admittedly, made a big mistake. But he doesn't even preach to her, or give her an assignment—"

She looked up at me and twitched her eyebrows. It felt good to see her feeling better. "He is so compassionate, so caring. Like he really understands how vulnerable we are. Women, I mean. We want so much to please the men in our lives, to keep them happy, that we all do things we regret, things those men get us to do."

I nodded.

"And I'm not trying to make her the victim or anything. She did what she did, and so did I. I see that. It was wrong, no matter who talked her into it, no matter who tempted her. She was guilty. But Jesus, he's, like, so kind. It's so unlike nearly anyone I have ever known. Because I think people are generally one of two ways. One set is condemning and judgmental and just writes you off as a jerk. Or a sinner. Or whatever. And the other is like, 'Oh, it's okay. Don't worry about it. It's nothing.' Like they excuse everything.

"But Jesus doesn't excuse her sin. He makes it clear she's forgiven and there's no condemnation, but at the same time he's firm about the fact she needs to get her life together and stop doing these kinds of things. It's so . . . refreshing. It's real. Man, I wish—"

She stopped and looked away, wiping her eyes again. When she came back to me, she said, "I wish I had a person like this in my life."

"You do," I said gently.

"I know—you, Jesse, and I'm sure there'll be many others, but—"

"No. Jesus. He's in your life. You can know him as intimately as those disciples back then did. Here, and now. In fact, in some ways, you can know Jesus now even better than they did back then. Because he's inside you, in your heart, talking, listening, conversing, encouraging. Even the disciples didn't have that in quite the same way until after Jesus was gone from their lives physically."

"Really? I mean it really is that way?"

"Of course. Even Jesus told them that having the Spirit in their hearts would be better than having him with them physically. When the Spirit finally does come upon the disciples at Pentecost, they're transformed from these scared little lambs into a pack of lions. Peter, who before Jesus was crucified, was so afraid of being found out as a disciple that he denied he even knew Jesus. And not to Roman soldiers, or people in authority. But to slave girls. To regular guys. He was so ashamed. But look at him in the book of Acts later. He's no longer afraid, no longer doing everything wrong, although he still makes mistakes. But that's it. Jesus is in you now, and he will never leave you. He's always there, at the drop of a prayer."

She sat very still. Then her face lit up for the first time since we'd met. "Do you have any idea how incredible this is?"

"What?"

"Jesus being there and not condemning you. Forgiveness. Confession of sin. Knowing God won't drop you. I mean, for years I've beaten myself up about the most minor things, let alone the major ones. I've had people hate me for years for things I've done to them. At one point, my mom and I weren't speaking for months because of something I said to her. A little slip. But God—he's like the one who should be the most mad—and all he says is, 'You confessed it. It's forgiven. Let's get on with the real stuff.' That totally blows my mind."

I laughed. "Why should God be hard about it? Jesus paid for it all by dying a horrible death on the cross. He took it all away. When God looks at you, he doesn't see you as a sinner, flub-up, joke, idiot, whatever—he sees his child with the same affection he has for Jesus himself. In fact, he sees you as if you were as perfect as Jesus. So while sin is serious, God doesn't want us to make more of it than it is. 'Okay, you sinned. So does everyone. It's forgiven. It's all covered by Jesus' blood. Now get up and go out there and do the important things I have for you today, and quit obsessing over whether I still love you or not. That can never change. Got it? I love you forever. You belong to me. You're part of my family. And I will never give up on you, no matter how many times you blow it."

She gazed at me and shook her head. "You make it so easy to understand."

"Believe me, it's not me. It's the Spirit. I have a 70 IQ normally."

She punched my shoulder playfully. "Do not!"

"Okay, it's 180, but don't tell anyone."

"Isn't there a commandment about not lying in there, too?"

"Fine. I had some good professors. What else can I say?"

"I could listen to you all day. I bet you're a good preacher."

I smiled. "Thanks for the vote of approval. But there are plenty of people who find me quite boring."

"They're the ones with the 70 IQs then."

We had a good laugh, and I moved the conversation on to other things—her family, her divorce, her business. When Jesse and Doug arrived awhile later, it must have looked like Julie and I had solved all the problems in the universe. She was beaming, full of new enthusiasm, and it thrilled me to see how quickly God brought her out of the darkness of despair and fear and back into the light of hope and joy.

Doug was especially surprised, but he didn't ask many questions, and we decided to plunge right in after the usual updates on Jesse's marriage, Doug's mom and son, and other things. No major changes, but both men indicated good things were happening.

One thing I noticed, though. Julie said nothing, but I sensed her tightening up every time I started to talk. I realized she expected me to blurt everything out about what she'd done. I finally turned to her and said, "Would you come with me a second?"

She got up and followed me over to the counter. I said, "Look, I'm sensing something, maybe I'm wrong, but I want to assure you I will never bring up what you told me with anyone. That's between you and God. If you want to talk about it to anyone, that's your privilege. But it's confidential between you and me."

She gazed at me. "Really? You won't tell Doug and Jesse?"

"No one."

"But why?"

"Why should I? You confessed it. God forgave you. It's gone. As far as God's concerned, it no longer exists. I can show you that . . ."

"From the Bible." She grinned. "Of course. You can give me all those verses later. But for now . . ."

She put her arms around me and hugged me, then whispered, "Thanks. That's what the Devil was telling me before I told you. That if I told you, you'd be blurting it out to everyone what a loser I was."

"Sounds like the same Devil who works on me."

Julie shook her head. "This Christianity thing is really blowing my mind."

"Hey, what just happened is the way it's supposed to be. It doesn't always happen that way."

"You mean Christians and gossip?"

"Right."

"I understand. I guess that's why you have to build relationships, to know which ones you can trust."

"Very good."

We returned to the table and both men looked up. Julie beamed and Doug said, "What, did you two just fall in love or something?"

"Christian love," Julie said. "But now I think we should get on with it."

The Free-Will Issue

I took a breath. "So now you want to know what God says about free will and how he can keep things going his way despite our obstreperous determination to do what we want?"

Doug nodded. "It's a biggie for me."

Jesse shrugged. "I'm not sure I get it, but I'm here. So let's dive in."

I mentioned how Doug and I had talked about this issue somewhat in an earlier session. "I showed how our choices in life are motivated by many sources—experience, upbringing, heritage, our bent to sin, and so on. But this issue is a little different. In it, we're asking, How can God be in charge of the world literally, down to the very things we do today and tomorrow, while at the same time we sense and feel no pressure from him, no one 'coercing' us to go one way or the other?"

"It's quite a problem," Doug mused. "One I've thought about before and finally came to the conclusion it just couldn't really be that way. Of course, I decided God couldn't really be in the picture at all, and that we all do as we please, to our own peril at times."

"That's how many regard it," I answered. "But just think of what this truth of God's sovereignty—that's the theological word for it—does for us in real life. If God is really in charge of the world, of events, of what happens, then—what?"

"Wait a second!" Doug said. "I thought you said Satan ruled the world."

"Yes," I said, encouraged he'd remembered that point. "Satan rules in the sense that the world system—all the subtle ways it entraps, and entices, and destroys us—is run by him. He can stir up our natural desires and turn them into addictions, lusts, motivations that mess up our lives. He's also head of this phalanx of demons he sends out all over the earth looking for people they can tempt, deceive, and keep away from finding out about God. That's all very true.

"But God stands in the background, moving and working to make his plans the ones that actually happen. Satan can't even touch a Christian unless God gives him permission. You may remember this from the first two chapters of Job, where Satan complains he can't smite Job because God put a 'hedge' around Job and all that was his. I believe the same kind of hedge is around each of us. To be sure, God does lower the hedge at times, giving Satan more freedom to work us over, but that's rare, and only in God's plan and purpose. It's always designed to help us grow spiritually, never to destroy us."

"So," Julie said, "there will be times in our lives when it will be a terrific battle just to keep our heads above water?"

"Sometimes. Just remember that God is in charge of even that. And the great thing is that nothing can touch us in life—not a drunk driver going out of control on the highway, not a burglar getting into our home and stealing us blind, not losing a computer on a trip, nothing happens in life that God doesn't allow into our lives for his purposes."

Doug shook his head. "Can you show me some of this in the Bible? I mean, I'm not sure I see it."

"Okay. Open your Bibles to Ephesians, chapter 1." Everyone flipped pages and even Jesse had a Bible with him this week. I helped them all find the text, though Doug found it on his own. "Okay, let's read verse 11: 'In him we were also chosen, having been predestined according to the plan of him who works out everything in conformity with the purpose of his will.'"

"Oh, boy, does that open a whole can of worms," Doug said.

"You mean predestination?"

"Exactly."

"Okay, I don't think we need to get into a real deep pit about this," I said. "Let me give you the plain, easy version. All predestination means is that God engineers and orchestrates the circumstances of our lives to make sure his outcome is what occurs. What I mean is, for instance, with Julie last week. Before Julie ever lived, in fact the Bible says before God ever created the world itself, God made sure the circumstances would arise in Julie's life that would lead her to that moment of faith."

Julie gazed at me, her brow wrinkled. "But it just happened by chance. I was hardly thinking about it, and then, bam! God kinda just hit me."

"Right," I said. "That's it. God didn't force you. He didn't smack you and say, 'Believe, idiot, or I'm done with you.' No, he planned everything needed to get Julie to that place in her mind and spirit. He made sure not only that you would have the opportunity, but he did it in a way that guaranteed you would make the right choice."

"But how?" Julie sputtered. "It just felt natural. What if I had refused? What if I never even brought it up?"

"Sure, that might have happened. But if God really wanted you in his family, then he would have used that experience and others to lead you to the same thing later, at another moment he had planned."

"So what if I'm not someone he wants?" Doug asked. "Where does that leave me? Did he plan that I wouldn't ever believe?"

I nodded to indicate I understood his question. "It's a tricky issue. But this is what I believe. God comes to, speaks to, touches all people at different times in their lives. He gives every person many opportunities to believe. But no one will ever believe unless he 'opens' that person's heart. Let's look at another passage, in Acts 16:14. Go ahead, read that one, Doug."

Doug read, "One of those listening was a woman named Lydia, a dealer in purple cloth from the city of Thyatira, who was a worshiper of God. The Lord opened her heart to respond to Paul's message."

"See? God 'opened' her heart. He made sure she was listening, and then somehow he worked deep inside her spirit so she would respond positively. Here's another one, Acts 13:48. Paul was preaching a message to the Jews, but they rejected it. So Paul told them he now felt free to go to the Gentiles. The next verse says, 'When the Gentiles heard this, they were glad and honored the word of the Lord; and all who were appointed for eternal life believed.' There you have it again, this 'opening' process, this 'appointing.'"

Doug motioned with his hand, but I said, "Let me show you a couple more and then we'll talk."

I turned to John 15:16. "Here, Jesus is speaking to the disciples on the last night of his life before his crucifixion." I read, "'You did not choose me, but I chose you and appointed you to go and bear fruit—fruit that will last. Then the Father will give you whatever you ask in my name.'

"Here we have the idea of God choosing each of us. Why he did that, I'll get to in a second. But here's one more. In this passage in Matthew 22, Jesus tells a parable about a king who gave a wedding feast for his son. He sends all these people out to invite the guests. However, many of the guests offer excuses and some of them actually beat and kill the king's messengers. So the king

becomes enraged and orders his servants to go out onto the high-
ways and invite everyone they meet. This they do. A great feast
occurs, but then the king notices one fellow not wearing 'wedding
clothes.' The king throws that person out. Then Jesus says, in verse
14, 'For many are invited, but few are chosen.' What, then, do you
think these things mean?"

Doug scratched his head, Julie peered down at her Bible, but
Jesse looked up brightly. "It means if you become a Christian, it's
'cause God selected you. He picked you out. And it's not because
you're anyone important, or that you never done nothin' wrong.
Or anything like this. It's because God just decides he wants you."

I smiled. "Good insight."

"That ain't all," Jesse responded. "This predestination thing,
the way I see it is God makes sure each of us gets there, the ones
he chooses. He 'calls' everybody. He gives them all a chance. But
they make excuses and even mistreat his servants. Kind of like Mus-
lims beating up on the Christians over there. Or the Hindus. Or
whoever. And those people were invited, but they didn't come.
However, God saw he had to do something more to get these people interested. So he goes out and just starts choosin'. And everyone he chooses, they come. But every now and then, someone
shows up at church or whatever, who hasn't really made his peace
with God. That's why he ain't clothed in the right suit. So God has
to deal with him. Although, I think Jesus shoulda gave that guy one
last chance, I guess it's still up to God."

I stared at Jesse. "You're gonna be a theologian someday, Jesse."

"Yeah, I'm gettin' this down." He paused. "But the really beautiful thing about this is that God isn't gonna lose any of us. Not
one. Not the ones who trust him and love him. He just makes sure
they not only have the chance, but that they take it. I don't know
how he does that exactly, but I don't think, like you said, it's anything forced. We ain't robots about it. But I kinda think it's beautiful, really. And it's makin' me wonder if I'm chosen, too."

"You know how you find out?" I gazed at Jesse evenly, trying
to fathom what really went on in this trucker's mind.

"How?"

"By making the decision. By trusting him, like Julie did last week. That's the only way you'll know."

Julie said, "So it's like no one knows who's chosen or anything until they cross the line. So it's like we should just tell everyone and figure God will sort it all out."

"Precisely," I said, marveling at how astute these folks were becoming. "That's it. We should never exclude anyone, no matter how bad, evil, or hateful they are." I turned to Julie. "Frankly, when I first met you a few weeks ago, I thought you were hard as a rock. I never could have predicted your conversion, ever, let alone when you did."

"I know," Julie said, grinning widely. "It's so cool. It's like all of a sudden I just saw it all in my mind—God's love, Jesus dying for my sins, all of it. And I wanted it. I didn't care about all those years of being an atheist, all my gripes, all my questions—which I know now he will answer sooner or later—I just realized I had to do it then, or I might never do it. So I thought, go for it. And I did. And I'm so happy about it."

Julie glanced at Doug, as if imploring him to make the same decision, but he simply looked away.

"So the reality is, and you'll find this all over the Bible, that God has planned everything in your life—first to get you into his kingdom, and then to help you learn and grow and do the great things he wants for you. Here's another verse, one of my favorites. Just listen."

I opened to Ephesians 2:10, and read, "For we are God's workmanship, created in Christ Jesus to do good works, which God prepared in advance for us to do."

"Just think about that one for a second: God has prepared all kinds of opportunities, situations, events, conversations, and so on, where you'll have a chance to do good for someone. It's not only his way of making your life an adventure and fun, but also so one day he can reward you for all those wondrous things you did in this life."

Julie's hand banged down on the table. "Wait a second! Hold it! You mean to tell me that God has placed all these cool things in our lives to do, and then at the end he's going to give us a reward for doing just what he intended us to do?"

I laughed. "Saying it that way is beautiful, but that's it. Maybe later we'll get into some of the ways God intends to reward us. And I'll let that idea just simmer for a while. The truth is, God has plans for heaven and eternity that will literally knock our socks off. There's a writer—C. S. Lewis—heard of him?"

"Sure," Doug said, and Julie nodded. Jesse shook his head no.

"Okay, great Christian writer and you should read as much of his stuff as you can. One series of novels for kids I'd recommend is The Chronicles of Narnia, the first one of which was recently made into a tremendous movie."

"I know some people who saw it," Julie commented.

"Now that I think of it," Jesse said, "I took my son to it."

"Excellent," I answered. "Anyway, at the end of the last book, Lewis has some killer lines. This is after heaven has started and all the earthly battles in Narnia are over, the good guys have won, and the bad guys are all dealt with. The series of seven books is about to finish. So there Lewis writes, 'And for us this is the end of all the stories, and we can most truly say that they all lived happily ever after. But for them it was only the beginning of the real story. All their life in this world and all their adventures in Narnia had only been the cover and the title page: now at last they were beginning Chapter One of the Great Story, which no one on earth has read: which goes on forever; in which every chapter is better than the one before' (C. S. Lewis, *The Last Battle*, p. 184).

"That about sums it up. We just haven't seen anything yet. But let's get back to this sovereignty/freewill issue. How do you think God pulls this off without violating our own sovereign will and right to make our own choices freely?"

"Seems like a contradiction to me," Jesse said.

"It's flat impossible," Doug said.

"But if the Bible says it, shouldn't we at least give it a hearing?" Julie asked.

Dilemmas, Contradictions, and Antinomies

You're getting close," I said. "Actually, this is what theologians call an 'antinomy.' In theological terms, it means you bring together two or more equally true ideas that appear mutually contradictory. The antinomy is that both statements are true and right, but our human minds, because it appears illogical, can't see how that's possible. There are many of these in the Bible. How can the Bible be the inspired Word of God, without error, and yet written by fallible people who, we know, could not possibly have written it without error? Or, how can Jesus be completely human and completely divine at the same time? Or, how can God be one God yet also a Trinity of three distinct persons?"

"Man, I've thought about all those," Doug said.

"Right. In our minds, we can't reconcile them. In the sovereignty/freewill debate it seems to us either God is in absolute control of everything, or else we have total freedom to make any choice we want. Both simply can't be true at the same time. One has to bow to the other. God makes us do what he wants, or else God allows us to let it all rip and has no idea what happens next.

"The trouble is, the Bible teaches both. So how can it be?"

Doug shook his head. "One more of those impossible things."

Julie said, "There has to be some explanation."

"There is. And the explanation is we can't explain it. It works in God's mind somehow, but our minds are a little too restricted, limited by *our* logic, to make it compute. So ultimately, we take it by faith."

"But isn't that a cop-out?" Doug asked.

"Why? Because we can't figure out something logically, because there's a mystery to it, we shouldn't believe it? Think of it this way: In the Bible God reveals many things we just don't understand. Like in the book of Exodus, when Moses is up on the mountain receiving the Ten Commandments, the people of Israel go crazy, get Moses' brother Aaron to fashion an idol-god for them, and then they have an orgy in front of this golden calf Aaron made. God is so enraged, he tells Moses he will destroy all of Israel for their sin and start over with Moses himself as the new leader. I mean, God looks like he's gone off the deep end on this one. And then Moses just starts talking and he talks some 'sense' into God, eventually making God back down and forgive and forget about the idea of starting over."

"This is in the Bible?" Julie said.

"Right. And there are many other things like this. God does something that not only makes no sense from what we know about God, that seems to make God look bad, very bad, like a lunatic."

Julie's eyes were popping, but Doug smiled. Jesse just looked stunned.

"How do we deal with such things?"

"It's a big reason I just don't believe the Bible," Doug said.

"Touché. And for many, that's precisely it. It's just too much. So they reject the whole Bible. But look at it this way. If the Bible is just a human book, written by people who tried to tell the story of what they saw, probably embellished it at times, weren't really concerned too much with the implications of what they wrote, then so what? God's a meanie in their eyes. Who cares? It's all gibberish anyway. But—and this is a big *but*—if the Bible is the Word of God, given to us by him to show us everything we need to know about him, then we approach it very differently. We have to ask, 'Okay, this is one of those times God really looks crazy. So what's up? He must be trying to teach us something with this, or it wouldn't be in here. Clearly, he's not worried we'll all haul off and call him a mental case. At least not all of us. So what's the deal?"

Julie sat very still and erect, and both men leaned forward, transfixed again. No one said a word.

"The truth is that every one of those situations teaches us something wonderful and beautiful about God, if we'll just look beyond the bald words on the page. If we're to take the Bible as God's Word, then we ask, 'What's God trying to show us here?' instead of saying, 'Obviously, God's an idiot and malicious to top it off, so I'm outta here.'

"Take the situation I just mentioned where Moses talks God out of destroying Israel. There're at least two times this happens. Moses appears to be the coolheaded, calm, and collected person here, and God the frazzled loon. But what could God be showing us? For one thing, sin makes him mad. Especially sin on this level. A whole nation who had witnessed all kinds of miracles, whom God had literally fed day by day and saved out of slavery—these people, who know God loathes idolatry more than just about anything, who were also given the Ten Commandments long before in God's actual voice from Mount Sinai, these people just sashay off, and not only worship the idol, but get falling-down drunk and have an orgy on top of it. How would you react and feel?

"So the thing I see here is that God has real feelings, just like we do, except his feelings are never sinful. God gets angry about sin. God feels pain and hurt when he sees people reject him. God weeps with us when we face horrible circumstances that nearly destroy us. Jesus wept when he saw the grief on Mary and Martha's faces at the burial site of his friend Lazarus. Even though he would raise Lazarus from the dead in a few seconds, he still wept for the pain and hurt his beloved people experienced.

"Name any honest, nonsinful emotion and you can bet God has felt it. The love he offers us is not just practical love, doing love, blessing love, but emotional love. I suspect Jesus was probably a hugger in some ways. And the portrait of him in the Gospels is of a person who felt deeply and realistically."

"Boy, that changes a lot for me," Julie said.

"How so?"

"Well, it's like I realize now God is not just this stone-faced guy up there organizing things and making sure his world goes like clockwork, but he's real, he understands me, he feels for me when I'm scared, or discouraged, or just torn up."

"Jesus is the picture. Look at him, and you see what God is like, on every level."

"It's kind of a mindblower," Jesse commented.

I glanced at Doug, but he seemed lost in thought for a moment.

"A second thing this reveals to me is that prayer changes things. There are several places in the Bible where it says God never changes his mind. He never 'repents' of anything he's done. Then there are other places where it says just the opposite, like in Genesis 6:6, where Moses writes that God 'was grieved' he had created humanity. What's the deal?

"To me, the bedrock truth is that when we pray, when we ask God to do something in our world, he takes action. In the case with Moses, we see the prophet asking God not to destroy Israel, and God relents, even though only seconds before he sounded about to smash them all flat.

"What's the truth there? That prayer changes things. That prayer works. That it can even change God's mind in some sense, probably not the way we do, but on some divine level. So we should pray about everything—from when we can't find our keys to when we're about to make a life-changing career decision. God wants to be part of all of it, and to act on our behalf."

Julie said, "So it's like, if we don't pray, God might not do anything?"

"Right. And if we do, he will. That doesn't mean he'll always do precisely what we want, but he will do what's right, and what will truly help us."

"Here we are once again, and you're blowing my mind," Julie said.

"Good, because with God in your life, it'll be happening on a daily basis."

Everyone laughed except Doug.

"The third thing I see here is simply that God is mysterious. We can't fathom everything about how he could act like this. It's part of the mystery of who God really is.

"There are plenty of new things to learn, and there are things we may never comprehend in this world. For instance, one of the things Doug brought up in our initial discussion was how God had ordered all these genocidal murders in the Old Testament. Well, I checked that one out and there are only a couple of places where God ordered the Israelites to exterminate a whole nation—men, women, children, cattle, and every other living thing. We see this order from God via Samuel to King Saul in 1 Samuel 15:3. But if you look at the context, you see God had a reason for this. The people in question here, the Amalekites, were a vengeful, murderous people who tried very hard to exterminate Israel when they first came to Canaan under Moses' leadership. These people determined that their mission in life was to annihilate Israel, much like you see many of the Arab nations saying today. So God ordered Saul to wipe them out.

"Now I have to ask you—doesn't it make sense? These people were committed to Israel's extinction. So God, after many years, in which he undoubtedly gave them a chance to repent, finally gave up on them and gave the command. To me, it's simply an intelligent strategy for protecting and defending your own people."

"I guess I can see that," Doug said. "But there are other places where God's judgment is just so out of proportion to what was done wrong in the first place."

"What ones are you thinking of?"

"Like Ananias and Sapphira."

I turned to Acts 5 and instructed the others to do so. After explaining about how all the people in the church sold property and gave the proceeds to the apostles to help the needy in the church, we learn that this couple did the same thing with a valuable lot or something they owned. They presented it to Peter with some fanfare, implying this was everything they'd been paid, as others had already done. Peter confronted first Ananias about his lie, and Ananias was struck dead on the spot. A little later, so was his wife, Sapphira."

I read at the end how 'great fear' (v. 11) came upon the whole church. I then asked, "So what do you think was God's point here? Was this overkill?"

Julie said, "They were lying about it, clearly."

Jesse nodded. "And they was pretendin' to be these big givers when in reality they was just hypocrites."

"But there are many hypocrites in the church," I said. "Many tell lies. God doesn't slay them at the moment of the lie. So why here, in this case?"

Doug said, "I just think Peter should have given him a chance to explain, or repent, or something."

"Good thought. But let's look at it a little closer. First, I'd say from the context, it appears Peter *did* give him that opportunity. He says, 'Why has Satan filled your heart to lie to the Holy Spirit?' Clearly, the Spirit must have warned Ananias and his wife about what they were doing, and they deliberately took Satan's side. I really don't think this all happened in a vacuum. The God I know would have been talking to this couple through their conscience, through the Spirit, perhaps even through their friends in the church. I don't think God blips people out without warnings galore and other methods to get them to change their minds."

"I know it's true," Julie said. "I've seen it all over my life in the past. As I've thought about it now, I realize many times God spoke to me when I was about to do something wrong and tried to deter me. I just refused to listen. But something else happened too: The more I did something wrong, like my affair with Dave, the less I heard that voice."

"You hardened your heart," I said. "That's how the Bible puts it. God warns people of sin initially, but if they keep doing it, eventually that voice gets drowned out."

"I seen it," Jesse said.

"The point with this couple is something else, even more important than giving them a chance to repent. Any idea what it is?"

No one spoke.

"It often happens in the Bible. When God starts something new in human history—here, it's the beginning of the church, he is often severe in his judgments. Often, the first time a certain sin is committed, God is very blunt about it. We see this with the people of Israel when they sinned with the golden calf. God punished them severely then. But later, he lets other things go by with hardly a slap on the wrist.

"Similarly, in the book of Joshua, Jericho was the first city to be vanquished. God warned Israel not to take anything inside the city, no gold, no animals, nothing. Everyone obeyed except one man named Achan, who hid several things in his tent. When Joshua discovered the sin, Achan and his whole family were punished by stoning.

"So when God begins a new work in the world—in the case of Ananias and Sapphira, starting the church—he has to set the rules very firmly in the minds of the people. Sin is serious. It won't be tolerated. So he gives them a first tough lesson. This one. Later, he's much easier on people."

"I seen that. With my boss," Jesse said. "When I first started workin' there, he was real tough, very particular, fining me and stuff when I did things wrong. But after a while, he lightened up and now we have a good relationship. I think a lot of people do that kinda thing."

"Sure," Julie said. "In my own business, when I hire new employees, I try to be stern with them at first. To set the boundaries. To make clear how we operate. But as they prove themselves, it usually turns out we become friends and have a good working relationship."

I nodded. "That's it. You see it perfectly. But there's another time when God is tough on people, too. Any idea?"

Doug said, "I was thinking of when Moses hit that stone with his staff and God punished him by not letting him go into the new land. Moses died without ever setting foot in the land of milk and honey. And others. Like Samson. Just for letting his hair be cut, God took away all his powers. There're others: King Saul in the case of the Amalekites, and then King David, when he took a census and God ended up exterminating seventy thousand people through a plague. I mean, speaking about overkill."

"Good—you've pinpointed it. With people in leadership positions, God requires much more. The same sin committed by an average guy might get a sharp word. But when a leader does something he knows is wrong, God can get real harsh. Moses knew he wasn't to strike the rock. Samson understood as a Nazirite he could never have his hair cut, and King Saul was specifically told to kill all the Amalekites. King David knew the law said not to number the people to find out how many could serve in the military. All of them were severely punished. God had to make a point, and he made it well, however unfair we might think it was, in our twenty-first-century mind-sets of letting boys be boys, and so on. We can make free choices about anything. But we are not free to avoid the consequences, including God's judgment if necessary."

Doug stared directly at me. "So that's it? That's your great explanation?"

I returned his gaze. "It's not perfect, but that's the way I understand it. There may be others with better insights, I'll readily admit that."

"But seventy thousand innocent people? And for something King David did, not them."

I shrugged, trying to be conciliatory. "Maybe that's one of the ones you'll want to ask God about when you get up there. I have many such questions."

I gazed around at the others. "Look, I'm going to be real honest. You're going to find many things in the Bible that throw you. About God. About Jesus. About his people. About his laws. Once again, you have a choice: to say, 'I see the problem. I don't know the answer, but I'm open and willing to hear it and study it through,' or to say, 'It's one more proof the Bible is a load of horse manure.'

"Many have taken each of those routes. I for one will take the first. And look, if you could dissect and understand everything about God and the Bible, you'd have to be greater, wiser, and all-knowing like God. Sometimes there are just things you have to take by faith, like this freewill/sovereignty thing, like predestination, like these other problems. We are not all-knowing. In fact, Paul wrote in 1 Corinthians 13:12: 'Now we see but a poor reflection as in a mirror; then we shall see face to face. Now I know in part; then I shall know fully, even as I am fully known.'

"We simply don't know all the facts. If God had wanted to explain everything about everything in the Bible, we'd have a book the size of the *Encyclopedia Britannica*. And that would just be on Genesis 1. Even Peter wrote that Paul's writings were often 'hard to understand.' If that was how Peter felt, who walked with Jesus on earth, wrote at least two books of the Bible, and probably was the mentor behind the gospel of Mark, how can we expect to do much better?

"There are passages in the Bible that have befuddled me for years. I study them now and then, return to them, puzzle over them, and usually reach the conclusion I just don't know the right answers. That's what it means to live by faith. You are 'sure of what we hope for and certain of what we do not see,' as Hebrews 11:1 says, but it's only assurance and conviction, not seeing it in daylight. I have never seen God's face. But I know he's there. I see him everywhere I look. But as for his face, not been there, not done that.

"It's a simple truth about Christianity that you'll just have to get used to: It's a life of faith, not of sight. You're in the tunnel. You may see a glimmer of light at the end, but you'll be in the tunnel till you awake in Jesus' arms in heaven. And that's what we all have to live by."

Everyone just stared a moment.

"Well, I'm convinced," Doug said sarcastically, slapping his hands on the table.

Julie turned to him, "If you'd give him a chance, a real chance, you might find it's all very different, Doug."

"Oh, so you're the great, wise teacher now?"

Julie's eyes fell. "I don't know a lot. But like that blind man Mark told us about in the book of John, I know I was blind and now I see. It may only be a glimmer, but I know it's there. And it's the greatest glimmer I ever saw. I'm going to run toward it for the rest of my life, and that's all I care about."

Doug stared at her, saying nothing. Then Jesse said, "I think I'm really close to doing something about all this, I want ya to know. I'm not sittin' here just pretendin'. This is really gettin' me, in a good way. Don't be surprised if I come in here soon just like Julie and cross that line in the sand."

"I'm praying for it," I said quietly.

"Can I do something?" Julie suddenly asked.

"Sure. What?"

"I want to pray for Jesse and Doug here, and some others. I really feel like I want to do this. Right here and now."

"Go ahead," I said. "I'm with you."

Julie, Jesse, and I bowed our heads. I wasn't sure if Doug did or not. Julie prayed, "Jesus, I know you love me, and after last weekend I realize how great that love is. So thanks. I'm feeling really amazed and happy and I'm just floored that all this has changed so fast in my life. But I want to pray for Doug first. I know how skeptical he is and how he's been hurt before, which he believes you did to him. So please, show him something, just one thing that will convince him. That's all I ask. And for Jesse, the 'man of insights' I'm calling him, I pray that you'd draw him in, too. Quickly. And if possible, save his marriage and everything else. You know about all those others I'm hoping for too—my kids, my mom, friends, relatives, coworkers, Dave. Even him, Jesus. I pray that you do that opening-the-heart thing with him. Just don't let him seduce me again."

She stopped, then said, "That's it. Thanks for hearing me. I love you. Amen."

We all opened our eyes. "Darn," Jesse said, "you're as good a pray-er as Mark here is. And already."

"I've been doing it like 24/7 so—"

I laughed. "Just remember, prayer is never a performance, a means to impress others who are listening, or even a way to manipulate God. It's just open, honest conversation with him. Keep it that way, and you'll always find him listening and answering."

"Yeah, I found that out, too," Julie said. "Let me tell you about it sometime. But now I have to go. I'll see you all next week. And Mark, this Sunday, your church. I'll be there."

She left in a whirl and Jesse, Doug, and I stepped out into the sunshine. Doug was solemn, but much as I wanted to say something that would knock him out of whatever it was he felt, I just squeezed his shoulder and said, "Hang in there. God is still there."

He nodded and left. Jesse turned to me. "How about I take you for a ride on my bike?"

I stared at him a moment, then said, "Let's do it."

We both straddled his Harley and were off. He took me out on the interstate and we roared along, the breeze in my face and nostrils like sweet savors.

CHAPTER 12

The Problem of Hell Is Actually a Tremendous Encouragement and Motivation

We Press On

The next Monday, Julie already sat at a table sipping a latte when I arrived. She looked up and smiled and I sensed the problems of the previous week had disappeared. We made small talk until Jesse arrived.

"Where's Doug?" I finally asked when he was ten minutes late.

"He's struggling," Julie said quietly. "I think he's really fighting God about this. I think my conversion just floored him in a way I never expected."

She stopped. "I think you should know something about him. I wish he would tell you, but I don't think he will. And please don't tell him this. But I think it's the big thing blocking him from crossing the line."

I thought I knew what she was about to say, but I simply let her continue.

"Years ago, when I first met Doug, we had an affair."

She paused and waited as if she thought I might pounce on her, but I just returned her gaze without flinching. "I was vulnerable, my marriage was in the pit, and I needed someone. First, we just started talking. Then it became, well, you know. It lasted about a year, then I guess Doug got tired of me and I ended up in a divorce. I was as lost as a goldfish in the deep, blue sea, but Doug is not the kind of guy to hang in there long. So, over the years, he's had a number of affairs, and he's in the middle of one now. His wife doesn't give a rip as long as he brings home the bacon and lets her do what she wants. For all I know, she may have her own boyfriend somewhere out there. I've encouraged him that God'll help him with all those decisions once he makes a commitment. But he just says he's not convinced of what you've told us, and he just feels you're a great debater and if he had someone who knew the Bible as well as you, he thinks you'd be on the ropes in seconds."

I shrugged. "A lot of people think that. If they just had someone who really knew his stuff, all these Christian, biblical arguments would be debunked rather quickly. The problem is that there simply aren't people like that. Because the facts are on our side, not theirs."

Julie nodded, her blue eyes looking pained and worried. "He's been reading some books by several atheists. I can't remember their names. One's a big evolutionist."

"Richard Dawkins?"

"Yeah, that sounds right."

"I've mentioned them here—remember when we talked about my friend's daughter?"

"Oh, right."

"I know their writings well. There are three who recently had big best sellers claiming to blow Christianity to smithereens. Dawkins has a book called *The God Delusion*, with all his so-called "facts" proving God can't possibly exist. Sam Harris is another one, whose books, *The End of Faith* and *Letter to a Christian Nation*, purportedly show all the fallacies in Christianity. A third one by Christopher Hitchens has the rather nasty title *God is Not Great: How Religion Poisons Everything*.

"All four of these books appear very convincing until you really study what they're saying and compare their arguments with the known facts about the Bible. Then they all crumble. I remember when I first picked them up, feeling a little nervous, like within them were the words that could ultimately throw my faith into the toilet. I half expected them to reveal certain new findings by evolutionists, or some texts discovered in old tombs, that would completely annihilate the resurrection of Jesus, or the inspiration of Scripture, or the existence of God.

"But when I finished them, I just sat there and said, 'Lord, these guys have nothing. They haven't proved anything. In fact, they're less than proofs, they're just emotional diatribes that twist the truth and supply no real facts to back up their arguments.'

"Nonetheless, I suppose for people who simply refuse to find out the truth about the Bible, God, Jesus, and so on, it's probably enough to make them feel they need not give them a second look."

"Yeah, he told me he wishes dearly he could get you in a room with one or all of them," Julie said. "He thinks you'd be torn to pieces."

I sighed, wondering how I might do up against such people. "These guys are professional debaters and have been fielding their positions for years. I've never really debated much. I know how easy it is for debaters to control an argument with emotion, ridicule, and straw-man arguments. You really have to be on your toes with them."

She sighed. "I just wish . . ."

Jesse and I gazed at her. Suddenly, her eyes filled with tears. For all the hardness she exhibited when I first met her, I found she felt deeply about things, and even more so now that she'd become a Christian. "It's so hard to see a dear friend reject everything you know is true."

"You *know* it's true?" Jesse said. "You don't just *believe* it's true?"

Julie glanced at me. "I don't really know how to explain it. Maybe Mark can say something about that."

"There's a great promise Jesus gave the disciples," I said. "It's in John 8, verses 31 and 32. It says," and I read from my little pocket Bible, "'If you hold to my teaching, you are really my disciples. Then you will know the truth, and the truth will set you free.'"

Julie slapped the table. "That's it. That's what I was looking for. Yeah, that's so true, Jesse. When you meet Jesus personally, when he becomes real to you—I don't know how that works either, but—he shows you deep in your heart. You don't just believe anymore in some sense like it's something you can question and worry about that it might not be true, but you know in your deepest heart it is the truth. And it does set you free. You stop worrying about hell because you know you're going to heaven. You aren't so concerned about surviving and ending up bankrupt because you know God's there. You feel secure in his love and presence.

"That's what's been happening in me the last couple of weeks. When I first took that step of faith, I believed all Mark said was true and so on. But now deep down I know it really is absolutely true in some weird but real sense."

"That's another verse you should learn," I added. "Listen to this one from Paul in 1 Thessalonians 2:13: 'And we also thank God continually because, when you received the word of God, which you heard from us, you accepted it not as the word of men, but as it actually is, the word of God, which is at work in you who believe.' And here's another one from Jesus, talking again to the disciples, in John 14:23: 'If anyone loves me, he will obey my teaching. My Father will love him, and we will come to him and make our home with him.' The true Christian has God living right inside him. That reality is best expressed again by Paul in Romans 8, verses 15 and 16: 'For you did not receive a spirit that makes you a slave again to fear, but you received the Spirit of sonship. And by him we cry, "Abba, Father." The Spirit himself testifies with our spirit that we are God's children.'"

"That's what I'm experiencing," Julie said excitedly. "It's like God talks to me all the time, telling me he loves me and he'll lead me and when I'm down or something, he even kind of encourages me. It's incredible."

I grinned. "Believe me, it gets even better. But let me give you one more verse, this one from 1 John 4:6: 'We are from God, and whoever knows God listens to us; but whoever is not from God does not listen to us. This is how we recognize the Spirit of truth and the spirit of falsehood.' Do you see?" I asked. "God doesn't just expect us to believe in some far-off way where we struggle along and hope against hope it's all true, but we're never really sure or anything. No, he comes right down into us and speaks and convinces us of his truth. It's very personal. To be sure, there are times when God may seem distant and to have disappeared from your life. I think we've heard a little bit about that recently when Mother Teresa's letters were published, in which she wrote of her doubts and fears quite honestly. Christians know we all face moments of doubt and fear and even the feeling we might be all wrong about everything we believe. But ultimately, God will deal with even those questions in our lives through that personal touch of his, and we are brought back to our more normal confident and persevering position."

"Wow!" Julie exclaimed. "That's it. How amazing this book is," she said, pointing to her Bible. "It's just chock-full of stuff that strikes right where you have need."

"Why not?" I asked. "God didn't write a computer technical manual for us. He gave us a book we can use to deal with all the difficulties in life. That's the Bible. It's not some deep, unfathomable tome no one can understand or use for real life. It touches us right where we hurt."

Julie shook her head. "I so wish Doug would find that out. You too, Jesse."

"I'm workin' on it, believe me."

I turned to him. "What do you think is holding you back?"

He gazed back at me, then shook his head. "It's stupid, but I admit it's really bugging me."

"Well, spit it out," Julie said. "That's what we're here for."

Jesse, mountain man that he is, took a deep breath like a giant suction machine. "Okay, I don't think I can live without some things that I think if I become a Christian, God will take away."

"Like what?" I asked.

He shook his head. "You're gonna laugh."

I smiled. "You may be surprised by what the Bible says."

He nodded. "Okay, here goes. For one, I don't think I can give up beer."

I started to speak, but he held up his hand. "Let me give ya all of it. Second, I could never stop ridin' my Harley or hangin' out with those guys. And believe me, they ain't anywhere near Christians. Third, if I do cross the line, as Julie says, I'm afraid they'll all laugh at me. You know, 'Oh, look, Jesse's a big Christian now. He don't drink beer. What a tough guy!' I know it's dumb, but it matters to me. But that's it, except for one more, and it's a biggie."

Both Julie and I waited.

"This is more in line with what you been teachin' and all. But the problem is about hell. If I do become a real Christian, then I guess I gotta believe most of the people I know and even love are goin' there. And I probably won't be able to do a thing about it, knowin' them and how they hate the Bible and Jesus and all that."

I knew my face had a grim look on it, but this was serious and I knew I had to give Jesse some hope.

"So that's it," he said, splaying his hand diffidently. "Guess you didn't expect none of that."

I smiled. "You're asking about things all kinds of people ask about, Jesse. I don't fault you for any of it. But let me take the easier stuff first. The one about hell is a biggie, but I think even for that you're going to find this is good news."

He gazed at me. "You do that, and I'm in."

"Well, that's a great challenge."

"I've been thinking about that, too," Julie said. "It really scares me."

"Good," I said. "That means you're thinking. Okay, first about beer. The Bible does not really say much about alcohol except that it's a sin to get drunk. But drinking for pleasure, the taste of it, and even some happy feelings I don't think is condemned."

I flipped to Proverbs 3:10. "Here Solomon speaks of how God blesses people: 'Then your barns will be filled to overflowing, and your vats will brim over with new wine.' Clearly, Solomon believed

God's blessing involves having a good grape crop with which to make wine."

I turned to the book of Ecclesiastes and read, "'Go, eat your food with gladness, and drink your wine with a joyful heart, for it is now that God favors what you do.' That's in Ecclesiastes 9:7. And Proverbs 31:6 says, 'Give beer to those who are perishing, and wine to those who are in anguish.' Clearly, the Bible is not against wine, which in those days had to be alcoholic to prevent it from going bad because they did not have pasteurization or refrigeration for grape juice.

"There's also a passage in 1 Timothy 5:23 where Paul advises Timothy, 'Stop drinking only water, and use a little wine because of your stomach and your frequent illnesses.' So it's not like it's outlawed.

"However, it's very clear that drunkenness is considered a serious sin. I'll just give you a couple more passages. First, Proverbs 20:1: 'Wine is a mocker and beer a brawler; whoever is led astray by them is not wise.' And finally, Ephesians 5:18: 'Do not get drunk on wine, which leads to debauchery. Instead, be filled with the Spirit.' So you see, while it's okay to drink alcohol for fun and enjoyment, getting drunk is out."

Jesse shrugged and cocked his head with amazement. "Guess I could live with that."

"Second, about your Harley. We know that Acts 5:12 (NASB, KJV) says the apostles 'were all with one [A]ccord.' So apparently, they drove a Honda."

"Ha, ha," Julie mocked, but she was smiling.

Jesse grinned.

"The truth is I don't think God would ever condemn any of us for riding a Harley or any other kind of vehicle. The only thing he would want us to do is wear a helmet."

Jesse laughed. "Yeah, okay, that's good."

"And as for hanging out with your friends, the Bible specifically says God wants us to do that—to have an influence and possibly share our faith with them. In fact, that's one of the main ways God reaches out to the world—by converting one from a certain group, whether it's a beer-drinking crew at a local bar, a Harley-Davidson club, or the local Moose lodge. That's how God infiltrates the world and has an impact."

"So what was the passage for that?" Julie asked.

"Oh, here's one from 1 Corinthians 5, verses 9 and 10: 'I have written you in my letter not to associate with sexually immoral people—not at all meaning the people of this world who are immoral, or the greedy and swindlers, or idolaters. In that case you would have to leave this world.' Clearly, Paul did not want his readers to cut themselves off from such people.

"In another passage Jesus says, 'All authority in heaven and on earth has been given to me. Therefore go and make disciples of all nations' (Matthew 28:18, 19). Certainly to do that, you have to get out there and mingle with such people. Jesus himself hung around with so many of the bad guys—tax collectors, prostitutes, sinners— that the Pharisees constantly criticized him. But Jesus told them, 'It is not the healthy who need a doctor, but the sick. But go and learn what this means: "I desire mercy, not sacrifice." For I have not come to call the righteous, but sinners.' That's in Matthew 9, verses 12 and 13.

"Once again, we see that Jesus specifically went to those people because they were the ones who could admit they needed a Savior, whereas the proud Pharisees, who didn't believe they ever did anything wrong, just wrote Jesus off. They didn't think they needed such a thing as salvation."

"Okay," Jesse said. "That's good. I get all that. But hell is a little bigger."

I cleared my throat. "You sure you two are ready for this?"

"Definitely," Julie said. "I really want to hear it."

Jesse nodded. "Got to know about this one, I guess. So hit me with it, no matter how tough it is."

"Good."

The Reality of Hell

First," I said, "I guess I should show you why Christians believe there's a hell. Many people in the world today think it's just an old myth, or that we made up the whole thing. So let's just look at a few passages, although there are many."

Turning pages again, I indicated they should look at some things Jesus said in Matthew 23. "In this chapter, Jesus speaks against all the hypocrites who thought God had to love them and reward them because they supposedly kept the Law of Moses. In reality they didn't and that's why Jesus says this: 'You snakes! You brood of vipers! How will you escape being condemned to hell?' (v. 33). So, clearly, Jesus believes hell exists and is a place of punishment.

"Then in the Sermon on the Mount, Jesus says this in Matthew 7:21–23:

> Not everyone who says to me, "Lord, Lord," will enter the kingdom of heaven, but only he who does the will of my Father who is in heaven. Many will say to me on that day, "Lord, Lord, did we not prophesy in your name, and in your name drive out demons and perform many miracles?" Then I will tell them plainly, "I never knew you. Away from me, you evildoers!"

"Where does Jesus mean for these people to go? Hell, of course. "And one final passage, Revelation 20:11–15:

> Then I saw a great white throne and him who was seated on it. Earth and sky fled from his presence, and there was no place for them. And I saw the dead, great and small, standing before the throne, and books were opened. Another book was opened, which is the book of life. The dead were judged according to what they had done as recorded in the books. The sea gave up the dead that were in it, and death and Hades gave up the dead that were in them, and each person was judged according to what he had done. Then death and Hades were thrown into the lake of fire. The lake of fire is the second death. If anyone's name was not found written in the book of life, he was thrown into the lake of fire.

I gazed at the two of them, awaiting a response. When they just sat still and said nothing, I asked, "Need any more than that?"

"You say there are many other passages?" Julie asked, a tremble in her voice.

"Some say Jesus said more about hell than heaven in the Bible. I'm not sure about that, but it's probably close. God clearly wanted to communicate that the penalty for hating him, rejecting him, and so on is not a small slap on the hand."

"I can see that," Jesse said. "So what's the good part?"

Hell as the Only Real Justice and Retribution for Our World

The first thing," I said, "is that the reality and threat of hell is humanity's only real hope for justice for those who have committed all kinds of crimes in our world. Think about it. How would you feel if people like Hitler, Stalin, serial killers, and multitudes of others just blithely disappeared into some kind of 'final sleep' or extinction? Don't you want to see those people pay for what they did to so many? Shouldn't they be called to account for the horrible things they've done? Don't we all have an innate sense that longs to see such people forced to face their victims and reveal all the sordid things they did on earth that most of us don't even know about?

"The truth is that though some people do face justice in this world for some of their crimes, many others have escaped, thumbed their noses at 'the system,' and laughed all the way to the bank, to their next crimes, and to their lives of hell-raising and terrible treatment of the most innocent of people. Like those guys who raped my friend's daughter."

Jesse and Julie just stared at me, nodding, as if a bit astonished that I might say such things, let alone that the Bible affirmed them.

"The truth is, God assures us that no one really gets away with anything in this world. Sure, they may escape the noose, or the chair, or imprisonment, or even a fine. Many have been let off by lenient judges who think corporal punishment is outdated.

"But most of the time, even with life sentences and capital punishment, multitudes of people never pay for their crimes. Think of small children abused by nasty relatives. Think of people who were murdered and their attacker was never found out. Think of the twelve million people murdered by Hitler and sent to the ovens, the more than sixty million starved and destroyed by Stalin, and the millions in China killed by Mao Zedong (Tse-Tung). Wouldn't you be outraged to believe those three simply died and that was the end? Or that in eternity they received seventy-two virgins to keep them happy for their violent deeds? I think everyone of us desires to see God deal some real punishment to such people, don't you?"

Again, both nodded.

"When you think of it like that," Julie said, "I guess I really do agree. Those criminals deserve the worst. But what about relatively innocent people who never believe in Jesus, or God, who never make a commitment? The Bible says they also will face judgment and hell, doesn't it?"

I was already peeling through my Bible. "Okay, listen to this passage. It's in Romans 2:12–16:

All who sin apart from the law will also perish apart from the law, and all who sin under the law will be judged by the law. For it is not those who hear the law who are righteous in God's sight, but it is those who obey the law who will be declared righteous. (Indeed, when Gentiles, who do not have the law, do by nature things required by the law, they are a law for themselves, even though they do not have the law, since they show that the requirements of the law are written on their hearts, their consciences also bearing witness, and their thoughts now accusing, now even defending them.) This will take place on the day when God will judge men's secrets through Jesus Christ, as my gospel declares.

"Look at that statement: Paul tells us God has written his law on everyone's heart and every person will answer to him about how they obeyed or disobeyed it. Moreover, look at the last sentence: God will judge 'the secrets' of all the people. Nothing hidden will be left unknown. Have you considered the many times you have done something wrong in secret and no one ever found out? Well, one day, it'll all come out. For those who are Christians, all will be forgiven. But for those who have rejected Christ and his offer of forgiveness, they will not be able to cover up anything. It'll all be exposed in the light of day."

Julie literally shuddered. "I'd hate to think of what would be shown if I hadn't trusted Christ."

"That's one reason why trusting Jesus is so critical. It's the only way any of us can avoid being totally exposed and judged on that day. The question is, Is any of us really innocent? Anyone who thinks he is is fooling himself. Even the best among us—Mother Teresa, Billy Graham, whoever—all admit to being nothing more than plain sinners. Jesus once told the Pharisees this, in John 8:24: 'I told you that you would die in your sins; if you do not believe that I am [the one I claim to be], you will indeed die in your sins.' What do you think he meant?"

Jesse and Julie glanced at each other, then Jesse said, "I guess it means you'll die and all your sins will be right there with you. No forgiveness or nothin'."

"Right, and the whole creation will see all of them. I remember hearing a pastor tell us Judgment Day will be like all creation seeing a person's whole life on a movie screen. Everything each person ever did will be up there. Thus, when God makes his final pronouncement on your life, all creation will agree you got what you deserved."

"You mean that will still happen to me?" Julie said with a gasp.

I smiled. "Not at all. Listen to this verse from the Old Testament, Isaiah 44:22: 'I have swept away your offenses like a cloud, your sins like the morning mist. Return to me, for I have redeemed you.' And this one from Isaiah 55, verses 6 and 7: 'Seek the LORD while he may be found; call on him while he is near. Let the wicked forsake his way and the evil man his thoughts. Let him turn to the LORD, and he will have mercy on him, and to our God, for he will freely pardon.' And another, Isaiah 1:18: '"Come now, let us reason together," says the LORD. "Though your sins are like scarlet, they shall be as white as snow; though they are red as crimson, they shall be like wool."'

"From these and many other verses, we know that no Christian will ever have to face that kind of thing. It's all forgiven, over, wiped out, cast into the sea, not remembered by God anymore. That's the beauty of the gospel. You really are set free from the past, the present, and the future. You never have to worry about God embarrassing you in front of all creation, or anything like that."

Julie visibly relaxed. "Wow! You really had me frightened there."

"Hey, what would be the point of the gospel if it wasn't that way? Why would we even come to God and Christ if they didn't offer anything real?"

"But you're sayin' if I don't cross that line, I'm in grave danger?" Jesse asked.

"You are, my friend."

He nodded, his eyes dark and worried looking.

"But all you have to do is exercise your faith, trust him, and it's gone. Just like that! Whoosh! Like all your sins piled into the toilet and flushed forever."

Jesse sighed. "It does seem incredible."

"It is. And it was paid for in Christ's blood. But that's how much God loves us. He doesn't want any of us not to have a chance. In fact, in 2 Peter 3, verses 8 and 9, Peter writes, 'But do not forget this one thing, dear friends: With the Lord a day is like a thousand years, and a thousand years are like a day. The Lord is not slow in keeping his promise, as some understand slowness. He is patient with you, not wanting anyone to perish, but everyone to come to repentance.' God really extends his hand to everyone, inviting us to come, get this problem worked out, and all will be well."

Julie looked like she'd swallowed a cat and then found out it was actually a piece of chocolate. "Boy, I'm really glad I did that. I didn't know any of this."

"Not many people do. We don't explain these things like we used to. Not that I'd want to go back to hellfire-and-brimstone preaching, but people just have no comprehension of how horrible hell is and what God is offering instead."

"You said there were other good things about hell," Jesse said, a little nervously.

Hell Is Tremendous Motivation

Let me just say the fear of hell drove me to Christ, perhaps more than anything else in my life. I was twenty-one years old. I had written off Christianity, having been raised in a church that didn't really preach the gospel or anything remotely connected to it. But I was terribly afraid that if I died I would go to hell.

"I think the Bible makes clear that God impresses this fear on every person. Why? To motivate them to seek him, to talk with him, to get the situation worked out. Anyway, that fear made me honestly seek God. I didn't want to die and go to hell. I didn't know Jesus was the answer at the time. But I did know that anxiety remained deep within me, no matter what friends told me, no matter what my professors said. In fact, several thought I was a real idiot because of my fear of death and hell. It was a primary motivating force pushing me to find out who God was and what he could do for me."

"I agree," Julie said. "With my affairs, even though everyone said they were okay, everyone had them, no one would condemn, deep down I knew something terrible awaited me in the future because of them. I couldn't even say where that knowledge came from; it was just there."

"Listen to this verse," I said. "In Romans 1, Paul lays out a very specific indictment against people who sin willfully and wantonly. He speaks of several judgments God enacts against people, sending them deeper and deeper into self-destruction and debauchery. Then Paul ends the chapter with the words, 'Although they know God's righteous decree that those who do such things deserve death, they not only continue to do these very things but also approve of those who practice them' (v. 32).

"Look at that 'righteous decree' idea. It means that every person knows the truth about God and what kind of conduct he condemns. But those people, although they know they could be judged for it, continue doing such things anyway, and even try to get others to do them."

"How I know that," Julie said.

"Yeah," Jesse added. "I know everything I ever got into—booze, drugs, sex, hatred, prejudice—was pretty much pushed on me, or at least encouraged, by my friends. I mean, most people don't just walk into that stuff. They're persuaded to do it. Am I right?"

"Absolutely," I said. "And the persuaders will be judged even more harshly."

"So really, hell is meant to lead us to Christ, not make us hate him for it," Julie said.

"Right. In fact, just about everything God does in a person's life is designed to get them to find out about and face the truth. It's his top concern in every life. I believe God orchestrates the events of every life to bring that person to faith. Of course, not all will do so. But I really believe he tries.

"Now to another thing we have to remember."

Hell Gives Dignity to Jesus' Death

Think about this. Jesus died a horrible death on a cross to pay for the sins of the world. God says believing in Jesus is the only way we can escape his final judgment. But what if he said, 'Well, if you don't believe in him, the punishment is a time out.' Or, 'If you reject him, it's not that big a deal. I'll just make you listen to a lot of lectures for a while in heaven and then we'll let you go.' Or, 'Actually, it's okay. We understand. Go and have a good time.'

"Does any of that make sense? Why would Jesus even have had to endure that awful punishment and die that awful death if hell was just a little time spent in jail or a little whack on the behind for our crimes?"

"I see that," Julie said. "It's like if we weren't really escaping from something terrible and lethal, why would we ever listen to God, or believe, or anything?"

"Correct. God knows how to motivate. And if he can't motivate us with his love and his tenderness, he shows us his stern side and scares us into believing."

Julie smiled and Jesse shook his head. "Yeah, I can see that," he said.

Hell Means We're Accountable for Our Lives on Earth

I guess another great truth hell points to," I said, "is that everything we do in this life has consequences. We are accountable, not only to each other, not only to the police or the judge, not only to the Supreme Court, but ultimately to God. That's a much higher accountability, and God will make it stick, unlike most of the various levels of justice we find in our world.

"I mean, I recently read about this man in New Hampshire who physically and sexually abused this little girl from like the age of five on, for years and years. When the man was finally caught and put on trial, the judge turned out to be one of those nut cases who doesn't believe in justice, just in 'helping' everyone become all they were meant to be. He gave this criminal three months' probation.

"As you have probably guessed, it set off a firestorm. In the end, I think the judge raised the sentence to one year in prison. This man's disgusting deeds got a year in prison, and probably less with parole and so on. Does that outrage you?"

Julie nodded her head slowly. Jesse said, "That's the kinda guy I'd like five minutes alone with in his cell. I'd make sure he never did that kinda thing again."

"Wouldn't we all? But in this unjust, fallen, twisted, and full-of-crazy-people-in-power world, that's all we get. Suicide bombers think they'll arrive in Allah's heaven to a grand reception and seventy-two virgins. How would you feel if that's the way this world really was? Murder a bunch of infidels and their god says, 'Bravo. Have a blast for all eternity.' It really makes no sense that people actually believe that, but they do. And they commit the singularly worst crimes in our world—killing people in the name of their god. Even though Allah isn't the God of the Bible, nowhere near it, that's what they believe."

Jesse said, "With them I'd like a whole hour in that cell."

We all chuckled. But I shook my head. "What if that really was the way our world worked, though? What if Islam really was the truth? Not only would all of us Christians be in grave trouble, but if we did tumble and convert, what crazy things would we be required to do, supposedly at the command of that god? Anyway, the point is that God's hell emphasizes the fact you haven't really gotten away with anything when you commit sin on planet Earth. One day, you will answer for everything."

Jesse perked up. "So it's like, when you know God's there and he's watchin' you, you sit up and take notice when you're about to do something bad. You start to think stuff like, 'Hey, God knows about this and I could be in trouble if I do it. So I ain't gonna do it.'"

"Precisely." I smiled at Jesse. "Good explanation. As I've told you before—"

"I should be a preacher."

"Right."

He grinned. "You know, you're scaring the heck outta me, but at the same time it's kinda good to realize these things. Because now I can do somethin' about it. Before I was just a dumb cluck doin' bad things and not thinkin' about how much danger I was in. Although I guess I really knew deep down, I just wouldn't listen to it."

"Correct. You guys are really getting this."

Julie shook her head, wonder in her eyes. "What I'm seeing is that hell is the great divide. On one side is heaven, forgiveness, God's love and goodness, and all that. And on the other side is judgment, pain, misery, and so on. But there's one thing I don't get. Why should the penalty be so stiff? Can't God give a lighter sentence? I mean what if you really didn't do that much bad in your life? What if you really were a decent person, but you just didn't get it about Jesus?"

"Good question. But think about what it's really all about. What do you think is the ultimate issue?"

"What kinds of things you did in your life?" Julie asked.

Jesse nodded. "Yeah, whether you believed or not."

"Yes," I said, "that's a big part of it. But the ultimate issue is whether you want to have a real relationship with God. Do you really want to live with him forever in heaven? Do you really want to listen to and have to obey all his laws and rules? Do you really want to worship him and love him for all eternity?"

"Yeah, I see it," Julie said. "A lot of people would look at that and go, 'Yuck. Get away from me.'"

"Precisely," I said. "People don't reject salvation because the facts aren't there, or they don't completely understand it, or they just don't care. No, the real issue is they don't want anything to do with God. They don't want anyone telling them how to live their lives. They don't want God around to point out any mistakes or errors. They just want him gone. 'Get out of my life, and I'll be fine,' is what many of them think, even if they don't voice it. And what is hell then?"

Julie's eyes went wide. "It's the one place where God isn't. Nothing that's his, nothing of his creation, nothing that will remind them of him will be there." She sat very still and shook her head. "I just never saw that before."

"That's it," I said. "Hell is God saying, 'Okay, you don't want to have anything to do with me? You don't need me, or care about me? You don't want to acknowledge anything I've ever done for you because you think you did it all on your own? Fine, then I'll put you in a place where you'll be totally free to do your own thing forever—alone, and without a single blessing of my grace, love, creation, person, or kindness.'"

Julie looked triumphant. Jesse looked aghast. "No beer. No Super Bowl. No nothin'!"

"Right. Total darkness. No water, so you'll always be in a state of raging thirst. No food, so you'll face constant and painful hunger. No sleep, so you'll feel tired and wrung-out all the time. And no sex, but always wishing for it. You'll be in a constant state of wanting all these things. That's why I believe the Bible says hell is like a fire. What happens when you're so thirsty you can barely stand it?"

"You feel like you're on fire," Jesse said.

"And hungry for anything to eat?"

Julie said, "You go nuts. You'll chew on cardboard."

"That's why I think the Bible often says hell is screaming and gnashing of teeth. Not because God is doing anything to them. They just don't have anything from God, and they need it. They can't live without it. But they'll have to because they have no power to create anything for themselves. So the agony will only increase."

Julie shook her head. "So it's like people who go to hell are only getting what they want—for God to step out of their lives forever?"

"I think so," I said. "It's sad, but that's about it. I really don't think God is into making them suffer. Some may imagine he will stand over them with a whip or something. No, I believe he'll simply abandon them to themselves. Plus, they won't be able to hurt anyone else in the process, even those in hell, because they'll be totally alone."

"It's so awful. I so don't want anyone I know to go there," Julie said. "Except some people." She smiled. "But really, when I think about it, I don't even want Hitler to go there. I want him to repent and find what I've found."

Hell Motivates Believers to Tell the World about God

That's another aspect of why hell is so important. As believers we know what will happen to people who reject Christ, so we should be all the more determined and hopeful of converting them. That drives us to pray for them, to engage them in conversation, and hopefully to show them the same kinds of things I've shown you."

Jesse shook his head. "It's really frightening. But I'm not sure it's enough. Won't some people still reject God even if they know all this and just refuse to accept it?"

"Sure. But they won't have an excuse. When they stand before God, the main reason will be quite apparent: They simply hate God, and for no real good reason."

"I've got to get out of here and start telling people," Julie said. "This is so scary. And some people I know are old, near death."

"It's a powerful motivation," I said. "But many, many Christians just don't care enough to tell anyone about it. Maybe they don't realize how terrible hell will be for those people. Or maybe they're scared those people will yell at them. Or perhaps, they just don't give a darn. That's sad, but that's our world. Even Christians remain sinners, despite God's forgiveness and work in them."

"It's so sad. And to think I was headed there, too," Julie said.

"And that's the final incredible thing I want to throw at you."

Julie and Jesse gazed at me. "There's more?" Jesse asked.

"Get into the Bible, you'll find more about everything I've told you. We've just, as the cliché goes, 'scratched the surface.' But think about it for a second—what is probably the greatest thing for us as Christians about the reality of hell?"

"It makes me appreciate what Jesus did for me," Julie said quietly.

I slapped the table hard. "Excellent!"

Hell Shows the True Beauty, Grandeur, and Grace of Salvation

When you look at what hell is, how horrid it is, and when you as a Christian see that's what you've just escaped from, it makes you realize how great salvation is. It shows the true beauty of it. It proves the goodness and greatness of all Jesus did.

"What do I mean? The contrast is so tremendous. On the one side, total darkness and despair. On the other, light, freedom, joy, peace, fun. On the hell side, pain, regret, guilt, horror at what you've done and rejected. On the other, forgiveness, along with the company of God and all the people you've ever loved, forever and ever. All the saints of all the ages. The time and power to explore and learn everything about God's creation. And of course, above all, the opportunity to be with Jesus, learn from him, listen to him, walk with him, party with him. Forever and ever and ever. Can anything be any more beautiful?"

"Amazing, just amazing," Julie said.

"But there's also the grandeur. Look at how God has crafted salvation. Anyone anywhere at any time can express faith in him and be delivered. From the smallest child to the oldest woman, from the most hardened criminal to the most decent but flawed saint, from the sharpest, most educated professor to the hopelessly handicapped person whose mental abilities are slight. From the richest king to the poorest peasant, it's equally available to all. God has made salvation simple: Believe in my Son. God has made salvation universal: You don't have to do anything but accept it. No program of keeping intricate rules, no impossible list of rituals. Just come as you are and receive it."

The two students simply looked more astonished than ever.

"Finally, God has also made salvation the ultimate act of grace. It's totally free. You don't have to give money. You don't have to perform some grand miracle or deed. You don't have to become a hero, climb a mountain, follow some fancy system of man-made principles that lead nowhere and have no real authority. No, all you have to do is say, 'I accept it. I admit my sins. I believe you died for me. Thank you.' And you're in. There's no reason to struggle or argue or fidget or worry or make demands. It's all there at the point of faith."

Jesse and Julie sighed. Both sat quietly. Then Julie got up. "I have to find out where Doug is. I really wish he didn't miss this one. But I wrote down every verse and I'm going to corner him and make him listen. I'm so scared for him. I just have a terrible feeling time is running out for him, like this is his last chance."

"Be gentle, Julie," I said. "Be loving. But remember, it's his decision. You can't make it for him."

"How I wish I could." She gathered up her things. "So what's the assignment?"

"Go tell someone what you're learning," I said. "I'd like to hear what happens."

She nodded and whisked out. Jesse got up and shook my hand. "You may be hearing from me in the next day or so."

"I'd love to talk more."

He just blinked, then gathered up his things. Without another word, he walked out to his Harley. As I watched, I prayed for all of them, plus several others I so wished would cross the line: relatives, friends, people I'd known since my youngest years. How desperate we Christians should be to get the word out about hell! But how much *more* determined we should be to tell the world the good news: God offers them a complete escape and everything else, and all they have to do is believe in his Son.

How could it be less difficult and less complicated?

CHAPTER 13

Everything in Life Counts before God, and Incredible Rewards Await Those Who Believe

I Try to Connect

I tried to call Doug several times, leaving messages at his office and house. Finally his wife answered. Carolyn immediately became angry and defensive when she found out who I was.

"I don't know what you've done to him," she seethed into my ear, "but he's angry all the time now, nasty to me and the kids, and he's changed in a way I can only track down to his talks with you. So thanks. Thanks a lot."

Not sure how to respond, I finally said, "Please just tell him we have a real encouraging talk coming up and perhaps he should think about being there."

"I will not," she said tersely. "You tell him. He has a phone."

Then she slammed the phone down in my ear and that was it. The thought occurred to me that if this was what Doug had to deal with on a daily basis, no wonder he blew his top. I continued to try to connect with him, to no avail.

Rewards Galore

Meanwhile, I kept thinking I really needed to give Julie, Jesse, and Doug, if he showed up again, some real encouragement about the future of our world, heaven, and so on, especially in light of the terrible consequence of hell for those who rejected Christ. My mind naturally turned to the kinds of rewards God promises to give those who love him in eternity.

As I reviewed the Bible on the subject, I began cataloging the different types of blessings God promises to give his children in heaven. First, there are those things that come simply with salvation, regardless of anything we ever did on earth or failed to do. They were things like:

1. Eternal life (Romans 6:23).
2. Forgiveness for everything we ever did or will do (Isaiah 1:18).
3. Adoption into God's family as a full brother or sister of Christ and all the rights of an heir (Galatians 4:4–7).
4. The power and presence of the Holy Spirit in our hearts (1 Corinthians 12:13).
5. Intimacy with God and his friendship forever (John 17:3).
6. Guidance, strength, and help from God for anything and everything we encounter (Isaiah 41:10).
7. Assurance of salvation and the "witness" of the Spirit that we are God's children (Romans 8:14–16).
8. The right to have our prayers heard and answered (1 John 5:14, 15).
9. Spiritual power for every situation and circumstance (2 Peter 1:3).
10. God's loyal, perfect, and unchangeable love (1 John 4:16).
11. Freedom from fear, prejudice, hatred, worry, and all other negative emotions in the world (1 John 4:18).
12. The promise that God will be with us and will get us safely to heaven (Philippians 1:6; Jude 24, 25).
13. Every spiritual blessing (Ephesians 1:3).
14. A home in heaven (John 14:1–3).

And that's only the beginning. I remember, while attending seminary, reading Dr. Lewis Sperry Chafer's list of more than thirty things like these that happen to us the moment we trust Christ. It astonished me God offered so much to us simply for expressing faith in his Son. But it was true. If people hearing the gospel had any idea of these realities, I can't imagine any but those with the hardest of hearts not admitting it was an amazing "package," to put it in modern marketing terms. Unfortunately, not only do many in our world summarily reject such truth, but they consider it worthless drivel.

What God Offers to Those Who Follow Christ Diligently

A second category of rewards is that of things God will give to those who have made discipleship and commitment to obeying Christ a priority. Again, the list is enormous, but here are a few of the things Jesus and others spoke of that will gain great rewards:

1. Leaving family, homes, and other things to serve God gains "a hundred times as much" (Matthew 19:29).
2. Showing hospitality to those who speak for Christ wins accolades and more rewards (Matthew 10:40–42).
3. Those who invest their talents and treasure in the kingdom of God will find their treasure multiplied in heaven (Matthew 25:14–30).
4. Helping believers who are hurting, imprisoned, hungry, naked, and so on wins God's approval and more (Matthew 25:31–46).
5. God offers a crown of righteousness to those who have "longed" for Jesus to come back (2 Timothy 4:8).
6. God gives a crown of life to those who endure trials (James 1:12).
7. To those who build on the foundation of Christ laid by the apostles, God promises even more (1 Corinthians 3:10–14).
8. God offers the "crown of glory that will never fade away" to those who lead others well for God's kingdom (1 Peter 5:2–4).

9. Enduring persecution and rejection by the world wins greater blessings, too (Matthew 5:12).
10. Praying without fanfare and in private also has a real reward from God (Matthew 6:6).
11. Giving in secret to charity and the church gains more blessings from God (Matthew 6:3, 4).
12. Spiritual fasting without telling others—more rewards (Matthew 6:17, 18).

And even more:

13. Good deeds to others (2 Corinthians 5:10).
14. Being kind and loving to your enemies (Luke 6:35).
15. Building God's church and leading people to Christ (1 Corinthians 3:8).
16. Preaching the gospel (1 Corinthians 9:17).
17. Serving your employers well (Ephesians 6:7, 8).
18. Keeping confidence and trust in God (Hebrews 10:35).
19. Enduring disgrace in public because of your commitment to God and Christ (Hebrews 11:26).
20. Rejecting false teachers (2 John 7, 8).

All these things win great approval, commendations, gifts, blessings, and awards in heaven—personally from Christ and God the Father.

For Overcomers Only

Finally, there are a number of rewards listed in Revelation 2 and 3 for people who have persevered through difficult times and problems in the church. They are called "[those] who overcome" (2:11), and the rewards are as follows:

1. For keeping your first love for Jesus, the right to eat from the tree of life in heaven (2:7).
2. For being faithful under persecution unto death, the crown of life (2:10).

3. For rejecting teachers who try to lead churches into idolatry and sexual immorality, the hidden manna, the white stone, and a new name (2:14–17).

4. For rejecting false teaching, the right to rule with authority and the "morning star" (2:24–28).

5. For enduring to the end of life, confessing that person's name before God (3:3–5).

6. For persevering in doing good, keeping God's Word, and not denying his name, becoming a "pillar in the temple of God," writing on him a special, personal name of God and the New Jerusalem (3:10–12).

7. For remaining "hot" in your commitment to God's kingdom, the right to sit with Jesus on his throne (3:21).

Of course, some of these gifts and rewards are a bit obscure—the "hidden manna" and the "white stone"—but clearly they are tremendous gifts, and those who receive them will be greatly blessed.

While my lists aren't exhaustive, they are good beginnings, and they are realities we can look forward to as we anticipate actually living in heaven with God and Christ.

I was preparing these remarks for our next meeting. But perhaps I should have prepared a little better for what was about to happen.

Back at Starbucks

Jesse arrived about the same time I did, and we talked about his situation with his wife for a few minutes. He seemed upbeat and I thought he might tell me he had accepted Christ, but he said nothing about that.

Then Julie walked in with a younger woman next to her, resembling Julie slightly, though with blonde hair, a number of piercings on her ears and nose, and a tattoo of a rose on her left shoulder and a serpent on her right forearm. Julie introduced her immediately: "This is my daughter, Donna Lynn, but she goes by D.L. Guess I blew it when I named her. She's never liked it, so please call her D.L."

D.L. stood there looking amused but with an underlying tension I realized might prove interesting the same way Julie had been.

Everyone ordered coffees and drinks and I asked D.L. what she did for a living. "I'm living off Mom at the moment," she explained, "going to Maple Woods Community College, hanging out, and getting my licks in before I settle down and become totally middle class."

We all smiled and Jesse said, "You're ahead of me, then. I'm still down there among the lowboys."

D.L. grinned and said, "I like your bike. Mom pointed it out coming in."

Jesse said, "I can't afford a Hummer, so I figured a Harley was all right since it started with an H, too."

D.L. turned to me after that, though, and said, "Okay, I want to know what you did to my mom."

Julie eyed me and raised her eyebrows, indicating this was the whole reason for her visit.

"If anything's been done, your mom probably did it to herself," I said, "under the supernatural power of the Holy Spirit."

D.L. grimaced. "Yeah, I heard all about it. I guess the main thing for me is she's actually nice now. Not always running around with that idiot Dave, and no more cussing, drinking, and pot. I mean she smoked pot, of all things, at her age. Now she doesn't even smoke Kools anymore."

I just tried to return D.L.'s piercing gaze. When she appeared to be done, I said, "What has your mom told you about it?"

Frustrated, D.L. exhaled dramatically. "It's all Jesus did this, Jesus did that, praise Jesus, hallelujah, amen, I'm born again."

"But I want you to understand, honey," Julie broke in. "It's not me. It's God. He's working in me to clean up my act."

"Right," D.L. said, giving her a skeptical look. "And I'm wondering when you'll start screaming at me again to clean up my room, to stop bringing those smelly boys by, and to not stay out till six in the morning."

"I told you," Julie told her, glancing at me for obvious help, "I'm trying to be more understanding. I know what it's like to be where you are. Right now."

"Yeah, right." D.L. looked back at me. "So this Jesus stuff—he's, like, real? Is that it? He's out there and he can fix everything? Is that what it's all about?"

I cleared my throat. "It's not that he promises to fix everything today or tomorrow. Clearly, he's done some amazing things in your mom's life. Many people, even devout Christians, find all those temptations she has managed to give up—"

"Except Dave. At first, anyway."

"Right. Well, I've talked to her about it, and I think she's not letting him in the house anymore, correct?"

I glanced at Julie, who I was afraid might have to confess to more compromising situations. She just nodded.

D.L. said, "He was a loser and I'm glad he's gone. He didn't like me, anyone could see that. And I thought he was just using Mom. Now she gets it. But I'm just wondering how long that will last till she falls for someone else in a week or two."

"D.L., that's not fair," Julie cried. "I'm trying to do the right thing."

"Yeah, write me about it in ten years. That's what matters to me."

I held up my hand. "Look, I think you all need to understand something. God does not expect us to get everything the first hour after we accept Jesus. It's a process. A long process. In Hebrews 12:1, the author tells us to run our race with endurance. It's life-long. I've been a Christian for thirty-some years and God still surprises me with things I need to work on, to change, to get right. Many times, I resist, and it takes some real persuasion on his part, but—"

"Like what?" D.L. said. "Tell me one thing that has happened recently."

I knew of several things I wasn't sure I should talk about, but then I thought, *What's the point if I can't be honest with these folks?*

"Fine. Here's one. Several months ago, after receiving these come-on e-mails for a long time about all kinds of porno sites on the Internet, I finally gave in and decided to take a look at one. It was totally stupid and I'd resisted so long, I wondered why I did it then, but that's the way the Devil works. He keeps hammering away until you give in, or he finds something else to trip you up with."

I looked around at the others and Julie's eyes were almost popping out. Jesse looked like someone had just kicked him. But D.L. was leaning forward, staring at me intently.

"Look, I don't need to go into the details. I got an eyeful at the site. I didn't have to pay anything and there were all sorts of lurid pictures of things I never could have imagined. It was all more of a come-on, but for a few minutes I just sat there and stared. But then, the Lord hit me and whispered to me to run. I closed the Web page, went into my computer and cleared the history so my wife wouldn't find out about it, and just sat there trembling.

"What I didn't expect was how powerful the temptation over the next few weeks would become. I felt a constant push to return to the site and see if they had any 'new' stuff up. I really had to fight it off. At times, I even stood up, left my computer, and went for a walk. At one point, I did some things with spam-blockers that all computers have, and it stopped a lot of the come-ons. But I realize now how easy it is to slide into porn. I'm still fighting it. The urge is there at times. But so far, I've been able to resist. I just had no idea how powerful the temptation would get after I finally gave in that once."

D.L.'s gaze never left my eyes. "So that was it? One time, and now you're free from it?"

"Far from it," I said. "The temptation always returns. When I'm sitting at my computer and a little bored, the thought inevitably hits: *Why don't you check out that site? You have a minute. No one will know. There might be something good there.* It blows my mind how such stupid enticements can work you over. Somehow, though, I shove those impulses out of my mind and do something else immediately. If I don't, it keeps slamming at my psyche."

D.L. turned to her mom. "This guy admits these kinds of things to you, and Jesse here?"

Julie nodded and Jesse said, "He's a pretty complete sinner, if you ask me."

We all laughed, even D.L.

She said, "Okay, what's your spiel for the day?"

"Wait," Julie said. "I have to tell you some things about Doug."

I steeled myself.

"I finally broke down and called him several times. He wouldn't return the calls, but I caught him last Friday and he talked. He's going through some tough stuff and he finally told me about it. His mom's really sick from the radiation treatments and in a lot of pain. He can't stand that. His son Gabriel has suddenly turned very hostile and his girl had an abortion. Gabriel feels real bad about it and chewed out Doug for not being in his life, and he just disappeared last Wednesday afternoon. Doug hasn't seen him since."

I sat there trembling and full of remorse. Why hadn't I tried harder to call Doug, offered some support? I knew the reason. I feared what he'd tell me, based on what his wife had said.

Julie shook her head. "That's not all. He said you've been filling him with all kinds of lies about God and the Bible, and he's through with it. He's all into these atheists now—we talked about them last time—and he thinks they're right. He feels you skewed everything, snowed him with your knowledge, and tried to make him feel guilty. So he's through with it."

I wanted to scream. "What do you think we should do?" I finally asked her, feeling like I'd completely blown it.

Julie's lips set into a line. "I think he's feeling conflicted, and convicted, probably confused, too. He really thought you praying for him and his mom and Gabriel would do some miracles. Now he feels like it's all a scam. He thinks God doesn't care about him and his family because God doesn't exist. His last words were, 'We're all in this alone, and we might as well face it. God is just our hope for a Superman who will step in and fix our lives. It isn't going to happen. It's all a crock.'"

Closing her eyes for a second, she shook her head again. "I don't know that there's anything anyone could say to him that would turn this around. It's like his heart has turned to concrete."

"All I know to do is to keep praying," I said, feeling defeated and hopeless.

"Yeah," Julie said, "but I don't think he'll be back."

"Let's just pray for a second," I said, my voice trembling. I didn't want anyone to see I was near bawling.

I spoke a rather perfunctory prayer, suddenly feeling depressed inside and thinking, *Who am I kidding?* I also sensed this could be a real test of Julie's faith and Jesse's desire to make the final commitment.

When I finished, everyone looked up as if they expected me to have the answer to this one. I quickly turned to Jesus' parable of the sower in Matthew 13, explaining the situation about the seeds of God's Word falling on different kinds of soil, or hearts. I showed them how on the rocky soil, the seed took root, but then withered when the sun became too hot. Then I read Jesus' words in verses 20 and 21: "'The one who received the seed that fell on rocky places is the man who hears the word and at once receives it with joy. But since he has no root, he lasts only a short time. When trouble or persecution comes because of the word, he quickly falls away.'"

I looked around at the three faces, Julie's and Jesse's sad, and D.L.'s just shocked. "It's sad but true there are many people out there who hear the truth of the gospel and get all excited, even accept Christ, and seem full of energy and commitment. But then suddenly something bad happens and they not only doubt the whole thing, but ultimately just give it all up. Strangely enough, at the moment I've been reading a biography about the Beatles. I loved their music.

"Anyway, some years ago I heard that sometime before he was murdered, John Lennon expressed faith in Christ. Several articles in a magazine I read—*Christianity Today*—detailed what happened. Lennon experienced a lot of pain in his life and he wanted out of drugs, out of his bad lifestyle. He was terribly addicted to heroin, as well as other drugs, drinking, and so on, and had a killer temper. He wanted out. He wanted to be free from it. So he started watching these famous evangelists on television, including Billy Graham and others. Oral Roberts actually wrote him several letters, and supposedly Lennon even made a call for prayer to Pat Robertson's '700 Club.'

"But then suddenly things turned in his life and he shucked the whole thing. No one was sure, except one person wrote that Yoko Ono was heavily into the occult and she used spells and a shaman to derail him.

"Perhaps that's true, I don't know. It really saddened me to read all that. Everyone had a favorite Beatle back in the early days, and John was mine. I thought he was funny, and cool-looking, and very smart. I'd always sort of rooted for him to become a Christian after I became one.

"Alas, I guess it was not to be. He may not have really believed, just been looking for a miracle. When it didn't come, he gave up. It happens, like Jesus' parable states. I'm not saying that's where Doug is now. To my knowledge he never truly 'received' the Word, or Jesus. But he became rather enthusiastic for a while. The truth is, though, you just never know how God is working in someone. All this could be happening to force Doug to face up to some hard facts. Anyway, I think the best course is to keep praying and not give up on him, even if he continues to be hostile."

"But how much should we take?" Julie said, her eyes glimmering slightly. "I didn't tell you, but he called me a number of insulting names, really nasty stuff. I was taken aback. And I'll admit I'm hurt, too. We've been friends for many years."

"Gabe and I were friends for a while, too," D.L. said. "But when he started in with this new girl, we just drifted apart."

I shook my head sadly. "Just don't give up. Here's another story from Jesus. Just keep it in mind as you pray and think about this." I turned to Luke 15 and read to them the three parables there, about the lost sheep, the lost coin, and the lost son.

When I finished, Julie said, "This is how God really feels, like that father waiting for and hoping his son will come back?"

"Yes. That was the whole point. The Pharisees had made the common people feel like rejects. They gave the people so many laws and regulations that they naturally thought all God cared about was our keeping these petty little rules. They thought when God saw you breaking one, he'd raise his big stick and whack you one."

Julie and Jesse laughed, but D.L. once again had that combination skeptical/amazed look on her face.

"But that's not how he feels at all, as these parables show. In the first two, he goes after the sheep and the coin, and searches till he finds them, then rejoices over it. In the case of the son, it's a bit more complicated. You can't just retrieve a son like a sheep or a coin. Perhaps Jesus wanted to show God's real heart for his Son through the father in the story. But look at what happens when the son does come back, remorseful and willing to become a slave. The father gives him the favored cloak, the ring that signified full sonship, and a kiss welcoming him back. And then he throws a huge party in the boy's honor. The boy has wasted everything, completely blown it. But the father doesn't even seem to care. All that matters to him is that the boy has come to his senses and returned.

"I think it's the same way with Doug. He may think God's deserted him, or doesn't care, or doesn't even exist, but God has plenty of patience and can do the impossible. Doug may yet come to him."

"I'll pray for it every day," Julie affirmed.

Jesse appeared stunned, though. "This is how God feels about me?" he asked as if unsure.

"Absolutely," I said. "He wants you to come home."

"But I was never there to begin with."

"It's a parable, idiot," Julie said gently, with a smirk. "Not everything will fit."

Jesse nodded. "Okay, I get it."

We all sat there staring into space, so I said, "Then I guess you'll want to hear about all these rewards God has for us."

"Go for it," Julie said.

I ran through the different lists I had prepared before our meeting. When I finished, Jesse was squinting at me, his face dark. Julie shook her head, writing furiously on her little pad. But D.L. just stared at me, her eyes no longer hard, but more curious than anything else.

"So God's going to give these things to my mom, and anyone else who follows Jesus? Is that it?"

"Right," I said. "Some things are contingent on obedience. Others are, as I said, part of the package of salvation."

"So it's not like you go up there and sit on a cloud and play a harp?"

I shook my head. "One more of those famous lies the Devil tells everyone. And it's a great one. If that was what heaven was really like, surely no one would want to go there. They'd prefer hell. Surely, that would be more fun. But, seriously, the Bible never even suggests that weird idea."

"I always thought it would be like a giant church service," Julie offered. "All of us bored out of our minds for years and years. Everyone screaming in their brains, 'Please let me go to hell.'"

We all laughed.

"It's all part of Satan's program to delude us into thinking God is this skinflint, really offering us nothing but pain and suffering all our days. But the Bible says clearly that heaven will be so incredible, we can't even begin to imagine. In fact, because we can't imagine it, the Bible doesn't say much about what it looks like or is like physically."

I thought for a second, then said, "But there are inklings. Look at this passage. It's one of the clearest statements about heaven, although it doesn't describe streets of gold (but that *is* in there)." I flipped to Revelation 22:1–5:

> Then the angel showed me the river of the water of life, as clear as crystal, flowing from the throne of God and of the Lamb down the middle of the great street of the city. On each side of the river stood the tree of life, bearing twelve crops of fruit, yielding its fruit every month. And the leaves of the tree are for the healing of the nations. No longer will there be any curse. The throne of God and of the Lamb will be in the city, and his servants will serve him. They will see his face, and his name will be on their foreheads. There will be no more night. They will not need the light of a lamp or the light of the sun, for the Lord God will give them light. And they will reign for ever and ever.

I gazed about at my three listeners. "Does that sound like pain and suffering? Boredom? Not worth looking forward to?"

D.L. Speaks Up

Julie and Jesse just nodded, their jaws hanging slightly. But D.L. said, "This is real? This is in the Bible?"

I pointed to the passage.

"Then how come no one ever told me this stuff?"

Julie looked like she'd just swallowed a grasshopper, but she said, "I was an idiot, honey. I never made us go to church and learn any of this. I'm just finding these things out now, too. But you can avoid a lot of the pain I've gone through in life by trusting him now. You're only twenty-one, and I'm forty-six. So if you make the commitment, you're twenty-five years ahead of me."

D.L. eyed me again with those cool blue eyes of hers. "So if I do what Mom did, do I have to get rid of all my hardware?"

I didn't know what she meant till she pointed to the piercings.

Smiling, I said, "I don't think those kinds of things matter much to God, although he does say we should treat our bodies like a temple. But most temples have a lot of ornaments, too."

D.L. laughed for the first time. "And I don't have to erase my tattoos?"

"Who knows?" I said. "Maybe having those kinds of marks of your generation will make your friends sit up and listen to what you have to say better than, for instance, if I or your mom started lecturing them with our too-white skins."

D.L. didn't understand. "You mean I would have to tell my friends I've accepted Jesus?"

Julie patted her hand. "You don't have to, honey. But you'll want to, if it's anything like what I've experienced."

D.L. nodded thoughtfully. "And God won't make me be a missionary to Salt Lake City or anything, will he?"

I laughed this time. "Now, I've heard of new Christians worried God will call them to darkest Africa. But never Salt Lake. I don't know. Do you have an interest there?"

"I have a Mormon friend, that's all." D.L. turned to her mom. "And you won't make me go to the same church you go to if I don't like it?"

Julie shook her head. "I guess it's okay however you feel. But I did go to Mark's church last week, and I liked it. I hear it has a good singles group both for people my age, and the younger set."

"'College and Career,' they call it," I said.

D.L.'s face remained unreadable. "And I won't have to carry around a big Bible everywhere I go?"

I showed her my pocket Bible. "There's nothing that says you have to carry a Bible with you at all times," I said. "But if you wanted to, just to have it available, you can always get one of these little ones you can slip into a pocket." I had noted she didn't carry a purse.

"Okay," she said with a shrug. "I'll do it."

I sat there stunned, but Julie said, "This is serious, honey. It's not like you try it out for a week, then go off and join the Buddhists. And it doesn't mean everything in your life will suddenly become perfect. You know what happened with Dave and me."

"I understand that," she said. "It's a relationship, right? You and God are friends? He's there, with you everywhere you go? And of course he forgives you and all that?"

"Yes, but you have to understand," Julie said, "Jesus died for you. He's not going to be your buddy. He's your Lord, your God, your Savior—"

I listened until Julie turned to me. "Am I off base here?"

"No, you're right on," I said. I looked at D.L. "You understand Jesus died for your sins?"

She nodded. "Right. Mom told me all that the other night."

"And you understand he's not just the only perfect human, but God in human flesh? He's not just some real smart guy who did a lot of miracles and stuff? He's God?"

"Yeah, I get that. I mean, who could do all those things if he wasn't?"

I smiled. D.L. was turning out to be as sharp as her mother.

"And you realize a lot of people in your life may not much like your new beliefs and commitments?"

D.L. nodded again. "You mean some of them may ridicule me and put me down, and even just walk away? Yeah, I get that. Like Dave. It's not that big a deal. There are a lot of people I wish would just leave anyway."

Julie nodded knowingly. "I can name a few. But, D.L., you realize that some of those may be the very people God wants to use you to reach."

D.L. nodded. "Yeah, yeah, yeah. I'll be the girl Billy Graham. I get all this. Let me say the prayer or whatever. I want this to be done. I need to get God working in me about some things I really wish I could stop."

Julie said, "I'm not going to ask."

We all laughed. This was turning out more astonishing by the minute. And then the real bomb fell.

"I'm ready, too," Jesse said. "I gotta do it. I gotta stop puttin' it off. If I can't drink myself silly anymore, tough. There are a lot more important things in life than Budweiser."

We all laughed again, and I led D.L. and Jesse in a prayer. Jesse finished it off with an Ayyyy-men.

D.L. said, "Whew! I'm glad that's done."

Julie was in tears and stood and hugged her daughter. "I can't believe you did this," she said. "I can't believe it was that simple."

D.L. said, "Well, the same God was working in you the last few weeks, he's been working me over, too. I just knew after I saw the change in you that this was what I was looking for. I decided with you if it lasted for two weeks, it had to be real. Because nothing good ever lasted two whole weeks before."

"Thanks a lot." Then Julie said, "Astonishing the way he was working you over, and you didn't give a clue." They both sat down, then jumped up as we all gave Jesse a big hug. The people in Starbucks must have thought we were all nuts.

Then Jesse remained standing and said to those who looked on, "Hey, people, I'm a biker, a cusser, a drinker, and I been in jail. But I just found Jesus and it's great. You should think about him, too. That's what this is all about. And if you wanna come on over, feel free."

Some of the people chuckled, but most just appeared amazed.

We talked some more. The enthusiasm just seemed to go on and on. But finally, with reluctance we knew we all had to get on to our other responsibilities. Outside, we all hugged again.

D.L. commented, "I think I'll try to dig up Gabe and tell him about this. See if I can connect with him. And, Mom, you should talk to Doug again."

"Right."

"And then I got to talk to Becky, Erin, and Trini. Tonight. I got to get this done. I can't wait."

We took a minute to huddle and pray. Then they were off and I breathed a prayer that God would keep them close.

CHAPTER 14

Faith in Jesus Is the Final and Ultimate Dividing Line for Every Person, and It's the Most Perfect Expression of Our Recognition of Who He Is

The Problem of Jesus

Over the years, I have watched the news, the entertainment industry, and the media closely. It always stuns me how the media can rationalize anything about Islam, Buddhism, and other religions.

But when it comes to Christianity—yikes! The hostility is huge.

Oh, you can talk about God, even faith in God, so long as you don't identify him as the God portrayed in the Bible. But you simply cannot exalt Jesus as the Savior, as God incarnate, as the God-man come down to teach us and redeem us. Oh, you can talk about some milquetoasty kind of guy who loved everyone, didn't do much, said some nice words, and was a major hugger, even an environmentalist. But the gutsy, strong, terrible, ferocious, and demanding Jesus of the New Testament is totally off limits.

Jesus remains the eye of the hurricane for the secular world, for people of every religion except true Christianity—for anyone who does not embrace the living God. Such people continue to despise Jesus, sideline him, ridicule him, ignore him, and simply refuse to listen to anything he has to say.

Why is this? Why is it that our cuss words center around God and Jesus? Why is it that you can talk about anything, but get serious or solemn about Jesus, and people go ballistic? Why is it that Islam is always 'the religion of peace' despite numerous pieces of evidence to the contrary, while Christianity is the 'hateful, bigoted, and violent religion,' also despite evidence to the contrary?

The fact is we're in a war. The leader of that war against God is Satan. He is trying to populate his side with every imaginable person who will oppose God with him. He simply cannot let anyone know the truth about Jesus, since it's possible they will cross over to the other side. Every such loss for Satan is a true slap in the face. Thus, he does everything he can in the wider world to keep people from learning the truth about Jesus and his gospel. His pawns in that world are used to oppose every form of positive media about Jesus.

So the war will go on. And Jesus will always be a lightning rod for harsh words, nasty thoughts, and darker feelings.

The Group's Experiences

As I explained these things to Julie, D.L., and Jesse, who had all once more shown up at our table at Starbucks, they all agreed.

"The hardest thing for me," Jesse said, "was thinkin' about the hits I'd take from my friends if I believed in him. They'd be callin' me a sissy for sure, a religious fanatic, all that. Even more than my worries about beer and my bike, that was always in the back of my mind. I wouldn't even bring up Jesus to them except as a cuss word."

D.L. shook her head with recognition. "It was kind of the same for me." I noticed she looked quite a bit more striking today, having shed some of the dark clothing and the hardheaded air. "I thought Jesus would come in and make me do all these stupid things. Go to church. Become a goody-goody. Read the Bible. Carry one around all the time. None of those things would have worked with my friends. And already, I'm finding it tough going anyway. All three of my closest friends have pretty much told me to lay off the Jesus stuff or they were outta my life. It hit hard, so I'm trying to lay a little lower. But it's difficult. I so want them to find him."

It amazed me how committed she was already.

Julie concurred, but said something a little different. "For me, it was knowing I couldn't live the way I wanted to live. I really loved Dave, or so I thought, and the others, and adultery, and all those things were the fun things in life, the stuff I couldn't live without. But I knew if God was real, he'd say no to all of it. I couldn't face that. But after I showed up here and heard you and realized how much sense it made and that Jesus wanted to give me real life, not the hell I was living in, I knew I had to go for it regardless of what came next."

She laughed. "The funny thing is how unfulfilling all those things were. I guess Dave was a good lover and all that. But all I felt was guilt about it, and dirty, and ashamed. I couldn't look D.L. in the eye about anything. And I knew she had no respect for me about anything else I said or did. Even the good things."

"There were good things?" D.L. said with a smirk.

Julie gave her a tap. "In my mind, yes. In yours—"

"No, there were, Mom. But Dave and the others just clouded it all out. And I sure didn't want any of them to be my stepdad."

"How come?" I asked.

"They were dirtballs," D.L. said. "Cheating on their wives? How can you trust any guy who does that? At least Mom was divorced. But they were just crumbs. I could see, even if Mom couldn't, that they were only in it for the sex, too. First thing they wanted when they showed up at the house was to go up to bed.

Unfortunately, Mom, insecure person that she was, obliged. But then they practically ignored her. Watching TV, sports stuff, wrestling, whatever. And eating all our food. And then just disappearing back to their 'happy homes' after they were satisfied. I just don't know how Mom stood being around guys like that."

Julie hung her head a little. "People don't realize the insecurity of being a single, divorced woman with kids. They don't know how we long for attention and love, even that kind, corrupt as it is. You get to the point where you'll take anything, just a glimmer of hope of something better. That's what it's like out in the world."

I nodded.

Julie continued, "Remember that line from the movie *When Harry Met Sally*? Princess Leia—what's her real name?"

"Carrie Fisher," I said, remembering one of my wife's favorite movies which, sexual as it was, still had a good message, I thought, in the end.

"Right. And the other guy she fell for. Remember they're in bed in the morning and Harry and Sally finally consummated their relationship the night before and they both call them, because he's Harry's best friend and she's Sally's. They're both on the different phones and pour out their feelings. Carrie and her husband give them some advice, then hang up. They sit there for a second, then Carrie says something like, 'Don't make me ever go back out there,' explaining to him what agony the single scene had been for her. And I agree. It's cutthroat. It's war, every female against every other. I don't know what it'll be like now that I'm a Christian, but somehow I'm not worried about it. I know God's in charge, so . . ."

D.L. nodded. "I'm really just starting on it, but I see that, too. Course, I don't know how any clean-cut, nice, decent, Christian guy will ever go for me, but what the heck? Maybe there're a few out there with nose rings, too."

We all laughed.

"Well, you see the problem," I said. "Jesus is a major hurdle for many people. Let me just give you a quick study of what the Bible reveals about Jesus."

He Is God in Human Flesh

The biggest dividing point is the fact that he's God incarnate. The Bible is very clear, but I'll just give you a few verses that confirm this. Turn in your Bibles to John 14."

I pointed them to the classic verses in the passage of what is known as Jesus' "Upper Room Discourse," because he spoke it while the disciples gathered in the second-floor room of a house to celebrate the Passover together. I read the passage:

> Jesus answered, "I am the way and the truth and the life. No one comes to the Father except through me. If you really knew me, you would know my Father as well. From now on, you do know him and have seen him." Philip said, "Lord, show us the Father and that will be enough for us." Jesus answered: "Don't you know me, Philip, even after I have been among you such a long time? Anyone who has seen me has seen the Father. How can you say, 'Show us the Father'? Don't you believe that I am in the Father, and that the Father is in me? The words I say to you are not just my own. Rather, it is the Father, living in me, who is doing his work." (vv. 6–10)

Continuing, I said, "It should be clear that Jesus meant here that he is equal to the Father, who is God. 'You've seen me, you've seen him.' What could be more direct?"

Everyone appeared to agree, so I turned to another passage. "This is John 1:1: 'In the beginning was the Word, and the Word was with God, and the Word was God.'"

Skipping down to verse 14, I read further, "'The Word became flesh and made his dwelling among us. We have seen his glory, the glory of the One and Only, who came from the Father, full of grace and truth.'" I'm sure you can see from this that John was saying that the Word—who is Jesus—was God, from verse 1, and then that this Word became human, so there is just no one else who could have qualified.

"Later Jesus himself says this to the Pharisees in John 10, verses 28 through 30. There, Jesus tells them he will not lose any of his sheep, because the Father gave them to him and no one can snatch them out of the Father's hand. He concludes, 'I and the Father are one.' It sounds a little cryptic, right?"

Everyone nodded. "But look at his listeners' response: 'Again the Jews picked up stones to stone him, but Jesus said to them, "I have shown you many great miracles from the Father. For which of these do you stone me?" "We are not stoning you for any of these," replied the Jews, "but for blasphemy, because you, a mere man, claim to be God"'" (vv. 31–33).

I looked at the three earnest faces before me. "Does it need to get any clearer? The Jews plainly understood what he was saying. But if you need one more proof, try Matthew 26:59–66:

The chief priests and the whole Sanhedrin were looking for false evidence against Jesus so that they could put him to death. But they did not find any, though many false witnesses came forward. Finally two came forward and declared, "This fellow said, 'I am able to destroy the temple of God and rebuild it in three days.'" Then the high priest stood up and said to Jesus, "Are you not going to answer? What is this testimony that these men are bringing against you?" But Jesus remained silent. The high priest said to him, "I charge you under oath by the living God: Tell us if you are the Christ, the Son of God." "Yes, it is as you say," Jesus replied. "But I say to all of you: In the future you will see the Son of Man sitting at the right hand of the Mighty One and coming on the clouds of heaven." Then the high priest tore his clothes and said, "He has spoken blasphemy! Why do we need any more witnesses? Look, now you have heard the blasphemy. What do you think?" "He is worthy of death," they answered.

"If there is any definitive statement in the Bible where Jesus was asked point blank if he was the Messiah, God incarnate, the Son of God, this is it. What do you see here?"

Julie spoke up first. "They were trying to get Jesus on anything, just to charge him. But the issue for them came down to who he said he was. They considered it blasphemy, but if he really was God, then—"

"Yeah," D.L. said. "It's like you just can't avoid it after this. You either have to say, 'He really said he was God,' or you have to say the Bible was wrong. But you can't say it's not there. I never realized he actually said that. In fact, in high school, one of my teachers was an atheist, and he challenged us one day to show him from the Bible once where Jesus said he was God. Of course, none of us could, or even cared, but he said to us, 'The fact is, he never did. It's something that was dreamed up later.' So basically, he lied."

"Sure," I said. "Most of the stuff you hear from secular people about Jesus is wrong. Because ultimately Satan is behind it, and he doesn't want anyone finding out that Jesus claims to be God. If they discover that, a whole new set of questions arises: Then what do I do with him? Can I really just write him off as an idiot? Or a fraud? Etcetera.

"For me, though, the strongest statement of Jesus' deity is from the apostle Paul. He writes to the Philippians these amazing words:

> Your attitude should be the same as that of Christ Jesus: Who, being in very nature God, did not consider equality with God something to be grasped, but made himself nothing, taking the very nature of a servant, being made in human likeness. And being found in appearance as a man, he humbled himself and became obedient to death—even death on a cross! (2:5–8)

"If anyone missed it, that's about as direct as anyone can get. But the question is, 'Fine, Jesus said he was God. Others said he was God. His enemies admitted he claimed to be God. But how did he prove it? Aren't mental institutions full of people who claim to be God?'"

Jesus Not Only Said He
Was God—He Proved It

Julie said, "I was wondering about that. But I guess it's pretty obvious. He did miracles. What more did anyone need?"

"There's more than that, but yes, the miracles were a great proof of his deity. This is what Jesus himself said about them in John 14:11: 'Believe me when I say that I am in the Father and the Father is in me; or at least believe on the evidence of the miracles themselves.' And this one, from Peter in Acts 2:22: 'Men of Israel, listen to this: Jesus of Nazareth was a man accredited by God to you by miracles, wonders and signs, which God did among you through him, as you yourselves know.'

"No one could deny these things. The Jews tried to find ways of circumventing these proofs. They said Jesus cast out demons by the ruler of the demons, Satan. They said he performed miracles on the Sabbath, which proved he couldn't be from God, but was a sinner. Today, some people try to write off the miracles as psychosomatic healings, or that they were somehow faked. But there are just too many miracles, and too many different kinds: healings of people blind from birth, stopping storms with a word, walking on water, feeding thousands of people with a little boy's lunch, turning water into wine.

"The truth is you just can't read all these and come to the conclusion that Jesus, like some modern magician, completely fooled the onlookers. Even the hostile witnesses admitted these were real miracles. In Acts 4:16, the Jews gathered and tried to figure out how to stop the apostles, who performed miracles all over Jerusalem just like Jesus had. 'What are we going to do with these men?' they asked. 'Everybody living in Jerusalem knows they have done an outstanding miracle, and we cannot deny it.'

"Once again, we have even Jesus' enemies completely dumbfounded as to how to explain these things apart from Jesus being God."

"It's pretty convincing," Julie said.

"I think anyone who gives the Bible a fair read about this, without even having to believe the Bible is inspired by God, just decent history and reporting, will have to admit there is simply too much evidence. One miracle, two or three? Sure, you could write those off. But the Gospels are full of them."

Jesus' Words Have Lasted
More Than Any Other's

That brings us to another proof: Jesus' words. I would be willing to bet that all three of you, who come from secular backgrounds, could still quote some of Jesus' words." I looked around at them. "Anyone think of any?"

"Love your neighbor as yourself," D.L. said. "I always thought that was a great one."

"Yeah, and I always heard from my mom, 'Do to others what you would have them do to you.' That's one, right?" Jesse asked, looking around at us.

"It's in Matthew 7:12, the Sermon on the Mount."

"I've always liked the one that says, 'Let the little children come to me'" (Matthew 19:14; Mark 10:14; Luke 18:16), Julie said. "That always gave me a good feeling about him, like if I did come to him, he wouldn't be mean, or start bawling me out about all the bad things I'd done."

"Right, Mom," D.L. said. "And that one about light. 'I am the light of the world,' or something. Isn't that from him?"

"John 8:12," I said.

"Yeah, and love your enemies, too," Jesse said. "Although I never got it until now."

"Another verse from the Sermon on the Mount, in Matthew 5:44."

All three stared at me. "How do you know this stuff?"

I chuckled. "These are famous verses, some of the first ones I ever memorized. Believe me, you'll be doing the same thing, if you're going to take Jesus seriously."

"It blows my mind," Julie said.

"Okay, but here's probably the definitive one about Jesus' words, the power of them, the simplicity, the beauty, the comfort. In John 6, Jesus fed five thousand (or more) people. Afterward, he spoke a number of tough words about God's sovereignty, and a lot of people got disgusted and left. At that point, Jesus turned to his disciples and asked if any of them wanted to leave. Peter spoke up right away, saying in John 6, verses 68 and 69, 'Lord, to whom shall we go? You have the words of eternal life. We believe and know that you are the Holy One of God.' How many people the world over have found Jesus' words a comfort, a guard against fear and worry, an encouragement in the face of danger? The truth is that more than two billion people today claim to be Christians and most of them probably treasure Jesus' words more than anything else he did.

"I remember reading years ago about a young Chinese man who came to America for education and became a Christian. When he returned to China, he took some Bibles with him for his friends and relatives. When he gave his mother a whole Bible in Chinese, she wept. But then she pulled a slip of paper out of a pocket. On it was written John 3:16 in Chinese. The mother said, 'This has been my Bible all these years. This one verse. And now I have it all.'

"Think about that. If one verse sustained this woman in China, through persecution and hatred and everything else, how much more is a whole Bible? Now you can understand why people treasure it so. It's the Word of God, and has the life of God in it, as 2 Timothy 3:16 says: It's 'God-breathed.' It has God's breath, or life, in it."

The three returned my gaze with surprise in their eyes. Then Julie said, "After all, if he really was God, he would speak those kinds of words. Memorable. Life-changing. Radical."

"Exactly."

Jesus' Character Shows His Divinity

Another element of Jesus' life and deeds was his perfect character. Although they tried hard, no one could ever accuse him of any specific sin. They finally nailed him on blasphemy because he claimed to be God. Since he *is* God, it wasn't blasphemy. But since they didn't believe him, that was the only crime they could pin on him.

"There are many passages in the Bible that say Jesus was sinless. And he had to be, if he planned to die for the sins of the world.

If he had not lived a perfect life, if he was a sinner just like the rest of us, he would have had to pay for his own sins, not ours."

"Can you give me a passage on that?" Julie asked, her pen poised to write.

"Sure. Just a couple. We have to keep moving on this. Let's look at Hebrews 4:15: 'For we do not have a high priest who is unable to sympathize with our weaknesses, but we have one who has been tempted in every way, just as we are—yet was without sin.' And 1 Peter 2:22: 'He committed no sin, and no deceit was found in his mouth.' On several occasions, Jesus even challenged his enemies to show him what sin he had committed, and they couldn't. It always came down to him breaking some rule they'd made up about the Sabbath or something else.

"So you see, Jesus' miracles, words, and character all show he had to be God. But there are a number of other things in the Bible that prove this. I won't go into detail, but such things as:

1. The prophecies in the Old Testament that he fulfilled.
2. His virgin birth.
3. The continual opposition of Satan.
4. His worldwide influence that stretches to our times.
5. The transformation that millions, if not billions, claim he has caused in their lives.
6. The presence of the Holy Spirit in those who believe.
7. The influence and effect his followers have had on the world for good.
8. The world's inability to do away with him.

"Remember those words of John Lennon that got him into so much trouble, about how the Beatles were more popular than Jesus? I don't think Lennon really meant to imply that their legacy was anything close to his, just that in that time when Beatlemania raged the world over, people paid more attention to them than to Jesus. But Lennon went on to say in the same interview that Christianity would go, it would cease, and it would just die out. He even said he would be proven right about that.

"Besides him, numerous others have made the same prediction. Voltaire. Hume. Thomas Paine. Robert Ingersoll. And yet Jesus and his legacy continue on, change people's lives, and have an effect the world over. What can explain this other than that he truly was God?"

Again, everyone seemed to hang on my words, and it felt tremendously gratifying. But I continued, "There are two more things Jesus did that establish him as absolutely unique in human history."

Jesus' Death on the Cross
for Sin Is Unequalled

First, Jesus' death on the cross for the sins of the world was what he came for. He himself said, in probably the most famous verse he ever spoke, John 3:16, 'For God so loved the world that he gave his one and only Son, that whoever believes in him shall not perish but have eternal life.' Many times Jesus warned his disciples he had come to die. His words were important. The miracles proved his deity. But his whole purpose was to pay the penalty God the Father demanded as the just payment for sins. Jesus knew it and pointed himself to it his whole life.

"No other religious leader has pretended to die for the sins of the world. Most of them died peacefully and made no personal claims of deity. None that I know of offered to die a horrible death to pay for anything, let alone humanity's sins. The very idea of it is unique."

I looked from face to face, all of them eager and obviously wanting to know more.

"So can any of you think of anything else he did that sets him apart from every other person in all history?"

The Resurrection: The Ultimate Proof

They all looked mystified, so I didn't belabor it. "The fact that he not only died but rose from the dead. If he had simply died and disappeared forever, it would have meant nothing. But the Bible is clear that the resurrection is the final proof of Jesus' deity. Here are several verses:

"Matthew 17:9, Jesus speaking after the Transfiguration: 'Don't tell anyone what you have seen, until the Son of Man has been raised from the dead.'

"John 2:22: 'After he was raised from the dead, his disciples recalled what he had said. Then they believed the Scripture and the words that Jesus had spoken.'

"Acts 17:3, Paul to the Athenians: '[Paul was] explaining and proving that the Christ had to suffer and rise from the dead.'

"Romans 1:4: '[He] through the Spirit of holiness was declared with power to be the Son of God by his resurrection from the dead: Jesus Christ our Lord.'

"And finally, a big one, where Jesus himself says to John in Revelation 1, verses 17 and 18, identifying who he was: 'Do not be afraid. I am the First and the Last. I am the Living One; I was dead, and behold I am alive forever and ever! And I hold the keys of death and Hades.'

"It is the resurrection that animates everything else about Jesus. Through it, he conquered death and promises he will empower us to do the same when he raises us up from death. Without the resurrection, it all falls apart. Jesus is just another regular guy who did some incredible things and might even have a following today because of them. But who would really care? If he didn't beat death, what can he really do for any of us? Without the resurrection, Christianity is nothing more than a nice religion of dos and don'ts. Jesus is little more than a good guy who ended up paying with his life for his foolish claims to be God. The Bible is just another throwaway self-help book. Some people might find a little wisdom in it here and there. But basically, it's all pretty boring, and I'd rather read John Grisham.

"But with the resurrection, everything changes. Now we see and know that Jesus was no ordinary person. His gospel no ordinary idea. His book no ordinary book. As Paul writes in 1 Corinthians 15:19, if Jesus didn't really rise, 'we are to be pitied more than all' people. But if he did, we have the greatest message the world could ever hear."

I sighed and smiled at the group. "So that's why I believe Jesus was God. So the question is, why is faith in Jesus alone so important? Why can't Islam or Buddhism, or any other religion be regarded as having the same authority as Jesus and his truth?"

I looked from face to face. Julie spoke first. "In Jesus, God came to our planet. No one else could claim to do that, and I'm not sure any of them ever did. So if he was God, then why should he let anyone else be worshipped or followed or trusted about salvation? He's the only one who accomplished real salvation. All the others may have had some words of wisdom, but that's about it. Jesus made it possible for us to go to heaven."

"Very good, student Julie. You get an A."

"What about me?" Jesse said. "I think it's like God took all this trouble to make the truth about himself clear to us. Sendin' Jesus, havin' him explain things. Then dyin' and risin' from the dead. If God did all that, and all these others are just makin' it up as they go along, then sure, why shouldn't we admit it? He's Numero Uno. The Big Boss. We should recognize him first. It's a no-brainer."

"Nice, Jesse. Also an A." I turned to D.L. "What do you have to say?"

She looked thoughtful, narrowing her eyes. "Well, I see all of that, but I'm kind of worried about the people who have never heard of Jesus. What happens to them?"

I nodded. "It's a good question, and one worthy of an answer. Here's one verse that I believe is very encouraging." I turned to 2 Chronicles 16:9 and read, "'For the eyes of the LORD range throughout the earth to strengthen those whose hearts are fully committed to him.' What do you think that means?"

D.L. squinted. "Well, I guess it means there are people out there who believe he's real, and he cares, he knows who they are, and can get them the news about Jesus. Or else he can do something else. I don't know what."

"Right," I said. "Consider what we've talked about. We know God is perfectly just. He's love to the max. He cares about all the people on earth. He has great compassion. Don't you think we can trust him to figure out how to deal with those people?"

"Yeah, but if Jesus is the only way, then—"

"Right. But in Romans 2:14–16, Paul writes,

(Indeed, when Gentiles, who do not have the law, do by nature things required by the law, they are a law for themselves, even though they do not have the law, since they show that the requirements of the law are written on their hearts, their consciences also bearing witness, and their thoughts now accusing, now even defending them.) This will take place on the day when God will judge men's secrets through Jesus Christ, as my gospel declares.

"I believe this passage indicates God has written certain things on people's hearts. He's clearly talking about people who didn't even know the Jewish laws, let alone about Jesus. I think Paul indicates that God knows all about such people, and I think that if they express faith in the God they find in their hearts, it's quite reasonable that God will honor that faith.

"But the real point is that God will never allow himself to be accused of being unfair or unjust. So whatever happens with those people, we'll all see clearly what decision God makes about them and applaud it. I think it comes down to simply trusting that the God you know will deal with them righteously."

D.L. gazed at me. "I can live with that."

"The important thing," I said, "is that we do need to tell people what we know about him. It's the most important information anyone in this world can receive, and God has called all of us to get out that truth."

"I'm trying," D.L. said.

"Yeah," Jesse added. "I've talked to a couple of my guys. They listened at least. But I figure it took me forty-two years to find this out. So I ain't gonna put no deadlines on anyone."

We all laughed.

Julie, though, looked a little upset. "The only thing I don't understand is why God took so long to speak to me. If I had found all this out when I was a kid, when I did go to church on occasion, a lot of pain and horror in my life could have been avoided."

I glanced around at the others, and I could see that the same question was on their minds. "It's a question I began asking the day after I became a Christian at the age of twenty-one." I stopped and considered a second. "Maybe it's time you heard my testimony."

Julie leaned forward. "I've been waiting for this. I want to see if you were a worse sinner than me so I can tell everyone."

"Yeah," Jesse added with a grin. "You're such a goody-goody now, I ain't about to imagine all the ugly stuff you got into. But I bet you did."

My Story

Thinking I needed to keep things interesting, I started with the words, "Okay, here goes. Before I became a Christian, I probably ranked up there as one of the top happy-go-lucky-on-the-outside-but-torn-up-on-the-inside guys. The feeling intensified in college. I felt confused about many things—religion, politics, who I was, what I was supposed to do with my life, what happens when you die, things like that. I agonized for hours over those questions, and I always came up dry—not an answer in sight. I kept asking, 'What is the truth?' and everyone kept saying, with postmodern conviction, 'You make up your own truth. All truth is relative, and whatever is truth to you—hey, guess what?—that's the truth!'

"It made no sense to me. How could each of us believe diametrically opposed things—there is no God—no, there is a God; Jesus was just a good teacher—no, Jesus was God incarnate; the Bible is God's Word—no, it's the Bhagavad Gita—and all of us be right? I couldn't seem to get beyond the basic laws of logic about such things.

"Perhaps the thing that troubled me most was the realization no one knew me, really knew what I thought and felt, about nearly everything. I'd been in bull sessions where I let it all hang out, but frequently, because of the situation, or someone else present, I never really told the truth. I hid a lot. And what I did try to articulate often came out diffused and unclear. Was there anyone in my life who both knew me through to the deepest parts and also accepted and loved me for who I was?

"I didn't think so. Even with girlfriends I never truly exposed my deepest, rawest core. I couldn't risk it. What if I told the truth, the whole truth about myself, and everyone hated me for it? Or worse, laughed me to scorn? No, I could never risk that.

"About such things my friends seemed equally confused and in the dark, but at least most of them had set their sights on some career-type direction in life. One wanted to be a doctor, another a lawyer, a third a forester. I envied them for their certainty about what they should do with their lives. I kept thinking someone—God, an angel, a professor, Baba Ram Dass—would beam down out of nowhere and tell me, 'Mark Littleton, you were born to be a _____. Go for it.'

"It never happened. The confusion continued until, after graduation from college, I found myself having to begin to pursue something feasible as a career. But there was nothing I burned to do. Sure, I thought about being a teacher, becoming a poet, working in a college setting. But nothing beckoned me to 'come hither, young fellow, and find your dream.'

"Something else bothered me. I felt empty and guilty all the time. Everyone told me the guilt came from my church upbringing. Shed the religious commandments and I'd be okay, they assured me. But how do you simply shuck your past, your life, the stuff that's rooted deeply inside you?

"The emptiness—well, no one was really sure about that one. One of my friends simply said, 'Go get a girl in bed. That'll clear most of it up.'

"I remembered back in my elementary school days when the excitement of upcoming holidays just about killed me. Christmas, Easter, Halloween—I could recall the adrenaline pounding inside me with anticipation. But now even those things just seemed like one more day. Nothing stirred me. I had no passion. Nothing in my life made me sit up and take notice.

"During those college years, I became a picture of the happy hedonist—drinking, drugs, sex, skin flicks, other pornography—

and yet most of it left me feeling vaguely foolish and even a tad condemned. Much of the reason I pursued such things was because I simply felt bored. The weekend would come, I had to get out of my dorm room and have some fun, so why not drugs, why not beer, why not a roll in the hay? None of it fulfilled me, but it did ease the agonizing thought of having to sit in my room all weekend studying.

"The thing I worried about the most was death. What happened out there in the great beyond after your last breath? Where did you go? Was anyone out there like God, or did you just disappear from existence?

"No one seemed to know, not even my Methodist church friends. But they all assured me that whatever I wanted to believe was okay. My problem was that I wanted to know the truth so I would indeed be okay once death happened to me. I didn't want to believe something I'd made up; no I wanted the raw, unembellished truth, whatever it was.

"But no one knew what to say, except, 'Hey, you're young. What are you worried about?'

"I couldn't seem to shake the confusion, the emptiness, the boredom, the guilt, the whole stinking pile of rotten feelings becoming the sum total of my existence.

"Now, please let me assure you, at that time I wasn't a walking factory of philosophical questions. Most of the time, I just sailed along, stuffed the worry and the feelings, and went along with the crowd. But in the dark recesses of the night—with no one to assure me life was good, that I was okay, to be calm—I found myself obsessing over these things.

"I just wanted to know, Is there a God? What happens when you die? Where am I going? What am I supposed to be doing with my life? I wanted to be sure, to know what was true and right as clearly as I knew I breathed and ate. But it eluded me, and no one I knew had a grip on it, either.

"That summer after graduation, I became a Christian, almost without seeking it. Suddenly, many things cleared up in my mind as if by some supernatural magic I couldn't explain. Death, drugs, drinking, sex, guilt, emptiness—I began finding answers for these and other things in the Bible, a book that fascinated me. For nearly any question I had, I could find a consoling truth in its pages. And I knew it was true. Somehow, deep in my bones, far in the recesses of my mind, something had changed. I knew it was the truth. There was no question about it. It was what I'd been seeking all along, and it was as real as anything else in the world.

"What amazed me even more was the sense of joy about life that I felt in my deepest being. I sensed that Someone understood me through to the core, knew my thoughts, my dreams, my fears, and my darkest terrors, and he also knew how to guide me through the murk of this world. I felt fulfilled and directed, as if this Friend had materialized beside me and could offer me wisdom and insight for the adventure I felt I'd begun.

"Some time later, I would discover a passage in the book of Ephesians that described the mess that was my life prior to my becoming a Christian. In Ephesians 4:17–19, the apostle Paul says,

> So I tell you this, and insist on it in the Lord, that you must no longer live as the Gentiles do, in the futility of their thinking. They are darkened in their understanding and separated from the life of God because of the ignorance that is in them due to the hardening of their hearts. Having lost all sensitivity, they have given themselves over to sensuality so as to indulge in every kind of impurity, with a continual lust for more.

"Look at that description:

Futile thinking
Darkness in their understanding
Separation from the life of God
Ignorance
Hardened hearts
No sensitivity to right and wrong
Sensuality
Impurity and greed

"It describes to a tee me and most of my buddies when we were in college. I almost laughed at the comparison.

"Why do we find ourselves in this condition? Why do so many of us refuse to admit these realities up front, go through life like all of you say without really thinking about such things, and yet deep down wrestle with them daily, as I suspect most of us do?

"This brings me to the bedrock truth I believe God wants us to understand about our lives. The reason we feel confused, empty, worried, and guilty, and yet continue to pursue the things that compound the problem—the drugs, drunkenness, and so on—is something the Bible calls *sin*.

"So that's the ultimate answer to your questions. We're sinners and we want to sin, forget God, and live the way we want. In many cases, it takes God a long time to get through. We think we're having fun. We don't want anyone telling us how to live. But God works on us, through our consciences, through the church, through Christian friends, through the Bible. And one day it starts to make sense. But everyone is different. My son, Gardner, accepted Christ when he was eight. I also have a four-year-old named Elizabeth. I read her a story the other night before bed, and we started playing, and suddenly I said, 'So when are you going to accept Jesus, Elizabeth?' She stood on the bed, put her hands on her hips, and said, 'Not this minute.' I laughed. But she hears the gospel all the time. In church. From me and my wife. Even from Gardner and other people in her life. I'm confident when she's ready, she'll take that step.

"On the other hand, my eighteen-year-old, Alisha, now in college, accepted Jesus at the age of four one night before bed. But she never really became committed until last summer after a visit at a Christian camp. She'd been going in the wrong direction for several years, and Jeanette and I prayed for her constantly. One day, God broke through.

"You just never know when he will, either. Julie, when you showed up here with Doug and started shooting your taunts and questions at me, I thought you were a hard case, and would probably be impossible to reach. And then the next time you show up, you're ready. Same with D.L. Jesse, on the other hand, has been coming for many weeks, and it's only now that he says he is ready. And Doug—"

I stopped and glanced around. "We all have to leave Doug in God's hands. His hands are capable, and I believe he loves Doug. You just never know what God'll do. He always has some tricks we've never thought of."

"I'm really praying about him," Julie said.

"You have to be patient. There's a guy I've read about, George Müeller. He started these orphanages in England in the 1800s, and he was a tremendous man of prayer. There's a story about how he prayed for sixty years for this friend to come to Christ. The guy never came—until shortly after George died. And then he crossed the line. Why? Why didn't God answer George's prayer while he was alive? Well, God knows, and maybe he'll reveal the reason someday. But does it really matter? If you really trust and love God, you have to let him have his way in your life and the lives of others. I don't think there's any other way."

A hush fell over us and everyone seemed to be thinking. "I just have to keep praying," Julie said. "That's all I know. I suppose there are many people who prayed for me all these years. So who am I to go telling God how to run his world?"

"Good insight," I said.

"Yeah," D.L. said, brushing her blonde hair back. "I have to hang in there with everybody, just love them, and not give up. I guess it's really not up to me if they ever become Christians. That's really between them and God."

"Another good thought," I said. "You guys are learning fast."

Jesse sighed. "I just wish Jesus would come back now. I got so much trouble in my house. It would be kinda nice to just flash outta here and get up there and party."

"It's a big responsibility. But remember, God isn't interested in giving you lots of information about all these things. He wants to transform you, to make you like Jesus in character. And he has a lot of people for you to reach that none of us would ever have a chance with. God has a plan for each of you. Believe me, he's going to blow your mind. There will be tough times. There will be moments, even weeks or months, when you might feel God has vanished from your life. But it's all part of the process of him teaching you to fly."

"You always finish making me feel excited," Julie said. "It's a real gift."

"Well, if you want to know the truth, I really believe one of my gifts—and we all have several if not many—is encouragement. So that's what's coming through, I guess."

D.L. said, "I feel like there's just so much I need to learn."

I smiled. "And we have all eternity to learn it."

They all grinned.

We finally got up and headed for the door. Outside, we stopped and had another prayer huddle and then we all went our separate ways.

CHAPTER 15

Real Hope Resides in Jesus Christ—in Nothing and No One Else

True Tragedy

That Thursday, I received a call from Julie. When I picked up, I could barely understand her, she wept so hard. I knew it was she, and I tried to calm her, but every time she began to speak, the tears and pain flooded through again.

Finally, I got her calmed down. "What happened?" I asked.

"Doug," she said, and lost it again. Finally: "He's dead. He was killed. He's dead."

I sat there, too stunned to answer. My throat constricted, my face twisted, and I cried, "No! It can't be! He was so close!"

"I know," Julie sobbed. "He was out driving, his wife, Carolyn, told me. Gabriel came home with his girl and announced that instead of an abortion—he said he'd lied about it to see what his dad would say—they'd gotten married. Doug learned from the girl's parents—she was underage—that they gave the justice of the peace or whoever their permission with the words, 'Good riddance. Now let him try to control her.'

"Doug went nuts, screaming, kicking things, tearing through the house, and knocking over everything in the place. You know he collected those kissing dolls. He had them all in this nice display case. He opened it and smashed every one of them in his home office."

I closed my eyes and prayed for my own control in the midst of this.

"Then he stormed out. Apparently, he got so drunk, when he tried to drive home, he crossed lanes into an oncoming truck. That was it. It was over."

Julie's shaking voice told me she was very broken up. But who wouldn't be?

"All I can think, Mark, is that he's in hell. That's all I can think. And I can't stand it. I want to die myself. This world is a pit. It's the real hell. Why does God let these things happen?"

I spent the next few minutes trying to calm her with gentle words, no big theological explanations. Finally, I said, "When is the funeral?"

"Saturday."

"Okay, let me call Jesse. Have you talked to D.L.?"

"Yeah. She's really upset, too."

"What about Doug's family?"

"Carolyn won't listen to a thing I say. D.L.'s on the phone right now with Gabe. He's full of regret, feeling like he's responsible. The police are even saying it might have been suicide, Mark. I always heard committing suicide was a straight ticket to hell. Is that true?"

"No, nothing is a straight ticket to hell, except total rejection of Christ."

I could feel her emotion surging again. I quickly added, "Look, let's get organized here. I'll call Jesse and let's go to the viewing—"

"There won't be any. Carolyn has already had him slated for cremation, and she doesn't want to deal with anyone at the moment. There will just be a small funeral. But I think anyone can come. Even you."

I smiled sardonically. "Do you think I should go?"

"Yes, yes, definitely. If not for Carolyn and Gabriel, for us."

"Okay. Get me the details and then I'll call Jesse."

When I hung up, I went to Jeanette and told her about all that had happened. And then we both wept for what seemed like all night. I couldn't sleep or think. This was the kind of thing I never had any answer for, let alone a good one. And I knew I had to offer Jesse, Julie, and D.L. something, some vestige of hope. Was there any?

The funeral was short. Doug's partner gave a short eulogy, but it was quite clear no one knew what to say. The minister who gave "a few words" was, unfortunately, in my mind one of those lame types who really didn't believe much of anything relating to Christ, God, the Bible, or Christianity. He gave out a few bits of pablum— "Doug was a good man, we all know that. He's in a happier place now." And, "Your questions are warranted. Do not be afraid to voice them. But even God has no answers for something like this, for those of you who might have a belief in God." I stiffened up when he concluded, "We all know that no matter where Doug is now, he is happier. That's what I believe."

It wasn't that I necessarily believed Doug had ended up in hell, as Julie intimated, but I always felt funerals were a great time to give people the real hope of the gospel. Anyway, it was very quiet when everyone slunk out. Julie told me many of the people who came were Doug's clients, so I thought that was refreshing. At least they had shown some support.

Afterwards, I gave Jeanette a kiss and she drove home—we had arrived in separate cars because I thought Jesse and the others might need some kind of talk afterward. Waiting for me were Jesse, Julie, D.L., and, to my surprise, Gabriel, who introduced himself with his new bride, Lizzie. He wanted to come with us, too, to ask me some questions.

We quickly decided on hitting a local Applebee's since everyone felt hungry for more than coffee and sandwiches. When we reached the restaurant, the greeter led us to a table in the back, as I asked for somewhere with "a little privacy."

We Talk

Everyone took a seat, looking grim and depressed. I didn't really know how to jump into things, so when the server came it relieved me to be able to stick my nose in the menu. As we all studied the various dishes offered, Gabriel began sobbing. D.L. touched his hand, and Lizzie lay her head on his shoulder and spoke gently into his ear.

Finally, he looked up at me, real fear and pain in his hazel eyes. "I wanted to hurt him. I said bad things. I told him I hated him and the main reason I married Lizzie was to get revenge on him for being such a . . . well, you can imagine."

He sobbed again. "I'm just sorry. I'm so sorry. I wish I could take it all back."

Everyone looked absolutely unable to speak. Finally, I asked Gabriel to look into my eyes. He obliged. They looked just like his father's. In fact, he resembled Doug so closely, I could imagine Doug must have looked just like him at the same age.

"Your father was a good guy," I said to him. "I'm sure he understood that words spoken like that are not what you really meant. You were angry, and hurt, too. We all say things under those conditions that we wish we could take back."

"But if I didn't hurt him, why did he go out and—" He choked up again, muttering, "I killed him; I killed my father. No one can say anything. That's what happened, and I have to live with it."

"We've all done horrible things," D.L. said, still clutching Gabriel's hand. "But we can be forgiven."

Gabriel said fiercely. "By who? My dad? He's dead."

"By God," D.L. said. "And perhaps through God, by your dad."

I was surprised D.L. would have the insight to say something like that. "Look," she said, "I've been thinking about this ever since we talked on Friday. I found this verse—"

She glanced at me as if to make sure she was right. "It's in the Psalms. Last time we talked, Mark told us how the Psalms are such a great source of comfort and hope when you're messed up. So I just started reading. I got all the way up to here, Psalm 130, skipping some of those big ones."

She glanced at me and rolled her eyes. "Sorry, Mark, but number 119 is a killer."

"I understand," I said, letting a small smile come onto my lips.

"Anyway, just listen." The passage was specified with a book-mark, and she turned right to it, then read,

"Out of the depths I cry to you, O LORD; O LORD, hear my voice. Let your ears be attentive to my cry for mercy. If you, O LORD, kept a record of sins, O LORD, who could stand? But with you there is forgiveness; therefore you are feared. I wait for the LORD, my soul waits, and in his word I put my hope. (Psalm 130:1–5)

D.L. looked around at the group. "I thought it was really cool, and I guess I felt strongly that God wanted me to show it to you."

Gabriel stared down at D.L.'s Bible. "What does it mean?"

D.L. turned to me, but I said, "Tell him what you think."

Hesitating only a moment, she plunged in. "I think it's basically saying that the person who wrote this felt really guilty about some-thing, and he started calling on the Lord. Somehow God made him realize that if he started adding up everyone's sins, no one on earth would live another minute. But the writer saw that God forgives, and that gave him hope. And he just decided to wait till God gave him the peace he needed."

"God will give me peace about this?" Gabriel asked. "He'll for-give me?"

"Of course," D.L. said. "He's not the kind of person to hold things against us, no matter how bad we are. You know me. I was a hell-raiser. I made my mom miserable—"

Julie tapped the table. "Hear, hear."

We all laughed quietly.

"Really," D.L. said. "I pulled the same stuff on her that you did with your dad. And now, for the first time in a long time, she and I are friends again. I mean in a kid-mom sense. I'm not going to hang out with her at certain places. But most of the time—"

We all chuckled again. D.L. said, "Believe me, you're not drag-ging me to one of those Wrestlemania deals."

"What?" Julie exclaimed.

"Just joking, Mom. I know you'd much rather come to Mark's Bible studies."

It felt good for things to be lightening up.

Gabriel seemed to feel a little better as he said, "Well, I guess I have to give God and the Bible a point for that one." He looked at me again. "I think you really had my dad going, Mark. He came home from the meetings with a little bounce in his step. He looked happier. But then, I don't know, everything hit the fan. And he started reading those stupid books."

"The atheists?" Julie asked.

"Yeah, he just started shouting that you were such a liar. I didn't get it. He tried to show me what they said, but I didn't really care. I wasn't interested in that. I had my own problems. Anyway—"

Questions

Jesse looked at me. "Mark, we all talked 'bout this without you there. Sorry. But we got some questions now that this has happened. First one, where's Doug now? Second, why did God let him die like that? And—" He glanced at the others. "What was the third one?"

D.L. said, "How are we supposed to trust God after this, when this kind of thing can happen at any time?"

I looked around at them, trying to feign a confident look. "That's it? That's all you have? Well, here are the three verses to each of those."

They all stared at me, not laughing. "Okay, just trying to . . . well, forget it. Let's just try to deal with them one at a time. I'm going to give you more my opinion on these since obviously the Bible doesn't give exact answers about things like this."

The server arrived with drinks, and I took a sip of my strawberry lemonade, my favorite Applebee's concoction. Jesse leaned back in his seat clutching a big Coke. Julie had a coffee with her hands cupped around it, as if she felt cold. D.L. leaned forward, gazing at me with those inscrutable eyes of hers, a Coke in front of her. Gabriel kept his eyes down, and Lizzie kept her head on his shoulder, obviously totally in love. They shared a lemonade. I admit it was cute, and I thanked God they hadn't gone for the abortion, though I probably would not have counseled marriage at their young age. But who knew? If Jesus came into their lives, they might make it, carve out a life for themselves, and grow up to be strong Christians. I knew no one could ever discount that, even with the worst cases.

When You Lose a Loved One and Don't Know Whether They Had Real Faith

The first question is really, What do I believe about loved ones who die who never exhibited real faith? Do they automatically go to hell? Is there no hope for them? Is there any way we can gain some assurance from God that it might not be as bad as it looks? This is where we all stand with Doug. No one knows for sure what he believed, although some words and memories indicate he was pretty far away from God.

"So, here are my answers. No, I don't believe such people end up in hell automatically. So, second, I believe there is still hope here. And third, I think God offers us some real assurance in the midst of this. Let's look at a few verses."

I quickly found the passage in Luke 23 about the thief on the cross and read how Jesus had promised him he'd live in paradise after he died because of his last-minute act of repentance and faith (v. 43). I said, "No one knows what God might have communicated to Doug in those last minutes, even seconds, of his life. I have heard of many people confessing Christ on their deathbeds. My own father-in-law, a man with no faith through his eighty-six years, finally accepted Jesus just a few weeks before his death. I have heard of others professing faith just seconds before they died. The fact is, we just do not know how God operates in those last seconds."

Next I turned to a passage in Mark 10 and told them the story of the rich, young ruler, a man who sought eternal life but when Jesus told him to give away all his riches, he turned away sad.

Then I read verse 27: "'Jesus looked at them and said, "With man this is impossible, but not with God; all things are possible with God."'"

I glanced about the saddened group, but I did note brighter eyes and perhaps some hope in the wan, drawn faces. "The fact is, we simply cannot discount the grace of God, my friends. In his last seconds, for all we know Doug might have called on Jesus, and that would be enough to tie the knot of faith. That's what I always do with friends, relatives, and others who die without ever making a profession of faith that I can point to. I couldn't stand it right now to think they absolutely have to be in hell, so I trust God about it. We just have to leave Doug in his hands."

Julie nodded and said, "Good answer." But the others looked skeptical.

"Even more importantly, remember what kind of God we're dealing with. He's gracious, compassionate, loving, always fair, always just and right. However it ends up with Doug, no matter what happens, we will all see for ourselves that God was absolutely righteous and loving with him. Being hard and fast about things, saying, 'Well, Doug was a bad guy and he's in hell now because of it' just doesn't fly with me. The God I know would not show anything less than absolute righteousness about Doug and every other person who has ever lived and died without that all-important profession of faith we all wish they'd make."

"So once again, it's trust God, he'll do the right thing," D.L. said. She glanced at Gabriel. "I think I can live with that. Little as I know about God right now, I know it's true. He hasn't been hard on me at all. In fact, I'm even finding I like it when he points out something I need to get right."

"There are cases in Scripture," I added, "that show people converting at almost the last minute, besides the thief on the cross. A biggie is Manasseh, one of the most brutal kings of Israel, who committed genocide on his own people, to say nothing of all the idolatry and immorality he caused the nation of Judah to commit, so that they did evil in the eyes of the Lord. Yet, this is what it says later, in 2 Chronicles 33:10–13:

The LORD spoke to Manasseh and his people, but they paid no attention. So the LORD brought against them the army commanders of the king of Assyria, who took Manasseh prisoner, put a hook in his nose, bound him with bronze shackles and took him to Babylon. In his distress he sought the favor of the LORD his God and humbled himself greatly before the God of his fathers. And when he prayed to him, the LORD was moved by his entreaty and listened to his plea; so he brought him back to Jerusalem and to his kingdom. Then Manasseh knew that the LORD is God.

"Second Chronicles goes on to tell us Manasseh dedicated his later life to righting every wrong he had ever done. So in God's world, it's quite possible for even the worst of sinners to turn around. Not that Doug was that, but—"

Gabriel said, "I know what you mean. We're all messed up. I know. But I just never heard these things."

"Neither have most people," D.L. said. "That's why you're hearing it now."

"The fact is, Gabriel," I said, "never write off the power and love of God. He can do the impossible, and he does it every day. I never thought my father-in-law would convert, but he did. And Julie and D.L. here. When they walked in at those different times, I thought they looked hard as nails. I expected to be torn to pieces. And here they both caved within weeks of each other."

"Caved?" Julie said with arched eyebrows.

We all chuckled.

"Gave in? Accepted Jesus? Got born again?"

"That sounds much better," Julie said primly, and we all laughed again.

"You just never know how God will work. The hardest cases are, to me, often the ones he goes after first. It's his way, I guess, of—excuse my French—giving the finger to the Devil."

This time everyone laughed hard.

"Now that's one I'd like to see," Jesse said.

"Figuratively speaking," I said with a grin.

The Second Question: Why?

Now we come to the second question: Why did God let this happen to Doug? And the answer is, I don't know. You don't know. No one this side of eternity knows. We can say he was suicidal, he was sinning, he was angry and drunk, or that he was hurting and didn't know what he was doing, but that maybe, just maybe, he did call on God in those last few seconds of life. The fact is, though we might come up with answers of explanation, we can never be sure they're right. And if we come up with some answer that leaves us feeling strafed and beaten, that's definitely wrong, because we can't know for sure. I think it's better to leave that explanation in the hands of God than try to figure it out on our own."

Everyone nodded their heads, looking a bit surprised and even pleased with this explanation. I continued, "But I believe something else. There are several passages of Scripture that speak of God's judgment and how we will all stand before him and answer for what we did in this life. I believe those events will be witnessed by every person who lived, from every age. God will show all he did to try to turn people around, and we'll see clearly what each of them did in response. Thus, we'll know without equivocation why God makes whatever judgment he does. All of creation will not only witness those things, but applaud and recognize God's justice, fairness, and righteousness. That, I believe, is when God will show us everything."

"But I thought that was only for unbelievers," Julie questioned, looking concerned. "That we believers won't have to be humiliated for all the things we did wrong."

I nodded. "Correct. We're forgiven, and I don't think God will bring up anything we were forgiven for. But I do think somehow God will show how he worked in us to bring us to himself. I think that will be clear. And that happens at the 'Bema Judgment Seat,' not the 'Great White Throne' in Revelation."

"The Bema?" D.L. asked, looking confused.

I sighed, realizing again how one little truth from the Bible often required hours of explanation. "There are a number of judgments recorded in the Bible. Each one is different and involves different groups of people. The Bema, though, is the judgment that happens after Christ raptures all the believers of all the ages out of the world before the Great Tribulation. A *bema* was a little stand, a little like the one the medalists stand on at the Olympics. When we stand on the bema, Jesus will show off to all believers what we followers did with the gifts, talents, money, and so on that he gave us. It will be a celebration, not a denunciation."

Julie leaned back and breathed with relief. "Had me going there, Preach."

I grinned. "There's one more verse I think you should know about regarding this situation with Doug," I said. I turned to James 1:5, 6 and read it: "If any of you lacks wisdom, he should ask God, who gives generously to all without finding fault, and it will be given to him. But when he asks, he must believe and not doubt, because he who doubts is like a wave of the sea, blown and tossed by the wind."

"I've used this verse many times. What I believe it's teaching is that we should not ask why something happened as much as, What should I do now? That's where wisdom comes in. When we ask God for wisdom, he doesn't necessarily tell us why something occurred, but what to do now that it has. He gives us practical help. He will answer all the whys later, in heaven, when we receive our perfect minds and bodies and can fully comprehend his meanings."

Everyone sat silent, appearing to meditate on this answer.

Julie finally spoke first. "Well, it makes a lot of sense to me. I've been reading the book of Job the last few days, and the first two chapters really floored me. It looked to me like Satan challenged God to a bet, and God gave in and let him attack Job mercilessly to prove Job wouldn't waver in his faith. God won the bet, but I couldn't find anywhere that he told Job why everything had happened to him. In fact, at the end, when God starts laying out all those questions—Where were you when I created the edges of the ocean? and things like that—I realized God was saying, in effect, 'You're going to have to trust me about a horde of things in this life, Job-baby, and maybe this is the place to begin.' I actually thought it was kind of profound, because where do the 'why' questions stop? We could be like little kids, going why, why, why, like they do, with God twenty-four hours a day. We have to get on with real life sooner or later."

"Exactly," I said, happy they were all learning so quickly. "And there's one more verse I want to show you about this. It's the last verse in Psalm 27, which is a very positive psalm, but there are elements that are pretty harrowing, including David being surrounded by evil men, and even the prospect of his parents deserting him. He concludes in verse 14, 'Wait for the LORD; be strong and take heart and wait for the LORD.' Now what do you see there?"

Jesse lifted his hand, and I nodded to him. "Hardest thing on earth for me: waitin'. Bein' patient. I want to git 'er done now. I want the problem over and to git on with life. But it mostly doesn't work that way. You have a choice: to trust God and wait till he does whatever is needed, or to scream, shout, and stomp about."

Everyone laughed.

"Good line," I said. "I'll remember that one. But that's it. Wait. Be strong. Be courageous. God's going to act. He'll free you from your distress. He'll fix the problem. But maybe not right now. Maybe not this week, or this year, or this decade. All you can do is be patient and give him time to work, then hang in there while he does and don't complain, and worry, and scream about it all the time."

"It always seems to come back to trusting God," D.L. said quietly.

"Exactly," I said.

"Mark's favorite word," Jesse added, and I smiled.

Ultimately, Trusting God with the Hard Questions Is What Living by Faith Is All About

That brings us to the third question: How can we trust God in the midst of situations like this one with Doug? I mean, if that happened to him, what could happen to us? How do we know he doesn't have a murderer, a drunk driver, or an abuser waiting around the next corner with their eyes on us?"

Everyone nodded. Jesse said, "I'm a big guy, but I ain't no match with bare hands for even a little guy with a tire iron, or a gun."

"Right. And I guess all I can do is direct you to two powerful verses I always keep on the back burner for times like this."

Opening to Proverbs 3:5, 6, I quickly read, "'Trust in the LORD with all your heart and lean not on your own understanding; in all your ways acknowledge him, and he will make your paths straight.' Once again, I'll ask, what do you think this is all about?"

As usual, everyone looked around, expecting someone else to reply. Jesse finally spoke, scratching his head. "It says lean not on your own understanding. I think I get that. It's like my head is tellin' me somethin': 'You can't trust God.' 'Look at what he did now.' 'He's a mean guy.' And things like that. But you got to ignore that stuff 'cause it ain't true. The truth is that God knows what he's doin', and even if we don't we still have to trust him about it. And when we do that, it says, if we look to him like that, he'll 'make our paths straight.' Which means, I guess, he'll lead you through everything else that's gonna happen in your life."

"Very good, preacher man," I said, and Jesse grinned.

"Another A, guys," he said to the others.

"Really, though, doesn't it make sense?" I asked the group. "Of course the Enemy will be screeching all kinds of junk into our minds about this—'our own understanding.' I mean, what are some of the things you've found going on in your minds about Doug?"

Gabriel spoke first. "That I killed my dad. That I'm a murderer. That I'll always feel guilty about this forever, so I might as well go and off myself, too."

Everyone looked at him. Julie said, "Please don't do that. I couldn't stand it."

"It was in my head, that's all I'm saying," Gabriel offered.

"The truth is, Gabriel," I said, "no matter how nasty you were to your dad, he made his own decisions. You didn't pull the trigger on a gun. Your dad went off, perhaps hurting over what you said, but he is responsible for his part, as you are for yours. No one can make anyone do anything. We're all responsible for our own decisions. That's what the Bible teaches. And the truth is that if we confess what we did wrong, and ask God's forgiveness, he gives it to us. And that's the end of it."

Julie looked deep in thought.

"What is it?" I asked her.

"What I'm seeing here," she said, "is that really all of life comes down to trusting the things God says rather than anything from other people, your own mind, your best friend, and so on. If they contradict God about anything, they're wrong and he's right."

"Bravo," I said to her. "That's a bold statement. But that's also a bedrock truth. The Devil, the world, your own mind and desires, will speak all kinds of lies into your head, even ones that sound good and right. But you have to make sure what that person said matches or agrees with basic Bible doctrine.

"There's a great proverb about this, Proverbs 14:12. It says, 'There is a way that seems right to a man, but in the end it leads to death.'"

"Ooooh, seen that one, done that one," Jesse said.

"Haven't we all?" I asked. "Really, think about it. One of our biggest problems in life as mere humans is pride. We want to figure things out for ourselves. We want to solve our own problems, fix our little worlds. Why? Not only to get the credit, but to prove we could do it. To boast, 'Hey, I'm Superman. I can do anything. Just watch.' But that's the most basic sin from Satan, believing you can do whatever you want without God.

"But isn't that the ultimate arrogance? Even if you're Thomas Edison, inventing the lightbulb, the phonograph, and so on, you still have to ask: Who gave Edison his brain? His ability to solve problems and invent things? The time and money? Edison might say he did it, but he'd be wrong. Nothing he had or did could ever have been achieved without the outside support of God."

"It's like people who say they're self-made," Julie said. "They're fooling themselves. Everything they have is from God. Ultimately."

"Right. Paul says in 1 Corinthians 4:7: 'What do you have that you did not receive? And if you did receive it, why do you boast as though you did not?' This is about God's gifts. No one can claim to have earned them, or created them, or even found them on their own.

"Another verse is from Jesus, John 15:5. Here Jesus talks about him being the vine and we're the branches. He says, 'I am the vine; you are the branches. If a man remains in me and I in him, he will bear much fruit; apart from me you can do nothing.'

"Pretty startling verse, don't you think? Without Jesus, you can't do a thing! But that's it. Spiritually, we can't accomplish anything that lasts in this world. We have to depend on him for everything. And that's the ultimate truth about Doug. We can't trust our own thoughts and feelings about him. We have to trust God about everything, from beginning to end."

"I really see it," D.L. said. "I'm like always arguing with Mom about stuff. Sometimes she says to me, 'Just trust me on this one.' That's when I really get my back up. I want to think I'm right and I can do it on my own. And I'll go out and prove it. And then totally mess it up. Fortunately, most of the time Mom doesn't walk over and whisper, 'Told you so.' But it's there."

"Something we all do," I said.

Harder Questions

But what about if the Bible don't say nothin' about somethin' you might have questions about?" Jesse asked. "Like, still with Doug. I mean, God doesn't say anything directly about him."

"Of course not. But where do you get those answers? You ask for insight—from friends, from your pastor, from reading the Bible about other things, from seeking God in prayer, and so on. God doesn't only answer our questions through the Bible. There are many times he has spoken to me through a friend, even an unbeliever. There's a story in the book of Numbers about Balaam, a pagan prophet who, nonetheless, believed in the Lord. When he went wrong and God tried to stop him, God finally grabbed his donkey's mouth and talked to Balaam through the donkey. God spoke to Moses through the burning bush. Angels have appeared at times and told believers what to do.

"In the book of Daniel, a finger appeared and wrote on the wall at one point to tell King Belshazzar what was about to happen to him for his unbelief. God has many means at his disposal, so you can be sure if you need wisdom and ask for it, he'll get it to you by some means. You simply have to stay alert enough and open enough to hear it."

Julie nodded, then said, "It's just so sad about Doug. All I can say is that it's sad and my heart hurts."

The Comfort of God

"You have good answers, Preach," Jesse said. "And I believe them. But sometimes answers ain't what you need."

I had to agree and said, "Don't look now, but let me read to you a few verses from 2 Corinthians, chapter 1. Maybe this will be a good way to conclude this time together." I read the passage:

Praise be to the God and Father of our Lord Jesus Christ, the Father of compassion and the God of all comfort, who comforts us in all our troubles, so that we can comfort those in any trouble with the comfort we ourselves have received from God. For just as the sufferings of Christ flow over into our lives, so also through Christ our comfort overflows. If we are distressed, it is for your comfort and salvation; if we are comforted, it is for your comfort, which produces in you patient endurance of the same sufferings we suffer. And our hope for you is firm, because we know that just as you share in our sufferings, so also you share in our comfort.

"In several places in the King James Version of the book of John, Jesus refers to the Holy Spirit as 'the Comforter' (14:16, 26; 15:26; 16:7). That's because one of his main duties as the person who lives inside us is to comfort us when we hurt."

Julie looked pensive again, then she said, "But how does he do that? Right now, I just feel empty, and still a little despondent, despite all you've said. How is he comforting me, us, right now?"

"Look around," I said. "You have some friends right here. We're all speaking good, helpful, encouraging words to each other. We've given hugs and kisses to each other. We've offered our support and love. And we've looked at some biblical truths that have offered us hope."

Julie looked surprised. "You mean he's not just going to zap me or something?"

I laughed and so did Jesse.

"Really, does he need to do that? What would he zap you with? A couple ounces of comfort like a couple ounces of espresso?"

"I don't think so," Julie said with a grim smile.

"Right. He's not going to give us a drug. He'll send friends, people, counselors, helpers of all sorts. He'll point you to passages in his Word. He'll speak through the pastor in a sermon. You'll go buy a book on bereavement or something—there are a number of good ones I can recommend—and that will offer help, too. But God understands us, too. He knows we're emotional creatures. He made us like that. We feel things deeply, and a little zap from him isn't going to suddenly change our whole world. We'll have to work it through, day by day, trusting him. Gradually, even for long moments at times, we feel elation, understanding, even joy. But he doesn't expect us to get over some horrible event just like that."

Elijah

There's a guy in the Bible, Elijah—you've probably heard of him." I looked around and everyone appeared to agree, except Lizzie, who was mostly just loving on her new husband.

"Elijah staged this wild confrontation on Mt. Carmel in Israel, where he challenged the idolatrous priests of Baal to see if they could prove their god was superior (1 Kings 18:16–40). In the end, God did a huge zap, like we've just talked about. He sent lightning, igniting Elijah's sacrifice, and proving once and for all he was the true God. All the people bowed down, Elijah killed off all the false prophets, then ran ahead of King Ahab in his chariot to the city some forty miles away. There, the wife of the king, the one who started the whole cult in the first place, shrieked she wouldn't rest till she lopped off Elijah's head.

"What would you have done? Elijah had just staged the greatest miracle those people had ever seen. And yet, he simply hightailed it for the hills, terrified for his life.

"A few days later, though, we find him in the wilderness alone, fuming, upset, accusatory. So God sent an angel, put him to sleep, then fed him when he awoke. The angel did this twice, and in the strength of that rest and food, Elijah left on a forty-day jaunt, ending up at Mount Horeb (1 Kings 19:1–10), where he deposited himself in a cave and complained to God about all his troubles.

"After all this, God came to him and gave him insight into the whole debacle through several miracles. God sent four feats of power. The first three—terrific wind, a powerful earthquake, and a tornado of fire—were all majestic, but God wasn't in them. Last, God sent a 'gentle whisper' of sound (vv. 11–12).

"Now the question is, What was God trying to teach Elijah in his horror and terror and disappointment at the fact a revival never happened after the miracle?"

No one said anything.

"Pretty tuckered out, I guess," Jesse finally said.

"Discouraged, too, maybe in despair," Julie added.

"Really ripped, too," D.L. commented. "Like totally mad at God for not doing what he really wanted."

"All of the above," I said when no one said any more. "I think God was showing him that huge zaps like the spectacle on Mt. Carmel and the other miracles were not the way he normally worked. Rather, the 'gentle whisper' was the reality. God was telling Elijah he rarely worked on the large scale. Rather, most of his work occurred subtly, gently, like the murmur of a tiny voice deep in the hearts of people. But the fact is, God didn't come to him initially with that sermon, or even a Bible verse, or a warning. He let Elijah sleep and then fed him, then let him work things through in his mind for forty-some days. It was only after Elijah had time to rest and eat and sleep that God came to him with the message."

"It really says a lot," D.L. offered. "That's not what Mom does when I come to her with some problem."

Julie grimaced. "Yeah, I pull out lecture number 36."

"More like 1,000,002."

We all laughed.

"But seriously, isn't that the kind of God you'd want to relate to? When Jesus arrived at the tomb of his friend Lazarus, one of the first things he did was weep. He felt deeply. In fact, Psalm 116:15 says, 'Precious in the sight of the LORD is the death of his saints.' God doesn't take lightly what we go through on this earth. It hurts him to see his children suffer, and it pains him that he must often refuse to do the miracle that will fix everything because he knows that will not be the real answer. So he lets us go through trouble, hard times, pain, and even horror shows of enormous proportions.

"But for all of them, he promises he'll be there with us all the way through. He says he's there, he cares, and he'll listen, soothe, comfort, and encourage our souls. But what he will *not* do is give us lives on earth that have no pain, no difficulties, no tough times. If somehow he gave all of us Christians trouble-free lives, but the rest of the world had to go through all the junk, what would that say about him? What would it say about us? How will we learn true character if we don't go through trials that test character? How do you learn patience without facing irritations? How do you discover the power to persevere without actually persevering through disturbing situations?"

Jesse sighed. "It's like my football coach in high school. He made us work out till we were nearly dead. He pushed us to the limits. He forced us to bash our brains out against one another in practice. So that when we got out on the field, we were ready for the even harder tests of another team throwin' themselves at us."

"Exactly. God puts us through the wringer, like he did with Elijah. But then he comes and puts his arm around us when we're devastated and assures us this isn't the end."

Julie nodded. "I know he's here with me right now. I know it. I don't know how. But it's true. And I have to admit, that is tremendous comfort to know he's there, to know he'll get me to heaven intact."

The Great Truth: Where Else Can We Go?

A men," I said. "You're going to find a great number of verses in the Bible that you'll want to memorize or keep at your fingertips. Not only for yourself, but for those you'll comfort when the time is right to give them a verse. It's real pain and sorrow to me that this happened to Doug."

The words suddenly caught in my throat and tears burned my eyes. Jesse put his hand on my shoulder. "I so wanted to see him make the commitment," I managed. "And I thought all along, by his willingness to listen, that he was close, really close. But I just have to leave him in the hands of Jesus now. What else can I do? Whom else can I trust? Like Peter said to Jesus when he asked the disciples if they wanted to give up following him, 'Lord, to whom shall we go? You have the words of eternal life' (John 6:68).

"I guess that's what it'll always come down to. Where else can we go to get real hope in this world? Money? Fame? Glory? Popularity? Our name in the paper? The wisdom of the latest guru from the East?

"No, I now know there's no place but Jesus himself. He alone is the hope of the world. Without him, we have nothing."

Everyone stared at me, then Julie said, "You know, I feel a little better. I feel like I can trust God about this. I'll probably be crying again tonight, and tomorrow, but gradually I'll get past this. And God will still be there then, too."

D.L. pulled her blonde hair back over a silver-studded ear. "I never thought I'd ever be saying this, but I'm so glad Jesus pulled me out of that ditch. I didn't know Doug very well. But I still feel for him, and Gabriel here, and Lizzie, and Carolyn, and all of them. But now I know I have something to give them when they ask, when they're ready."

"What exactly is that?" Gabriel asked, his hazel eyes like stilettos.

"Jesus. I'll give you Jesus, because he can give you everything else."

We all stopped talking for a moment. Then I said, "You can give talks to people, the latest self-help books, a visit from Dr. Phil. Have them go on *Oprah*. Shower them with a Lotto jackpot. But in the end, none of those things lasts. It's Jesus—eternal, personal, the greatest Friend of friends—who can see them through everything."

I paused. "In school, we used to have a saying about ministry. Give a person a fish, and he'll eat for today. Teach him how to fish, and he'll eat for his whole life. Maybe I can retool that a little. Give a person the Bible, church, fellowship, books written by Christians, all that, and some people will do all right. But give them Jesus and they'll make it through right on into eternity. He's the key to everything."

Gabriel nodded, then stood. "I'd better get home. Mad as Mom was at Dad, she still needs comfort, too." He grabbed Lizzie's hand. "Thanks, Preach. I think I understand better about all this Jesus stuff. And maybe I'll soon be ready to take that step. I'll let D.L. keep talking to me, anyway."

"I'm glad to hear it," I said.

Everyone else got up and Jesse paid the whole bill—he said he wouldn't let anyone else do it. Besides, he'd gotten a bonus that week. "So it's all covered," he said. We headed out, then stopped in the parking lot for our little prayer huddle one more time. Everyone prayed except Gabriel and Lizzie, and then we all parted with words of love and encouragement.

I left feeling like much had been accomplished. There were, of course, many more questions, many more situations to talk through and dissect. But in the end, I knew God had it all well in hand.

With him out there and everywhere, I knew I could trust him to always do what was right.

And to be there with them, no matter what they faced.

Epilogue

A S YOU might guess, I would continue my studies with these new friends, as well as others who entered our part of the world. It's my hope I might do follow-up books about such things as basic apologetics questions, such as How do we know God exists? and Why do we believe the Bible is the Word of God? I may call it *All Those Big, Bad Questions: And How They Can Build Your Relationship with God.*

Others could follow, too, about *Big, Bad Christians* who often hurt the sincere and the innocent, and *Those Big, Bad Events in Church History* such as the Crusades, the Inquisition, the Salem witch trials, and others unbelievers use to try to prove Christianity is a flawed, nasty religion.

I hope you have found my answers and those that came out in the dialogue in this book true to the Scriptures. I also hope they didn't come off as standard responses without any new insights or ways of looking at God and his world. I know many of you will probably disagree with some of the interpretations, and that's fine. That's what walking with God is all about. He deals with us individually and no one person has a corner on the market of ideas, questions, and answers.

If you're upset about how things have turned out—I was told

repeatedly by those critiquing this book that they had earnestly hoped Doug would become a Christian in the context of the discussion—I can only say such devices were used in order to focus on some specific truth or idea that needed to be brought out. It's good if you enjoyed the underlying story in this book. However, this is not fiction in the traditional sense—a story meant to entertain and perhaps offer an insight or two.

No, my purpose was to look at the questions raised in the first chapter, and to seek and find satisfying answers to them.

I suspect all of us have faced similar tragedies to some of those in this book. To make everything work out perfectly seems to me to be an obliteration of reality. This world is not a pleasant place. The whole point of the evil, anger, and hatred that infests so many corners of our world is to make us long for the next, real, and perfect world God will create for us. Mistaken is anyone who thinks planet Earth as it exists now is the best God can do. This is, as C. S. Lewis wrote, only "the title page." The real story begins after this world has long disappeared from our interest and memory.

It's also my hope that if you are a Christian this book will have helped you become more grounded in your faith. I also hope it will give you ideas about how to explain to your unbelieving friends, relatives, and coworkers the great truths of our faith. There are so many misconceptions and untruths out there, it shouldn't be too hard to find many people who need to hear that God is not the big, bad being some people envision.

Finally, I hope that if you are not now a Christian this book will have been a step up the ladder toward real, dynamic, and enduring faith. Feel free to write me with more of your questions if you have interest. I will make every effort to answer any and all that come to me.

Thanks for reading this far. May God guide you on to your destination in heaven with joy and a great expectation that he will "rock our world," literally, every day, for all eternity.

Mark Littleton
mlittleton@earthlink.net
www.marklittleton.com